Christianity und   cie: F   )

In the middle of the seventeenth century religious belief and practice were intrinsic parts of everyday life and very difficult to escape. Professor Ward offers a brief, but comprehensible, account of Christianity in Europe between the Westphalia settlements 1648 and the French Revolution in 1789. The focus of the book, however, is not on the religious institutions themselves, but on policy, that is to say those things which conservatives and reformers, revivalists and missionaries, statesmen and peasants sought to change or preserve in their religious heritage. The book is organised around large European regions, for instance, central and north-western Europe (including Britain), southern Europe, and northern and eastern Europe, and within each chapter the political, social and intellectual events and influences of the times are discussed, thus allowing the reader to understand changes in policy in context. With its maps, glossary and guide to further reading, this will be a major aid to students of Christianity under the *Ancien Régime*.

W. R. WARD is Emeritus Professor of Modern History at the University of Durham. He has contributed to several journals and has written a large number of books including *Faith and Faction* (1993) and *The Protestant Evangelical Awakening* (1992).

New Approaches to European History

Series editors
WILLIAM BEIK *Emory University*
T. C. W. BLANNING *Sidney Sussex College, Cambridge*

New Approaches to European History is an important textbook series intended to provide concise but authoritative surveys of major themes and problems in European history since the Renaissance. Written at a level and length accessible to advanced school students and undergraduates, each book in the series will address topics or themes that students of European history encounter daily: the series will embrace both some of the more 'traditional' subjects of study, and those cultural and social issues to which increasing numbers of school and college courses are devoted. A particular effort will be made to consider the wider international implications of the subject under scrutiny.

To aid the student reader scholarly apparatus and annotation will be light, but each work will have full supplementary bibliographies and notes for further reading: where appropriate, chronologies, maps, diagrams and other illustrative material will also be provided.

For a list of titles published in the series, please see end of book.

Christianity under the Ancien Régime, 1648–1789

W. R. Ward

CAMBRIDGE
UNIVERSITY PRESS

CAMBRIDGE UNIVERSITY PRESS
Cambridge, New York, Melbourne, Madrid, Cape Town, Singapore, São Paulo

Cambridge University Press
The Edinburgh Building, Cambridge CB2 2RU, UK

Published in the United States of America by Cambridge University Press, New York

www.cambridge.org
Information on this title: www.cambridge.org/9780521553612

First published 1999

A catalogue record for this publication is available from the British Library

Library of Congress Cataloguing in Publication data

Ward, W. Reginald (William Reginald)
Christianity under the Ancien Régime, 1648–1789/W. R. Ward.
   p.   cm. – (New approaches to European history)
Includes index.
ISBN 0 521 55361 X – ISBN 0 521 55672 4 (pbk.)
1. Church history – 17th century.   2. Europe – Church history – 17th
century.   3. Church history – 18th century.   4. Europe – Church
history – 18th century.   I. Title.   II. Series.
BR455.W37   1999
274'.07–dc21   98–35140   CIP

ISBN-13 978-0-521-55361-2 hardback
ISBN-10 0-521-55361-X hardback

ISBN-13 978-0-521-55672-9 paperback
ISBN-10 0-521-55672-4 paperback

Transferred to digital printing 2006

Contents

Maps

Preface

To outline the religious history even of Christianity alone among religions in Europe in the century and a half beween the Westphalia settlements and the French Revolution in a volume of modest compass, and to provide at the same time the basic introductions to the politics and the religious technicalities of the period which modern students need, involve a great exercise in leaving important things out and carry the risk of a somewhat importunate virtuosity in general judgments; the reader is entitled to know what the author thinks, though (within the limits of space) not always to the grounds on which opinions are based. It is well therefore to come clean at the outset as to strategy adopted. A history of Christianity in this period ought in my view to be primarily a history of religious belief and experience, and, while not neglecting the history of the churches, has less to do with a history of the churches than those bodies commonly claim. Thus a major institution like the papacy appears here as an engine of policy rather than as an institution; and the same is true of the principal feature of its institutional growth, Propaganda Fide. Religious belief and experience are, however, deeply affected by the churches' political involvement. It would be nice to feature an *Alltagsgeschichte* of popular religious observance and its significance, but for huge areas of Europe nothing of this kind is available; and where a good deal of work has been done its value has been diminished by the rashness of historians in adopting a rather amateur anthropology for the occasion. Nevertheless where the evidence permits *mentalités* make their appearance. At the other end of the social scale eighteenth-century writers raised many important questions about the grounds of Christian belief, and some of these are approached in the longest chapter of the book. It would here be an advantage to have found more space for the history of biblical studies but this has not proved possible. Overseas missions, already altering the European churches, perforce appear only by implication or by side-winds. Nor has it been possible in this study to remedy the great neglect by historians of doctrine of eighteenth-century theology except as slanted towards questions thrown up by the Enlightenment.

There would be little virtue in attempting a study of this kind as a collection of encyclopaedia-style articles by nation or denomination (which are in any case available elsewhere). It is possible to treat the history of ideas from a single point of view; but on broader themes it has seemed best to work with large regional blocks, which have in the main to be politically defined. Even so a God's-eye view or even a pan-continental perspective is out of reach, and the book is largely written round an axis from Britain to central Europe. This is due partly but not mainly to the bias of the author's studies. It has the pragmatic justification that one distinguished contribution to this theme has been made by Sir Owen Chadwick from an Italian base, that the well-worn series produced by Fliche and Martin are written from a French viewpoint, and that a major history of the French church is expected from Professor McManners soon after this book is due to go to the publishers. Moreover the Cambridge University Press itself is contemplating a volume by another hand devoted to the French Revolution and the Church. Another angle therefore seems advantageous. The drawback with the standpoint adopted is that it is more suitable for the study of Protestantism than of Catholicism (then as now the majority party); but I think it is also true that in this period, as the Counter-Reformation ran into the sands, more new things were happening on a local basis in the Protestant world than the Catholic, and that many of the new Catholic developments can be profitably observed from a German standpoint.

The book therefore attempts to illustrate the balance between lethargy and vitality in eighteenth-century Christianity by sampling various aspects of religious life and attempting to sketch the main outlines of its history on a regional basis. One unwritten aspect of its history which might well prove to be an indicator of a much wider field is the fate of mysticism in the eighteenth century; grounds of space have compelled its abandonment here, but I hope to return to it later.

A book of this kind profits from the labours of many scholars, and the suggestions of friends and colleagues; it is proper here to thank the anonymous readers of the Cambridge University Press, who would doubtless have written a very different kind of book themselves, for much valiant assistance in remedying the limitations of the author's knowledge. To the Bishop Bell Foundation are due best thanks for encouragement and for financial assistance to a student excluded by retirement from many of the usual sources of research subvention. My wife, as always, has put up with the entire project with exemplary patience.

Glossary

Almost all the technical terms used in the text are explained on the first occasion they appear; a few which are explained on a later occasion may be traced through the index. The following terms, many of them referring to topics which it has not been possible to discuss in the text, fall outside both categories.

Apocalypse, apocalyptic A vision of the future, like that of the Revelation of John in the New Testament; a genre of prophetic writings, including the Book of Daniel in the Old Testament, but not confined to the Bible.

Armageddon The site of the last decisive battle on the Day of Judgment (Rev. 16: 16); hence a final contest on a great scale.

cabbalism The cabbala was the oral tradition handed down from Moses to the rabbis of the Mishnah and the Talmud; here it is the most important school of Jewish mysticism which flourished in Christian Europe from the late twelfth to the nineteenth century.

Cartesianism The mathematical and metaphysical doctrines of René Descartes (1596–1650).

chiliasm The view that Christ will reign with his saints for 1000 years before the end of world history.

curia The papal court and government; hence curialism and anti-curialism.

diocese The sphere of jurisdiction of a bishop.

eschatology The doctrine of the four last things – death, judgment, heaven and hell, first treated on a substantial scale in the Lutheran tradition by Abraham Calov (1612–86). Whereas apocalyptic reflects on the way to the New Age, eschatology is concerned with the end of the Old Age.

Laodicea According to Rev. 3: 15 the Church at Laodicea was neither cold nor hot; it became the archetype of lukewarm religion.

neo-stoicism The influence of Roman writers such as Seneca, Epictetus and Marcus Aurelius, came in the seventeenth and eighteenth centuries to exceed that of all ancient philosophers with the exception of

Aristotle. Neo-stoicism was given academic shape by Justus Lipsius (1547–1606) and his pupils, and continued to be important right through to the Enlightenment.

Paracelsianism Doctrines derived from the Swiss physician, chemist and natural philosopher, Philippus Aureolus Paracelsus (1490–1521). His view of the universe as a complex of sympathetic relationships long attracted alchemists, mystics, Pietists and Quietists who resisted mechanical views of human nature.

Remonstrants Members of the Arminian party in the Dutch church whose views opposing absolute predestination were condemned at the Synod of Dort (1618–19). Stripped of their offices and banished, they formed a Remonstrant Brotherhood which still exists.

Rosicrucian A member of a society alleged to have been founded by Christian Rosenkreuz in 1484, but actually appearing in 1614 in the circle of Johann Valentin Andreae (1586–1654), a court chaplain and General Superintendent of Württemberg. Members claimed secret and magical knowledge; more substantially they looked for a renewal of church, state and society on a Paracelsian basis. In a later phase in which the English alchemist and astrologer, Elias Ashmole (1617–92), was prominent, the movement became an influence upon freemasonry.

Socinianism A sixteenth-century anti-Trinitarian doctrine propounded by Laelius and Faustus Socinus (or Sozzini), Italian theologians, uncle and nephew. They denied the divinity of Christ, his atonement and the doctrine of original sin. Socinians were numerous in Poland and Transylvania in the sixteenth and seventeenth centuries, and were voluble in England from the 1690s.

Theosophy Any speculative system which bases a knowledge of nature on that of the divine nature. Apparently anticipated in 1 Cor. 2: 10, it is used in this period mostly with reference to Böhme and the complex of Paracelsian, Rosicrucian and cabbalistic ideas which attracted many opponents of Protestant Orthodoxy.

1 Peace and conflict: church and state in central and north-western Europe

Christian and non-Christian belief

In the middle of the seventeenth century religious belief and practice, by no means all of it Christian or confessionally organised, was interwoven with most aspects of life and was very difficult to escape. There were no doubt few who had Luther's vivid sense of the immediate and terrifying presence of God, but the time when a fine mystical soul like Gerhard Tersteegen (1697–1769), a slightly older contemporary of Wesley, could devote much of his ministry to assisting his fellows to 'realize the presence of God' (his most famous hymn in Wesley's translation begins 'Lo! God is here, let us adore') had not yet arrived. Many agricultural routines could be made to fit to the church calendar; many guilds were in one aspect religious associations with their own saints, banners, altars and processions; and if life could hardly be lived without some practice of religious rituals, formal or informal, death, which God had in store for everyone, was the crown and test of all that had gone before. Like matrimony, death, the great reaper, was not to be undertaken lightly or wantonly.

Between birth and death, the European peoples, Catholic and Protestant, found authority driving the parish harder, and seeking to break up the congenial mixture of religion and magic which had sufficed in the later Middle Ages. To get rid, in the one case, of superstition, and in the other of Catholicism and superstition, required a continual clerical pressure which was something new. In each case church furnishings were exposed to the new broom. One of the objects of Catholic pressure was to secure individual confessions, and the confessional box became the norm. On the Protestant side there was a determined attempt to concentrate the devotions of the people on the preaching service, and, by purging the churches of the familiar Catholic appeals to the senses, to exalt the Word of God read and preached. Over much of Protestant Europe this required almost three generations to complete, and was then often undone and recommenced as parishes changed hands during the wars. What was never completed was the effort to turn the family into an *ecclesiola* (a miniature church); much of what English Puritans called 'visiting' was

1

devoted to this, even to the reintroduction of confession by the back door. The Protestants, especially in Lutheran lands, reinforced their congregational solidarity with hymn-singing; but it illustrates the limits of our knowledge of the realities of popular worship, that congregations are known to have substituted their own less edifying lyrics for those in the hymn-books, a practice now impossible to assess. And if parish worship, slowly subsiding into a Protestant rut, became less of an entertainment than of yore, the rival entertainments of drinking, dancing, swearing, profligacy and rowdyism flourished invincibly.

There was less immediate change on the Catholic side, though besides the Council of Trent, zealous local reforming authorities were continually leaving their mark, and weeding out customary scenes which were now held to be damaging to the church. The Mass continued to be the centre of Catholic worship, though those who communicated more than three times a year were considered religious virtuosi. But just as the Catholic system depended less on the parish than the Protestant, so more of it went on outside the church than the Protestant. The veneration of saints was a Catholic characteristic at every level from the household to the nation, and in France the cult of relics reached extraordinary proportions. The church became more cautious in recognising the sanctity of individuals, but new religious orders were noteworthy for pushing hard in the corridors of canonisation. Pilgrimages also united all social classes and were great corporate celebrations. They had their Catholic critics, but limitation rather than abolition was the watchword. Places of grace were especially dear to the Catholic people. But all the time Catholic devotional practices were being subjected to clerical control, and Roman influences were supplanting regional peculiarities. And whether the institutionalisation of approved channels of grace, a process on the whole congenial to the modern state, would in the long run strengthen or weaken the faith of the flock remained to be seen.

Confessionalism and politics

Religious belonging, however, could never be solely a matter of the faithful and the parish. Israel had bequeathed to Christian Europe notions of corporate, covenantal, fidelity to God in which the symbolic role of the temple at Jerusalem had passed very fully to the various local religious establishments. Hardly any of these were efficient, but even the tiniest, like some of the minute establishments of Protestant Germany or of small Swiss cantons, were public statements of the relation of the community to God, and, as such, might at any time become a political issue. There was less difference on this point between Catholic and

Protestant states than appeared at first sight. The Catholic churches all acknowledged the universal headship of the Pope, and included religious orders with an international constituency; but all had conceded considerable rights to kings and princes, and city and cantonal governments, as the senior lay members of the congregation, while the popes themselves exercised secular authority over territories in central Italy. This inevitably embroiled them in the struggles of Habsburg and Bourbon for supremacy in the peninsula. And within the Catholic pantheon, different states adopted different celestial patrons, Poland the Virgin, Bohemia St John of Nepomuk and so forth. It was, moreover, Catholic states which had borne the brunt of the armed defence of Christendom against its external enemies, Spain against the Moors and Moriscos, Spain and the Republic of Venice against the Barbary pirates, Poland-Lithuania and the Holy Roman Empire against the Ottoman Turks; Poland against a Christian enemy external to western Christianity, Russian Orthodoxy. And, surmounting the cathedrals in the Kremlin fortress, the cross standing above the crescent still testifies to the ancient mission of Muscovy to put down Islam in the interests of Orthodoxy and Russian power. Nor were these conflicts, in which political interests and ideology could hardly be separated, a matter of the past. The Turks laid siege to Vienna in 1683; a fifteen-year struggle to force them back enabled the Habsburgs to lay the foundations of the Austro-Hungarian empire, and the final triumph of Prince Eugene over the Turks, sealed by the Peace of Passarowitz in 1718, had deep implications for the religious situation right through the Holy Roman Empire; the Habsburgs could not only continue a bitter struggle for the recatholicisation of Hungary with very little distraction from the south, they had enormously increased their political patronage and their ability to provide settlements for German peasantry, Protestant and Catholic. Moreover a great release of energies was accompanied by a powerful if covert temptation to turn away from the confessional divisions of the Holy Roman Empire to the creation of a dynastic empire in the Balkans. At the same time the power of Lutheran Sweden, which had reached its apogee in a great rescue operation on behalf of German Protestantism in the Thirty Years War (1618–48), was finally broken in a desperate attempt to supplant a nerveless Poland as a barrier against Russian expansion, an expansion short-sightedly assisted by the very Protestant states in north Germany Sweden had helped to save.

Confessionalism and coexistence

Thus politics and religion in the confessional sense could be mixed in very various proportions; but, whatever the proportions, it was very difficult for any state to tolerate religious dissidence at home, and, when full-scale confessional conflict occurred, as it had in the Empire in the Thirty Years War, the prospects of restoring peace were undermined by the fact that the interests of *raison d'état* and confessional survival were frequently at odds. In the Westphalia settlement (the treaties of Münster and Osnabrück) in 1648 a pacification was painfully achieved, the pain of the achievement being fully matched by the discord among posterity as to its worth. In particular the initial relief at the conclusion of a disastrous conflict rapidly gave way to a cacophany of mutual accusations that the terms of the settlement were being abused in confessional interests.

Two factors made a religious agreement hard to reach. The Lutherans stood out for the principle of equality, that is, equal status not for individuals but for the estates of both confessions in the Empire; this the Catholic party were determined not to grant, and the Lutherans had not only to swallow their disappointment, but to allow the recognition of the Reformed faith as one of the three religions of the Empire. The chief representatives of this last were the Elector Palatine, who had precipitated the outbreak of the Thirty Years War by his disastrous attempt to seize the crown of Bohemia from the Habsburgs, and the Elector of Brandenburg the Reformed ruler of an overwhelmingly Lutheran state. The second problem in getting a settlement arose from the extraordinary fluctuation in the fortunes of war. After the Protestant debacle at the battle of the White Mountain in 1620 a decade of disasters followed which, but for Swedish and French intervention, seemed certain to lead to the downfall of the whole Protestant interest, and led in fact to the recatholicisation of many territories. The diplomatic device of the peace settlement was to select a 'normal' year and guarantee that the religious profession of every territory should be for the future as it had been in that year. After immense wrangling the year 1624 was agreed, a date on the whole favourable to the Catholics, and it was possible to bring a fearful and destructive conflict to an end. This agreement has been described as 'the establishment of Protestantism', and it undoubtedly meant that if the armed might of the Counter-Reformation had been unable to dislodge the Protestants hitherto, it would be unable to do so again.

Limitations to the Protestant guarantees

There were, however, four very substantial limitations to this guarantee. In the century between the outbreak of the Reformation and the beginning of the Thirty Years War, events had on the whole gone the Protestants' way; in the century commencing with the White Mountain, the reverse was true, and to this the Westphalia settlement made little difference. The early successes of the Reformation had encouraged princes to climb on to a successful bandwagon; now they had every inducement to climb off. The chances of mortality brought to an end the Protestant line in the Palatinate in 1685, and the succession passed to a Catholic branch. Protestant princes unable to attain royal status within the Empire looked for crowns elsewhere; Brandenburg, Hesse and Hanover found them in East Prussia, Denmark and Great Britain without surrendering their Protestantism; but the head of the Corpus Evangelicorum (the Protestant fraction in the Imperial Diet), the Elector of Saxony, successfully pursued the crown of Poland, and, in order to get it was received into the Catholic Church in 1697 (retaining his headship of the Protestant body). The duchy of Württemberg passed to a Catholic in 1733. By the beginning of the eighteenth century almost every Protestant princely house in the Empire had one or two converts to Rome. The Protestant church establishments showed great tenacity in holding their ground when the princely house changed confession, and were assisted by the Westphalia provision about the 'normal' year; but the whole point of establishment was that the forces of authority should stand together, and an establishment without the head of state looked threadbare.

The second great limitation lay in the local implementation of the peace settlement. Even in an atmosphere of goodwill it would not have been easy to work legislation by reference to a date already a generation past when the peace treaties were signed. In fact the bitter Protestant experience was that, as at more exalted levels, the tide went pretty consistently against them, and even a century later, an enormous amount of the time and energy of the public authorities in Germany was still taken up with trying to implement what was supposed to be the fundamental law of the Empire. The constant disputes over petty local matters of status and convenience were among the things which generated a mentality of conservatism and pessimism in the German Protestant churches; they had sought security in an internationally guaranteed status, had hardly found what they hoped for, and could not see where to turn next. That their fears were not illusory was demonstrated in 1719. The scene (appropriately) was the Palatinate, now governed by a Catholic line. The great church of Heidelberg, the church of the Holy Spirit, was a mirror image of conditions in the Electorate as a whole. The choir was owned by the Electors who were buried there, and for forty years it had been used by the Catholics and separated from the rest of the building by a wall from top to bottom. This wall was now pulled down, and the Reformed were turned out, with specious promises designed to induce them to forego their internationally guaranteed status, and, prospectively, that large part of the ecclesiastical revenues of the Palatinate attached to the church.

Moreover, concluding that the glosses to the eightieth question of the Heidelberg catechism to the effect that the Mass was 'abominable idolatry' were not part of the original catechism that he was bound to maintain, the Elector seized all the copies he could find notwithstanding that his arms appeared on the title page. Politicians, especially in England and Hanover, were deeply convinced that the affair had been worked up by the papal curia to get the Emperor out of Italy and embroil him with England in Germany. This international dimension forced a local dispute to the very brink of war. At the brink the Elector yielded and the Palatine Protestants regained their rights. This retreat proved to be the end of the Catholic advance which had been going on for a century, unhalted by the Westphalia settlements. But this was more clearly perceived in the Chancelleries than among the faithful; among them the spectre of the ultimate Armageddon between Catholic and Protestant still struck fear to the end of the Seven Years War.

The third limitation upon Protestant satisfaction with the peace settlements was the confessional price which had to be paid. In effect the huge number of Protestants in the great triangle between Salzburg, Transylvania, and Poland were abandoned to the tender mercies of the Counter-Reformation. The Emperor was not prepared to make concessions in his family lands. In Silesia where there was a Protestant majority, Protestant worship was to be permitted in the duchies of Brieg, Liegnitz and Münsterberg-Oels, and the town of Breslau, three new 'grace' churches (i.e. churches built by special permission of the peace settlement) were to be built elsewhere, and the Protestant Silesian nobility of other duchies together with their subjects (and the remnant of the Protestant nobility of Lower Austria) were not to be required to emigrate on account of their adherence to the Augsburg Confession. They might attend services at frontier churches in neighbouring territories where the Protestant faith was established, hence the wearisome journeys in summer for communions abroad, and the line of frontier churches on the Saxon side of the Silesian border. These concessions proved to have an unexpected importance in the survival of Protestantism throughout the region, but they were all that were to be had. For Protestants in Salzburg, in Austria, and in Poland (once the land of liberty achieved) there was nothing. Nor was this simply a problem for those who had to endure it; in eighteenth-century New England Jonathan Edwards reckoned that the Protestant world as a whole had been reduced to half its peak strength. Why God should apparently desert his Zion was a mystery, and when 'showers of blessings' were finally encountered, not least in Edwards's own parish, they were greeted with relief as well as joy.

Fourthly and finally the Westphalia settlements did not preserve the central European heartlands of the Protestant world from the depredations of even one of the contracting powers. Louis XIV, who assumed personal government in France in 1661, pursued a long course of aggression along his eastern frontier, inspired at least in part by a desire to balance the gains ultimately made by the Habsburgs in Hungary; these gains left him with a dreadful reputation in the Empire. In 1689 the French ran amok in the Palatinate, and remained till the peace settlement of Ryswick in 1697. Behind the French troops the building of Catholic churches in this Protestant state recommenced, and in places Catholics were permitted to use Protestant church buildings. This was to use duress to make a nonsense of the normal year of the Westphalia settlement, and was held by Protestants to be not binding in conscience; the Catholics replied menacingly that Westphalia itself was an act of force in which they had been pillaged by the Protestants with foreign assistance from France and Sweden. This bitter confrontation poisoned the atmosphere of the Empire for half a century, and the Catholics substantially got their way. Clause IV of the peace of Ryswick provided that in the places the French now gave up Catholicism should retain its present status.

Peace and the papacy

This episode drove home the fact that the principal player on the Catholic side, the papacy, had been as bitterly dissatisfied with the Westphalia settlements as any Protestant, and had consistently refused to recognise them. The papacy had been abandoned by the German Catholic powers and so cut out of the most important peace settlement of modern times. From a Protestant viewpoint the Pope could still be a thorough diplomatic nuisance. Pope Innocent XII gave total support to Clause IV of the Ryswick treaty, and his successor, Clement XI, determined to uphold it at any cost in the next great peace negotiations at Utrecht (1713). His agent, Passionei, was prepared to buy off British backing for the German Protestants by dropping demands for the relief of Irish Catholics, but the Pope, still protesting against the Westphalia treaties, would have no compromise. In 1715 the Pope held a consistory to inform his cardinals of the balance of advantage and disadvantage to the Church. He found especial pleasure in the maintenance of Clause IV and especial pain in the failure of the Stuarts to regain the British crown, the confirmation of Westphalia, the recognition of a ninth electoral dignity (in the choice of the Emperor) in favour of Protestant Hanover, and the royal title of Prussia to the Hohenzollerns; most of all he complained that the suzerainty of the Holy See over Naples and Sicily had been overridden. His rallying-cry for combined action against the Turks fell on deaf ears. The papacy was of course often less aggressive in political practice than in diplomatic claim; but this consistory only confirmed the view of many hard-pressed Protestants that the Pope was indeed the Man of Sin who held the agreements which secured the peace of Europe as of small account beside the advantage of the church.

Confessional Armageddon?

The Catholic powers could not do without papal authority in the management of their churches, but continued to act independently of, or even against, the papacy. The paradox was that at a time when all the great churches offered a systematic theology guaranteed watertight against the attacks of opponents (what was known among continental Protestants as Orthodoxy), and, if possible, supported by the state, the course of events was inexorably undermining the absolute claims made by the confessional programmes. The Thirty Years War, an ostensibly confessional conflict, had shown innumerable examples of what was then known as 'indifferentism', as troops changed sides for pay, irrespective of their religious profession; and the peace treaties giving legal standing to the Catholic, Lutheran and Reformed churches, produced the situation, still characteristic of Germany, that it was possible to pass straight from a parish adorned with all the street furniture of Catholic devotion into one where no such thing was to be seen. Rulers continued to force or induce their subjects to change their religious profession; but as long as the Catholic world was riven by the rivalry of Habsburg and Bourbon, the nightmare of Protestant imagination, a fight to the finish between Protestant and Catholic, would remain a dream. Each side had to pick up allies from the other to meet the needs of the moment.

Protestants had indeed tied themselves in theological and metaphysical knots over this question at the Synod of Dort in 1617. The question there in debate, the issue between supralapsarianism and infralapsarianism (an issue which even in the Reformed world was, before the end of the eighteenth century, being admitted to be incapable of resolution), obtained its urgency from the demands of foreign policy. Dutch independence was still at that date threatened by Spain; that threat might be eased by alliance with France, but the French monarchy was itself at loggerheads with its Reformed subjects whose toleration was always precarious. Was it right to save the Reformed cause in the United Provinces by alliance with a power which would dearly love to end the Reformed cause in France? The supralapsarians held that God's gracious decree of election had been made before the Fall, and, in a sense, in anticipation of human waywardness; if therefore the object of creation from the beginning had been the fine flower of the elect Reformed congregations of the saints, then it would be sacrilege of the worst kind to treat the French Reformed as a diplomatic pawn to be sacrificed for the greater good of the Dutch Reformed. The infralapsarians, holding that God's decree of election was made after the Fall of Man, took the view that even the plan of salvation exemplified how God himself had (so-to-speak) to make the best of a bad job when confronted by human sinfulness, and, if God, why not the United Provinces? Perhaps mercifully, the Bible offered no absolutely cogent evidence for either of these views; nor did Calvin, since he had never been pressed on the matter. The upshot was that the Dutch fought their own corner, including three wars against Protestant England, but at the same time kept up generous financial and other support to struggling Reformed congregations in the Rhineland, the American colonies and elsewhere far down the eighteenth century.

The reconstruction of the Church of England

The Dutch also had a hand in undermining the wilder claims of the one great Protestant success story of the late seventeenth century, the reconstruction of the Church of England. During the civil wars (1640–60) the head of the Church, Charles I, and Laud, the Primate, were both beheaded, and Presbyterianism was introduced under pressure from Scottish armies, themselves later routed by Cromwell's troops. Bishops, cathedral chapters, church courts and the Book of Common Prayer were all abolished by parliamentary action, and in a purge of 'scandalous' and 'malignant' clergy, between a quarter and a third of parish priests were replaced by men of Puritan convictions. The tone was set by Cromwell's ideas of reform and toleration, and the bishops who were left kept a low profile and allowed their line almost to die out. It was not at all clear when Charles II was restored in 1660 who could speak for the (very Protestant and Reformed) Church of England of pre-civil-war days.

The decisive group were clergy and lay advisers, prominent among them Edward Hyde, later Lord Clarendon (1609–74), who had gathered round Charles II in exile in the Netherlands. They would have nothing to do with foreign Protestants, constantly warned the king against alliance with Presbyterians, and sincerely believed that nothing which destroyed the mitre could save the crown. Their dominant influence at the Restoration led to the adoption of a narrow Act of Uniformity in 1662, and the ejection of 1,700 ministers. With the political backing of a high-Tory Cavalier Parliament an exclusive settlement was created and made to work, and life was hard for dissenters. But none of the props of the new system was as secure as it looked. Some two-thirds of the clergy from the Interregnum continued to serve; they were not turncoats, but showed less initiative than either their predecessors or their successors in developing professional associations to further their work. This was serious at a time when the general public would attend church when there was a government drive to make them do so, and stayed away in droves when there was not. Lay magistrates in the counties would enforce the legislation against dissenters as long as they feared a sectarian uprising; but when they began to be alarmed at the international advance of Catholicism it was a different story. Moreover the Church had begun as a religious monopoly symbolised by the godly prince at its head. But Charles II left much to be desired as a godly prince, not least in his intention to secure indulgence for Roman Catholics and others, and the necessities of polemic against papists and Protestant dissenters began to edge the dominant party in the church towards the view which triumphed in the nineteenth century, that the bishop was the sacred symbol and that there was no reason why the boundaries of church and state should be coterminous. Moreover, although the Restoration had given rise to much imprudent veneration of the Divine Right of Kings, it had been an Erastian, parliamentary, settlement, and in 1689 Parliament was to exercise its own dispensing power in the Toleration Act. And when James II finally fathered an heir to the throne, the political parties, faced with the prospect of an indefinite Catholic succession, got rid of him in a remarkably slick operation; but only one bishop, Compton, signed the invitation to William of Orange to come to save the Protestant cause, while six bishops and 400 clergy were speedily ejected for refusing the oaths to the new government. There were snags with apostolic bishops as well as with kings by divine right.

The Protestant succession

But if in William III the Church of England now had a joint head (with Queen Mary) who was a Dutch Presbyterian, he vigorously put down a Catholic rebellion in Ireland and secured an exclusively Presbyterian establishment in Scotland. The position now was that the sovereign was an Anglican in England, and a Presbyterian in Scotland, and there was also a second-class establishment in England of those dissenters who were prepared to make the undertakings required under the Toleration Act. (For those who were not, such as Socinians and Roman Catholics, there was still no toleration.) But for the Church of England, with its apologetic awkwardly built on the Divine Right of Kings and episcopacy, there was worse to come. Queen Anne (1701–14) was acceptable as a loyal Anglican and a Stuart, but could not produce a surviving heir; the succession passed by the Act of Settlement to the Lutheran George I, Elector of Hanover; many clergy were guilty of treasonable talk and some became treasonably involved with the Stuarts, who would no longer dissemble their Catholicism. The fiction that James II had abdicated, and that his son and heir had not been born to him, but inserted into the royal bed in a warming-pan was now fully exposed; too many clergy were prepared to gamble on a Catholic monarch.

This fractious temper was born of a series of disappointments in the practical working of the Protestant constitution since the Revolution of 1688. The Toleration Act, limited as it was, put statute law and canon law (which aspired to bind the whole nation) out of step, and severely impaired the ability of the church courts to compel church attendance; and the lapsing of the Licensing Acts in 1695 and the total ineffectiveness of the Blasphemy Act of 1697, though not creating a free market in news and opinion, made possible open challenges to religious orthodoxy, and were among the things which created the impression in Germany that English scholars were of unusual critical boldness. Moreover in the first twenty years of the Toleration Act, more than 2,500 dissenting places of worship were licensed, and these confronted the clergy with the spectacle of an organised and dynamic schism. Add to this the facts that after the Toleration Act the business in the church courts – matrimonial, probate and tithe causes apart – declined rapidly, but bishops found the courts increasingly useful as a device for disciplining the clergy; that campaigns against occasional conformity and dissenting education proved fruitless; that a great Anglican counter-reformation planned to coincide with the beginning of the Tory Parliament of 1710 obtained very little parliamentary support; and that the clergy were among the financial losers as the bills came in for the great continental wars commenced (primarily for Dutch benefit) by William III, and one may understand why the clergy became restive. Moreover the accession of George I in 1714 brought home the perils of combining an apologetic for a national church with that of a godly prince by divine right. He was in the pocket of the Whigs. Many of the Whigs' wider ambitions fell victim to divisions within their own party, but their intentions were as unmistakable as the use they made of their patronage. Convocation was suspended and the high-church party which had made the most exclusive claims for the church went down before a faction which believed that neither ecclesiologically nor diplomatically could the Protestant cause survive in isolation from the Protestant world abroad.

Church and State in France

There was much in common between the churches of England and France, not only in their social make-up, but in the Erastian relations of Church and State. The liberties of the Gallican church were invoked as often in France as was the primitive character of the Church of England across the Channel, but what they meant in practice was the right of various privileged bodies to unimpeded access to the higher patronage of the church, and these interests varied with time. For the king there was no escape from church affairs. The revenues of the church, estimated in the later seventeenth century at 270 million *livres tournois*, were much greater than those of the state, and the clergy, whatever their mutual rubs and social differences, had a cohesion which the nobility lacked. They met in their own assembly every five years to vote the king a *don gratuit* in lieu of their exemption from ordinary taxes (the English clergy surrendered their right of self-taxation in 1664, and with it the main reason for existence of Convocation). Moreover the monarchy had been granted by Pope Leo X the appointments not only to the bishoprics, but to 700 of the richest abbeys; these were an enormous fund to keep the nobility quiet. Under Louis XIV's predecessors major statemen like Richelieu and Mazarin had built up tremendous fortunes from this fund; Louis wanted no more over-mighty churchmen (they made a comeback in the eighteenth cen-tury), but he had no scruple in easing his budget by treating the upper ranks of the church as a nursery of great diplomats. There was clearly room for considerable trade-off here among king, pope and clergy. The clergy were always rabid against the limited toleration still retained by the French Protestants, and here they were assured of the sympathy of king and papacy. On the other hand royal covetousness of church revenues might not be complacently received in Rome, notwithstanding that monarchy and papacy were generally at one in hostility to theological deviance. All parties in France were willing to plead old customs against the authority of Rome when it suited them, and the French church, which was undergoing one transformation under the pressure of Counter-Reformation zeal and another under the pressure of royal despotism and war, was curiously ready to cover its changes by an appeal to old liberties. Thus there were at various times and in various combinations an episcopal gallicanism, a gallicanism of parish priests (or Richérism), a royal and a parlementary gallicanism. Whether Louis himself changed is a question. A simple-minded Catholic who, like most of his contemporaries of whatever confes-sion, had little notion of toleration in any modern sense, his view of what was due to God combined easily with the need to consolidate his realm behind the rising trajectory of his power in Europe. Protestant, Jansenist, even the pope, might suffer if they got in the way of the cause.

Regalian rights

Take the case of regalian rights. In 1673, after the conclusion of one phase of expansion by the Treaty of Aix-la-Chapelle (1668), Louis set out to extend his episcopal rights to his new territories, seeking the nomination to certain women's abbeys, and to benefices without cure of souls in the gift of a bishop when the see was vacant. These were spiritual regalian rights and were new. Moreover, he wished to claim the revenues of vacant bishoprics, either for the benefit of the royal treasury or for pious works such as the conversion of Protestants. These were temporal regalian rights, long exercised by the monarchy in older parts of the realm, and had long occasioned friction between the clergy who disliked them, and the Parlement of Paris which wanted to see them universalised. For his part the king claimed as absolute monarch the complete disposal of all the property in the country, lay or ecclesiastical, and began to extend his rights by declaration, even nominating several abbesses without the agreement of the Holy See. He had extraordinary success in manipulating the clergy to submit. Two bishops, however, Alet and Pamiers, resisted and appealed to the Pope, and by the end of the 1670s Louis was in open conflict with Innocent XI, an opponent who proved worthy of his steel. The Pope would neither accept the theological backing for the king's position provided by the clergy (the Four Articles) nor institute bishops on Louis's terms. By 1688 thirty-five sees were vacant, and the clergy were exposed to a painful dilemma as to which master to serve. The French violated papal property in Rome and Avignon. Only under the next Pope, Alexander VIII, when war in the Netherlands was going badly for Louis XIV, did the king agree to a settlement: the Four Articles were not to be taught, the members of the assembly that produced them must write an apology to the Pope. In fact temporal regalian rights were extended to most of the country, and Gallican doctrines continued to be taught. Royal and episcopal gallicanism seemed in the ascendant; Parlementary Gallicanism remained to give trouble in the eighteenth century.

The affair of regalian rights was in the end a matter of mostly domestic consequence, a by-product of the rise of royal power; though the interest of the papacy in the matter, and the aggressiveness of French foreign policy gave it an international dimension. The issues raised by the Protestants, Quietists, and Jansenists, however, had a very broad bearing; and it is important not to succumb to a Franco-centric view of them all.

The Huguenots

The clash between Louis XIV and the Huguenots was implicit in the relations between organised religion and public life in Europe generally in the later seventeenth century, and it was made the more certain by Louis's personal unwillingness to brook dissidence of any kind, by his conviction that what France needed was a fierce monopolistic national Catholicism of the Spanish style, and by the calculation that anti-Protestantism was a platform on which pope, king and church could happily act together. Moreover, in 1629 the Protestants had lost the defences which had made them something of a state within a state; they should therefore be a softer target than of yore. And on a broader view, the Reformation in France had not so much failed as achieved a measure of success in the fringes of the country, not least in territories lately annexed to the body of the old kingdom of France. If, therefore, national union was to be the order of the day, Protestantism must be squeezed out. What Louis could not know, but has been made plain by the religious and political cartographers of the last two generations, is that in the long run it was precisely in these fringes of the country that religious practice, Catholic *and* Protestant, was to be most vigorous; and that in the establishmentarian territories of the old kingdom that it was to be most fragile.

In 1662 Protestant loyalty during the Fronde was rewarded in a royal declaration promising to preserve the full toleration granted in the Edict of Nantes. But Louis counted upon the increasingly stringent administrative application of the edict, rewards for conversions to Catholicism, and draconian penalties for conversions or relapses to Protestantism, not to mention the apologetic power of his own spokesmen, Bossuet prominent among them, to destroy the heart of the Protestant community. But even this did not satisfy. A 'Declaration of 40 Articles' in 1669 has been described as a real 'counter-edict' and formed the legal basis for the destruction of meeting-houses, restrictions on Protestant worship, marriages and burials, and administrative harrying of every kind. After the peace of Nijmegen (1679) Louis was at the peak of his power, and shed all inhibitions to embark on a course of savage violence, a course which enabled him as early as 1685 to revoke the Edict of Nantes on the ground that the 'best and greatest part' of his Protestant subjects had embraced the Catholic faith.

Huguenot reactions

How did the Protestant community react? Even before the final blow fell, many, as the King expected, professed conversion to Catholicism, from whatever motives. Many also emigrated while there was yet time. But very many had no skill or capital they could take abroad with them, and they had little option but to stay whatever the hazard; prominent among these were the Protestant peasantry of the Midi, who enjoyed more community solidarity than the business and professional elites of the Protestant movement, were tied to the land, and henceforth constituted a far more important part of that movement than they had ever done before. Each of these groups attained a considerable international importance.

Those who conformed exposed a problem of conscience which could never have been far from the minds of those threatened by French expansion into the Rhineland, and was debated in the United Provinces between two of the exiles from the moment of the Revocation. Pierre Poiret (1646–1719), who will concern us later as a universal salesman of mysticism, was the son of a cutler of Metz, and later a pastor in the Palatinate. Building upon an important mystical tradition, his 'charitable advice' to Huguenots exposed to compulsory conversion was to adapt to Catholic worship. Confessional hostility was not the will of God; the essence of the faith was love of God and self-denial; enough had already been sacrificed on the altar of Reformed shibboleths. Though a Huguenot and a war refugee, Poiret was not strictly a victim of Louis's persecution; his opponent, Pierre Jurieu (1637–1713) was all three. The son of a Reformed pastor and grandson of a theology professor at the Reformed academy at Sedan, where he himself became a professor in 1674, he had become increasingly anti-Catholic rather than anti-royalist as persecution had sharpened. On the devotional side Jurieu was a great advocate of the 'practice of piety' in the Puritan tradition, but he was a stout confessionalist and hoped to awaken the new converts to the virtues of Reformed corporate life as it was exemplified in the Reformed *assemblées* in the Languedoc. The increasing desperation of the confessional struggle in France drove Jurieu towards chiliasm as ferocious pounding drove the Reformed in Hungary. Within three years Louis XIV would be converted to Protestantism. From Poiret's viewpoint this was to crown error with absurdity.

The emigrants who had to escape by night, estimates of whose numbers vary wildly, have been the central feature of the traditional picture. They have been credited with ruining the economy of France to the benefit of the host countries, especially the United Provinces, Brandenburg and Switzerland, and with creating an international political mafia which blackened the name of Louis XIV, and helped to create the Grand Alliances which finally contained his power. Their interest really lies elsewhere. French luxury industries did not always thrive in the colder climate of north Germany, and some at least of the Reformed advisers with whom the Great Elector surrounded himself were justly suspected by the Lutheran Orthodox as being men of very little religion. The Dutch could not maintain their commercial and maritime supremacy with Huguenot assistance, and would have gained their supremacy in the international gathering of news without it. The Swiss, whose generosity in assisting persecuted brethren in the faith was legendary, did not care for some of the theology or some of the social airs which the Huguenots brought with them.

On the other hand the recruiting of the Huguenot diaspora created precedents for states which considered themselves underpopulated to recruit oppressed religious minorities, and familiarised states in the west with the need to mount rescue missions, a need which, in the next fifty years, recurred all too frequently. And whether these policies at a high level encouraged negotiations for church union (to help avoid the horrors of confessional brutality) or led to the reception of alien populations, the edge of confessional exclusiveness was blunted. The forcible (or even peaceful) assimilation of religious minorities – one of the main functions of religious establishments everywhere – was clearly much more difficult than governments and church managements thought. The result of Huguenot immigration in England is particularly instructive. Freed from the worst pressure, these irreconcilables found various routes into English society, some under the aegis of the church, others through the (mainly Anglican) religious societies, others as French Reformed. It is interesting that many were picked up by Wesley in his original stamping ground of the old East End of London; just as at a later date many of the next wave of Reformed refugees, the Palatines, were picked up by him in their settlements in Southern Ireland. In both cases great differences of confessional and theological tradition were readily overcome by the congenial ethos of a movement which was native but not hidebound.

Apocalypse and resistance

The final section of Louis XIV's dissenters were those who remained in France but refused to conform. The toughest of these were the mountain population of the Cévennes. Here Calvinism had penetrated early and deep, and those who adhered to it were prepared to make a fight. They were not *politiques*, were not led by politicians from the upper crust, and had already acquired from Jurieu's grandfather, du Moulin, an interpretation of the Revelation of John which explained their sufferings and offered imminent salvation to those who stood firm. Du Moulin calculated that the persecution of the True Church by the Beast (the Pope) would end with the resurrection of the two witnesses of Revelation 11 in 1689. This scheme could be readily adapted to include the Revocation of the Edict of Nantes, which marked the death of two witnesses, who would lie unburied for three-and-a-half years before their resurrection in 1689. These views were elaborated by Jurieu and clandestinely circulated in the Languedoc. What was happening there was to happen all over Europe where Protestant minorities came under the hammer; the people had to find some substitute for the church which was taken away from them, and in the Cévennes they found it, not at first in the family and small group religion which proved to be the key to survival in most places, but in illicit assemblies addressed by lay preachers who served very well, and in a continuity of religious experience, an experience now strongly tinctured by apocalyptic expectation.

The surprise they sprung left an indelible mark on the revival movements of the eighteenth century. In 1688 prophets appeared among them, a sign that the end of persecution was at hand; and they were children. To complete the guarantee of innocence they prophesied in their sleep. In thus embodying the dead-but-not-dead state of the two witnesses of Revelation they were figures of the true church; as their deliverance drew near their bodies became agitated. The first of these prophets was a sixteen-year-old shepherdess in the Dauphiné, Isabeau Vincent, the daughter of a new convert to Catholicism who had returned to the original faith of her parents. She sang, prayed and preached while asleep, and had no memory next day of what had passed. Soon there were many more like her, embodying, like the lay preachers, a continuity with the past, and prefiguring, as the preachers hardly could, dramatic new hopes for the future. Those hopes were continually deferred. 1689 came and went; the peace of Ryswick (1697) contained no concessions for Huguenots. But in 1701 there was a great revival of prophecy; hundreds of prophets were at work, many of them children with no recollection of normality in the Reformed world. When the dreadful revolt of the Camisards broke out in 1702 they were attached to the Protestant commandos who tied up 20,000 French troops for years, prophesied whether prisoners should be taken or killed, and committed acts of violence against persons and property. Although the revolt took place in the early stages of the War of the Spanish Succession its effects were religious rather than military. Governments did not much care for supporting rebels against their enemies, and although the allied navies were operating in the Mediterranean within reach of the Camisards for most of the war, it was not till 1710, when the revolt was petering out, that a miserably small detachment was landed to assist them. Prophecy produced a sharp division of spirits first among the Huguenots, then in the Protestant world at large. Their eschatology was what eighteenth-century English critics understood by 'enthusiasm', that is, the pursuit of ends without consideration of means. And when resistance was finally crushed, and the prophets were scattered to Geneva, the United Provinces and England, rejection was mainly their fate. On the other hand, the 'revolt of the children', that curious revival in the wake of Charles XII's invasion of Silesia in 1708, was a clear demonstration-effect of the child prophets of the Cévennes, and children were to play a prominent role in religious revival right down the eighteenth century. The 'Inspired' too, though numbering but a few hundred, had an amazingly prolonged after-history.

The Inspired

For the strange psychic phenomena and prophecies made under Inspiration proved almost indefinitely reproducible. In England they were still disturbing the early outdoor meetings of Wesley's ministry in the late 1730s. In Germany respectable theologians would not exclude the possibility that revelation might be mediated by such means; a notable fringe of doctors, professionally interested in the understanding of dreams and miracle cures, attached itself to the movement, and odd psychic gifts, like second sight, seem to have persisted among the German Inspired. When Max Goebel was carrying through the first major investigation of the movement in the late 1840s and almost all the Inspired were in America, he was astonished to find the American brethren sending home, twelve months in advance, modestly circumstantial prophecies of what was to happen in Germany in the revolution of 1848, which none of the German brethren believed would take place. In Scotland there was another circle (to be encountered shortly) of Protestant, episcopalian and Jacobite devotees of the French Quietist, Mme Guyon, and the Belgian enthusiast Antoinette Bourignon, whose own experience of persecution was a milder version of that of the Camisards. There it was discovered in 1709 that Bourignon had herself foretold the Prophets, and in due course the Scottish Quietists assimilated the inspirations and agitations of the French Prophets while the latter assimilated Quietist attitudes towards worship and prophecy.

Yet because the Prophets were soon rejected even by the French Reformed and the Quakers in London, they had to form a fellowship of their own, and in 1711 undertook a burst of missionary activity in the United Provinces and Germany, aiming first at scattered colonies of French emigrés. With these too they had little success, but they did much better with mystical groups, and aroused a good deal of interest among Pietists. Nevertheless the rival interest of the police and *Lumpenproletariat* drove them back into a little group of Reformed principalities in the Wetterau, near Frankfurt, where toleration was to be had for cash, and

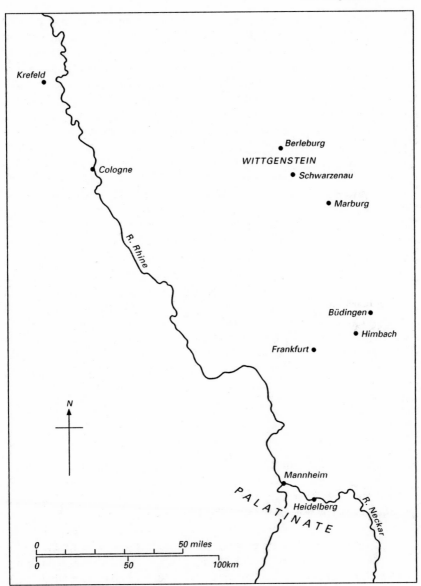

Map 1 The Wetterau

where various groups of Pietists who had fallen under the ban of anti-Pietist edicts at home, had taken refuge. As in Scotland, cross-fertilisation took place. Inspiration not only gave a new impulse to the separatists of the Wetterau, but countered their isolation and individualism; and led to the formation of prayer-fellowships with public and proselytising functions, which encouraged hymn-singing and writing. The result was that the Inspired not only left a considerable literary monument, the Berleburg Bible and a journal which interpreted the signs of the times, the *Geistliche Fama*, but undertook strenuous itinerant evangelism with a view to gathering in all the children of the Prophets, from among all sects and peoples. These took them right across Swabia and into Switzerland. Prophecy had now been transformed into revival, and the original hope of delivery from the tyranny of Louis XIV was transformed into the (equally illusory) expectation that the structure of authority in central and northern Europe had been so undermined that outbreaks of revival might be expected anywhere. But the importance of the French Prophets to the general history of religion in the eighteenth century lies not in the accuracy of their prophecies, nor even in the fact that they form a historical bridge between the millenarian sectaries of mid-seventeenth century England and eighteenth-century revivalists and Shakers. It is that in the geographical range of their activity they reveal the existence of a very widespread vein of millenarianism, even in circles like the Scots episcopalians where it would not have been expected. The eighteenth century was never the Age of Reason exclusively, and, in spite of alarms, was not yet the Age of Reason in any great degree.

Louis XIV and Quietism

If the history of French Protestantism was to show the limits of what could be accomplished by even a powerful and brutal state against religious dissidence, how did Louis fare in dealing with deviation within the Catholic fold? If the problem of the Huguenots, like that of the Protestants in central Europe excluded from the protection of the Westphalia treaties, was how to manage without a church, there were intellectually important minorities in Catholic France whose problem was having too much church, and especially too much church backed by too much state. It was this which brought the Quietist and Jansenist crises to a head in France, but the problems to which they sought a solution were so general as to give each of these movements an international resonance entirely beyond the reach of Louis XIV.

The theological polemic generated by the great controversies of the sixteenth century had led both Catholics and Protestants to develop a systematic and closely integrated presentation of Christian doctrine, hopefully guaranteed against the onslaughts of the other side, but in each case generating religious problems by its very complexity. The heavy (and verbose) dominance of the Word in the Protestant world sapped the vitality generated by the original rediscovery of the doctrine of justification by grace through faith independent of works, and evoked not merely the silent worship of Quakers but other ways of simplifying the union of the believing soul with Christ. On the Catholic side Tridentine Orthodoxy proved to be a burden on the great flowering of Counter-Reformation religious life, and a new impetus to finding ways of lightening or circumventing the weight of the church as a supernatural but institutional dispenser of the means of salvation. There was a great rebirth of mysticism, especially of the practical as distinct from the speculative variety; and within the field of practical mysticism was the growth of the view that meditation and discursive knowledge and the practice of the outer works commended by the church might improve the believer but not unite him with God; whereas the perfection of the Christian life, the union with God, was the fruit of contemplation (or intuitive knowledge). What was needed was the exclusive, disinterested love of God; even vocal prayer was an external work and a likely impediment. The ideal was continual contemplation. The roots of this direct route to God are to be found in the reform of Spanish monasteries in the sixteenth century; in the seventeenth century it had followers in north Italy; and in 1664 a blind Frenchman, François Malaval, published a kind of Quietist work, *La Pratique facile pour élever l'âme à la contemplation*, which called for the suppression of the believer's thoughts, affections, will and speech in the interests of listening to God.

But the real beginning of the Quietist movement came with Michael Molinos (1628–1717), a Spanish priest who spent most of his life in Italy. His fame rested on the instant success of his *Spiritual Guide* (Rome, 1675) which in six years went through twenty editions, appearing in Spanish, Italian, French, Latin, Dutch and German, and was circumstantially reported on in England in letters appended to a travel book by Bishop Burnet. The extent of the demand for the guidance Molinos offered was revealed when the Roman Inquisition raided his private archive of 22,000 letters. The raid itself was characteristic of the roller-coaster history of Quietism. For Molinos enjoyed the favour of the devout Pope Innocent XI, and cardinals beat a path to his door. Unfortunately he also incurred the hostility of the Jesuit order, whose asceticism was of a quite different kind and of prelates who did not care for the way groups of Quietists made light of ordinary props to devotion. Hence Molinos was arrested by the Inquisition in 1685; two years later sixty-eight propositions from his works were condemned, and he was sentenced to perpetual imprisonment. Thus from the beginning Quietism raised the question not only of the way to God, but of who should set the tone of Catholic piety in the late seventeenth and early eighteenth centuries. In the France of Louis XIV the close relations between the King and his Jesuit confessors in matters of religious policy guaranteed that Quietism would raise questions of authority in the state as well as in the church, the more so as a hapless woman, Mme Guyon (1648–1717), showed some capacity to pull wires at court. Alas! the modern interpreters of Mme Guyon, literary, theological or psychiatric, have achieved no more agreement than her contemporary critics.

Her life was one of almost unrelieved tragedy. Born Jeanne Marie Bouvier de la Motte to well-to-do parents, both of whom were in their second marriage, she was married at fifteen to a man of thirty-seven, and at twenty-eight was left a widow with three children. This was, however, the least of her troubles. M. Guyon had, not surprisingly, been perplexed by a wife who in 1672 contracted a spiritual marriage with the child Jesus, and endeavoured within marriage to live the religious life in the technical sense; and after his death his family did not take to the idea that the disinterested love of God justified the abandonment of her children. If she took refuge in the reconstructed diocese of Geneva, where the bishop was struggling to convert Huguenots and educate 'new Catholics', she found him unwilling to add a nest of Quietists to his burdens. If she migrated to Paris there was more trouble, violent attacks from Bossuet, the great preacher of his day, and prison sentences (including a spell in the Bastille); appeals to the king's consort, Mme de Maintenon, did not help. Mme Guyon was not without friends, but Fénelon, who stood up for her, found twenty-three of his propositions condemned in Rome. Only in 1701 did the French hierarchy decide that there was no purpose in imprisoning her further, and she soon settled in pious retreat near Blois till her death in 1717. Indeed one of the curious images of the early eighteenth century is that of Mme Guyon at the very end of her life holding court to Protestant episcopalian Jacobites from the north-east of Scotland. And this was mainly on the strength of appearing a victim of Papal and Bourbon tyranny, and a modest corpus of works, principally *The short and very easy method of prayer* (1685), *Spiritual Torrents* (1688) and her posthumously published autobiography (1720).

There was nothing particularly distinctive about Mme Guyon's formulation of Quietist doctrine. God enjoyed perfect rest in himself, and rejoiced in the contemplation of his own beauty and glory. It was to share this joy that he had created man for himself. The great grace of creation was not that it was created out of nothing, but that man being created in

the image of God's son, must, like him, be the object of God's most
perfect love, and framed to enter God's perfect rest. The highest stage of
the life of prayer was the wordless prayer of the heart, the pure effect of
the spirit of God within. There was no single route to this state of grace,
but *Spiritual Torrents* envisaged three general stages of the spiritual pilgrimage. The first was not specially passive: it embraced the active pursuit
of religious truths, strictness of life, and the exercise of works of mercy.
The end-product would be a religious life based on rule and method, not
unlike that of the young Wesleys. But some would penetrate by passive
contemplation to the second stage, where they would be joined by those
who from the beginning had had the spirit of God in their hearts, without
recognising what the object of their love was. For the distinction between
divine and human love was that the latter was directed to external things,
while the former could be found within in the recognition of the grace
upon grace, the gift upon gift which God had granted. In the third stage,
reached by some elect souls, God himself revealed within the believer the
distance separating him from the object of his desire; and God finally
ended the confusion and anxiety caused by this discovery by revealing
that the treasure sought by the believer was indeed within him and not far
away where he had sought it. Ecstatic astonishment followed. In all this
Mme Guyon continued to regard herself as a good Catholic, com-
municating every three days, but there is no doubt that she had found a
way of circumventing the institutional Catholicism of her day. Fénelon
himself solicited doctrinal judgment on the Quietists, and in 1694 got a
good deal more than he bargained on. Mgr Godet des Marais found her
guilty of four grave errors in asserting that human perfection was attained
by a continual act of contemplation and prayer; that in this state resorting
to acts of charity was of no avail; that the state of total indifference to all
that is not God was legitimate; and that perfection consisted in extraordinary prayer, at which every Christian should aim. Mme Guyon in short
was breaking free from the tried and trusted channels. Recent conservative Catholic opinion has doubtless gone to excess in charging her modest
blow for liberty with some responsibility for both the growth of eighteenth-century libertinism and the rigour of Jansenism. It has taken a
contemporary Carmelite to point out that only Mme Guyon's *Short way*
suffered serious official condemnation, that from a mystical standpoint
pure contemplation is preferable to action, and that interior prayer and
entire devotion to God's will are Christian attributes.

It was Protestants who took up the bait the Quietists offered and that
for three principal reasons. The heavy emphasis on the Word and the
forensic understanding of the doctrine of justification might seem to seal
Protestantism off from the mystical tradition, but they had not produced

all the results hoped for. Many were on the watch for new springs of spiritual vitality, their alertness sharpened by the creaking system of theological censorship which prevailed over much of Europe. In 1687, for example, August Hermann Francke, later the leading name of the second generation of Pietists but not yet converted, in order to assist a disputation on Quietism at Leipzig translated Molinos's *Spiritual Guide* and *Daily Communion* from the Italian into Latin, still the technical language of Protestant theology. Francke did not owe his conversion to Molinos, but he did approve his emphasis on Christ as the sole way to salvation, and his treatment of spiritual temptations. Moreover Molinos reinforced the vein of mysticism with which Francke had already made contact in the impeccable Lutheran source of Arndt, and sharpened his awareness of the vein of mysticism in Luther. What Molinos clearly did not do was to tempt Francke into ecstasy, melting into God, or self-emptying. For him the biblical images remained dominant.

Jakob Böhme

There were two other ways in which Quietism might find a Protestant reception. There were both dissident and conformist streams of mystical piety in the Protestant world. The first found its spokesman in Jacob Böhme (1575–1624), the shoe-maker of Görlitz, whose life was a protest against the Orthodoxies – Lutheran, Reformed and Catholic – which were fighting over the body of Upper Lusatia, and who died when it was finally incorporated into Lutheran Saxony. Böhme dabbled in Paracelsianism and offered an alternative science, religion and philosophy to those of the powerful Orthodoxies. That Protestant Orthodoxy could react against his mysticism and against Quietism quite as fiercely as the Jesuits, was illustrated in 1690 by the huge polemic of the Lutheran Ehregott Daniel Colberg, on *Platonisch-Hermetisches Christentum*, attacking the 'fanatical spirits' in successive chapters on Paracelsianism, Weigelianism, and Rosicrucianism, on Quakers, Behmenists and Anabaptists, on the followers of Antoinette Bourignon (the Belgian mystic), Labadie (a pupil of the Jesuits, who joined the Reformed Church and then went into schism from it) and Molinos. What this showed was that Böhme had offered a way of looking at things which had spread right across Europe into the Netherlands and Britain, had taken off to Pennsylvania, was now taking into itself the Catholic mystics who had fallen foul of the Church, and was in fresh demand by those anxious for some defence against the menace of Cartesianism. These views were also current among the religious radicals of the Wetterau, who (as we have seen) had been influenced by the French

Prophets. The chief of Mme Guyon's followers here was also an émigré Huguenot, Hector de Marsay (1688–1753), who lived to fight off the blandishments of Zinzendorf, the founder of the renewed church of the Moravians, who also in the early 1730s was reading Mme Guyon to his followers. Marsay was a man of considerable influence, and as late as 1769 one of Tersteegen's followers noted that 'in his style of teaching he was very like dear Mme Guyon and also led souls upon the way of mere faith and pure love through a total sacrifice to God and His will and through a basic dying to all things under the guidance of the spirit of Jesus, who was his one and his all'.

Peter Poiret

The Quietists, however, not only reinforced this kind of mystical under-world, they were taken up by the adherents of a major current of interdenominational piety. The key figure we have encountered in connection with the Huguenots; it was Peter Poiret. His search for religious certainty began by attempting to create a synthesis between Reformed theology and Cartesianism, a synthesis which creaked from the beginning. His first published work, *Rational Thoughts on God, the Soul and Evil in four Books* (Amsterdam, 1677), was a rather fragile attempt to use Descartes to combat thinkers such as Hobbes and Locke. Both in vocabulary and in substance mysticism began to show through, and already in 1676, before the book was in print, Poiret had been captivated by the Belgian mystic and separatist, Antoinette Bourignon, and was travelling with her to acquire her doctrine. When she died in 1680 he settled in Amsterdam, and when his own wife died in 1688 he removed to a small settlement of separatist Collegiants at Rijnsburg near Leiden, where he lived till his own death in 1719. This period was not, however, one of withdrawal. He published the works of Antoinette Bourignon in nineteen volumes, and wrote very successfully on a variety of subjects including the education of children. But he also developed his interest in Jakob Böhme, and above all in the French mystics. He avidly followed the great conflict between Bossuet and Fénelon, and published the complete works of Mme Guyon, clearly regarding himself as part of her defence after the defeat of Fénelon. But his output was enormous and underpinning it were his vast library of mystical authors and his index of their works, which was very nearly as complete as could be made at the time. Both were to be of first-class importance. They vastly enlarged his personal resonance, and put texts like the *Lives* of the Marquis de Renty, Gregory Lopez and Mme Guyon into the hands of readers as different in space and time as John Wesley, Suzanne von Klettenberg (who introduced the young Goethe to pietism), or, in the nineteenth century, Mme von Krudener and Schopenhauer, each of whom quarried in his or her own fashion.

Poiret's library passed to the greatest of his later contacts, Gerhard Tersteegen, and underlay Tersteegen's two great achievements: a personal life in which charm, sanctity and learning were equally balanced, and his principal literary monument, his three huge volumes of *Select Lives of Holy Souls* (1733–54; 3rd edn Essen, 1784–86). These thirty-four lives, all of them Catholic and divided almost equally between pre- and post-Reformation saints, were at first sight an odd production for a Protestant with no great sympathy for ecclesiastical pretensions, but they catered for more than the popular milieu of Rhineland mysticism from which Tersteegen sprang. What he spoke to was the tradition of 'true Christianity'. This term was supplied by Johann Arndt whose *Four* (later *Six*) *Books of True Christianity* (1606) constituted him the most devotional of Lutheran theologians, and a significant sign of the times to boot. For it is now clear from bibliographical studies that the Protestant world had never generated enough devotional literature to meet the effective demand and that what seventeenth-century Protestants relied on to stay them through a century of terrible trials was not Orthodox polemic, but medieval mysticism; and that mysticism was mediated through three chief channels, Thomas à Kempis's *Imitation of Christ*, the practical theology of English Puritanism, much of it also medieval in origin, and Arndt, who was very heavily dependent on the late medieval mystics. In Tersteegen's youth Gottfried Arnold in his famous *Impartial History of Churches and Heretics* (1699–1700) had endeavoured to demonstrate the historical basis of this 'true Christianity' among both the churches and the heretics they purged, the 'true Christianity' being the institutional possession of neither. What Christianity was all about, 'the essential truths of of the inward life – the complete denial of the world, dying to one-self, the basic virtues, God's leadings over his elect, . . . to unite them with himself, to reveal the miracles of his grace and love in them and through them . . . these are the truths of faith, based on God's word and on experience'. This last word was the key to the matter.

Poiret, Tersteegen and Arnold were none of them rich patrons indulging a whim to rescue a curious literature from neglect; they were catering for a market which was weary of the high orthodoxies, Protestant and Catholic, and ready for immediate reports of religious experience, however unfamiliar. If there was one thing calculated to make this kind of thing go with a swing in those circles in the west of the Empire where hostility to court mores in which the pace was set by French fashion was deeply ingrained, it was the combined brutality of church and state under Louis XIV against the devotees of experiential religion. There was a sense in which Poiret, inconsiderable as politically he was, played his cards more skilfully than the great Sun King. If he was going to pursue his special vocation, he chose the right base in the United Provinces; Reformed Bern threw up barriers against mysticism as high as those in Catholic France. And as the eighteenth century proceeded, experiential religion (not, it is true, mostly in a mystical mode) became more than the great seventeenth-century systems could cope with. Louis XIV, on the other hand, put his weight behind vested interests in the French church which he could never quite dragoon, and which had limited spiritual vitality; and in so doing he increased the venom of his enemies abroad.

Jansenism

The character of Louis's relations with Jansenism bore many of the same features; deviance within the Catholic fold was contained, but had an extraordinary after-history. In this case Louis wanted papal cooperation in putting deviance down and did not always get it. For this there were three main reasons: successive popes did not always treat Jansenists in the same way; they were, however, steadily resolved to keep decisions on matters of doctrine in their own hands; and finally Louis's original ruthless behaviour towards the Holy See put paid to any goodwill in that quarter with which he might have begun. After a clash in 1662 between the Pope's Corsican guard and the French ambassador's suite in Rome, Louis refused all apology, invaded Avignon, and threatened the Papal States. The Pope was finally compelled in 1664 to erect a pyramid in Rome to mark his undertaking never again to employ Corsicans.

The Jansenist question generated more problems of conscience for Louis's Catholic subjects than anything else; yet Jansenism originated outside the country. Cornelius Jansen, bishop of Ypres, died in 1638, his *Augustinus* being published posthumously at Louvain in 1640 and Paris in 1641. The main effect of the work was in France, where his friend, the Abbot of St-Cyran, had been building up a reform party on the basis of disciplinary and ascetic ideas and a theology of Augustinian provenance. By 1640 the chief elements of the party were the Cistercian convent of Port-Royal, in which the parlementary family of Arnauld was influential, and friends and admirers of St-Cyran, who favoured his attacks on the Jesuits and their laxist theology. In short, Jansenism, like Quietism, raised the question of who should set the tone in the Counter-Reformation, and for this reason incurred the inveterate hostility of the Jesuits. Still worse, a number of highly placed Jansenists were suspected of being involved in the Fronde, and not only did they believe that France should put the Catholic reconquest of Europe before the immediate interests of the

Bourbon dynasty, but Saint-Cyran opposed to Jesuit laxism a moral strictness which would have made Richelieu's foreign policy impossible. For this the great cardinal imprisoned him in 1638. Jansenism was not so much a party line as a way of approaching policy in the church; its adherents stressed the need for conversion under grace and (as a consequence) predestination. The moral force behind this view was provided by Antoine Arnauld's *Frequent Communion* (1643) which (again in opposition to the Jesuits) advocated abstention from communion until the penitent's contrition had been proved. Thus Jansenist and Jesuit took opposite sides in a quite serious problem of pastoral strategy. And although Jansen's *Augustinus* was condemned by a Papal Bull in 1643, the Jansenists as a group had support in the Parlement of Paris and minority backing in the Theology Faculty. The event was to show how difficult it was to put down an elite group even in a church with so powerful a central doctrinal authority as that of Rome.

In 1649 the syndic of the Faculty in Paris got his colleagues to censure a number of propositions, five of them said to have been drawn from the *Augustinus*, a decision endorsed, after further inquiry, by the Pope in 1653. A prolonged exercise of snakes and ladders in the church discipline followed. Jansenists replied that while the Church had authority in matters of doctrine, it had none in matters of fact, and that the condemned propositions were not in fact to be found in the *Augustinus*. To close that door fresh declarations in France and Rome were called for. The accession of Louis XIV began a period of severe persecution. Port-Royal still resisted; Louis, in a curious reversal of roles, asked the Pope in 1665 to provide a constitution and formulary and to command, *ex cathedra*, all ecclesiastics and nuns to sign it. This the Pope did by the Bull *Regiminis apostolici*, making it clear that the matter was one for him and not the French king and bishops to settle. It took a *lit de justice* to get the Paris Parlement to register the edict based on the Bull. Throughout the 1670s the Jansenist question burned low, while Louis's relations with Rome deteriorated on regalian issues, and when he began a fresh series of petty persecutions at the end of the decade, the Jansenists found themselves in the unfamiliar position of having the Pope Innocent XI and ultramontanes as allies, while Louis needed concessions from the Pope as the Pope did not need them from him. The king got the bishops to publish the Four Articles justifying his exercise of authority over the church and incorporated them into the theological teaching of the church in 1682. There were certainly many in the country who did not accept the articles, and all the more after Innocent XI had issued a scathing brief castigating the French bishops for their cowardice in surrendering the rights of the church, and began to block appointments to French bishoprics.

Innocent was equally unimpressed by Louis's claim to have extirpated Protestantism, and by press campaigns accusing him of favouring heretics in the shape of Quietists and Jansenists (though he had certainly considered making Arnauld a cardinal in 1680). At the beginning of 1688 Louis was secretly told that he was under sentence of excommunication. His response was to invade the papal territory of Avignon. France was not far from schism, but extreme measures were prevented by the death of Innocent XI in 1689 and Louis's involvement in a great European war. A compromise was reached under Innocent XII who extracted letters of apology from the French bishops and confirmed them in their sees. The King withdrew the order that the Four Articles be generally taught, and got most of his way with the *régale temporelle*. What now would happen to Jansenists who had been supported by the Pope and opposed the king's claim to regalian rights?

In fact the battle went on much as before, though (as was characteristic of Jansenism far into the eighteenth century) with different leaders and different issues. The reconciliation of the king with the Pope gave him ground for hope that Rome would support his efforts to put down the Jansenists and certainly put a final end to Port-Royal; in 1709 the Lieutenant of Police and his bowmen arrived to deport the last twenty-two contumacious old ladies, shortly followed by demolition squads and drunken grave-diggers (to get rid of the bodies in the graveyard) ostensibly to destroy the memory of the place for ever.

Harlay's successor as Archbishop of Paris was the Cardinal de Noailles, Wake's partner in the negotiations after the Utrecht peace settlement between the English and the Gallican churches, and also godfather to two of Zinzendorf's daughters. His appointment turned the conflict into a new course. In 1695 he had warmly approved a collection of *Moral Reflections on the New Testament* begun in 1671 by Pasquier Quesnel, a companion of Arnauld in exile. Quesnel was now found to be a moral and political danger, and in 1713 the Pope issued the notorious Bull *Unigenitus* which condemned 101 propositions from Quesnel's hoary work, not least his doctrines of irresistible efficacious grace and irreversible predestination. The Jansenists were not alone in objecting to a document which had condemned a book without the author being allowed to appear in its defence, by a Roman congregation, only one member of which understood the language in which it was written. Louis XIV had compromised the sacral character of the French monarchy by securing a condemnation of Jansenism as part of an implied bargain to put down Gallicanism in the French church. Protestants everywhere regarded the Bull as an attempt to make people affirm what they knew was not true, or repudiate what they knew was true; at all events the alliance of pope and monarchy was now publicly on the line, and Jansenism now subtly changed with it, becoming a shibboleth of those opposed to monarchical and papal power, of parlementary Gallicans defending royal power against the Pope and his royal ally, and of lower clergy resisting the bishops. The attack on Quesnel seems to have been launched by Jesuits hoping to discredit Noailles, an objective continued down to the present by conservative historians seeking to present him as a vacillator promoted beyond his capacity for services to Bossuet in the Quietist controversy; certainly it gave the Jansenists a respectable ideological cover and the prospect of respectable allies in the church among moral rigorists and enemies of the Jesuits. Half a century later the alliance of Jansenists and the Paris Parlement still formed the hard core of opposition to the Jesuits, and, contrary to every probability, was able to plot and preside over the destruction of the Jesuit order in France.

After the death of Louis XIV in 1715 the Regent Orléans reacted against recent policies, and promoted Bossuet's nephew to the episcopate from which he had been kept for years by the Jesuits. Pope Clement XI tried to hold up the consecration to force compliance with the Bull *Unigenitus* and was met by threats which sounded like schism; the Regent found the young king a non-Jesuit confessor, who, as Cardinal Fleury, was to achieve a political significance of a quite unexpected kind. Four bishops appealed against the Bull and were subsequently supported by Noailles. The French clergy were now divided into appellants and constitutionaries, the former being denounced by the Pope. The tension in the French church in 1718 encouraged Wake, the Archbishop of Canterbury, to see whether some part of it might not be detached from the Roman obedience, a total pipe-dream as it turned out. Indeed, the alliance of papacy and monarchy reestablished itself. In 1725 under Benedict XIII the Roman council designated *Unigenitus* as a rule of faith, and in the following year a national council turned against both the appellant bishops and Le Courayer who had written a vindication of Anglican orders as part of the push for union. By the end of 1729 only three appellant bishops remained, and as they died they were replaced by strong constitutionaries. Fleury set about purging the religious orders and theological faculties, and control was speedily re-established in the French church. Jansenism, it appeared, was now really *Richérisme,* a policy embodying the dislike of the lower clergy for the upper clergy with secular support in the parlements. In the end in 1756 Benedict XIV was brought to ease the rub by refraining from expressly describing *Unigenitus* as a rule of faith and by discountenancing the way in which people had been refused the sacraments in these disputes. The one loophole for discontent which had not been plugged occurred, surprisingly, in a Paris cemetery.

Saint-Médard

On 1 May 1727, when the controversies over *Unigenitus* were at their worst, a Jansenist deacon of saintly reputation named François de Pâris died in Paris. Two days later, when he was buried in the parish cemetery of Saint-Médard, crowds of worshippers began to flock to his grave, most but by no means all from the rather dowdy area round about. Here they witnessed apparently miraculous cures of otherwise incurable conditions, from cancerous tumours to blindness, deafness and arthritis, posthumously performed by the holy man. The publicity given to these cures led to the development of an unauthorised religious cult and to great notoriety for a hitherto undistinguished *faubourg*. The cult attracted adherents from all over Paris and beyond. By the summer of 1731 the flood of visitors had become unmanageable, and the scenes at the tomb had developed from pious devotions and occasional miracles to the frenzied convulsions of people claiming to be inspired by the Holy Spirit through the intercessions of M. Pâris.

These events obtained their special significance from the *Unigenitus* affair. Saint-Médard provided a rallying-point for the Jansenist party and their lawyer friends, and the miracles, if authenticated, might indicate divine sanction for their cause. As Wesley put it thirty years later, 'if these miracles were real, they would strike at the root of the whole Papal authority, as having been wrought in direct opposition to the famous bull *Unigenitus*'. They also struck at the root of both long-term and recent developments in the church. The whole trend since the Council of Trent had been to eliminate paranormal phenomena, many of them doubtless superstitious, in the interests of the church's institutionalised channels of salvation and grace. Saint-Médard offered a religion of popular participation and unpredictability. Unfortunately the miracles of scripture and the early church had played a major role in the apologetic of both Catholic and Protestant, and were now beginning to fit awkwardly into a well-ordered Newtonian universe. To rubbish the miracles of Saint-Médard with too great abandon might well create apologetic difficulties of a fundamental order.

By the summer of 1731 church and state were too provoked by the cult to leave it alone. Restrictions were imposed and in January 1732 the cemetery was closed. This evidence of ill-will simply confirmed the belief of the convulsionaries, as they were now called, that they had a mission of social and spiritual regeneration, and their efforts to fulfil it let loose a great wave of religious enthusiasm in the French capital. The fate of this Catholic version of the Protestant French prophets was not unlike that of its predecessors. The force at the disposal of the government was never enough to destroy the movement, which persisted throughout the century, but it was amply sufficient to prevent it from realising its aims. Repression had its usual effect of encouraging more eccentric behaviour, even what was called fanaticism in some quarters. The result was that the support which the movement had early enjoyed among opponents of the current policies of monarchy and papacy soon ebbed away, to reveal only too clearly that the convulsionaries were not seeking an alternative church, merely the old church broadened and revivified; and without the backing of the influential that was not to be had.

Nevertheless the convulsionary cult revealed a number of important things about the Ancien Régime in France. Monarchical absolutism had not put an end to the overlapping of jurisdictions in France, and eventually the restiveness of privileged bodies seriously undermined the monarchy itself. The interaction of royal, papal and ecclesiastical authority, and attempts by church parties to manipulate the complicated system in sectional interests, had not helped the monarchy and had clearly created a popular impression that at the official level the redemption of the people was not a major object. It is thought that Louis's backing for church authority as he understood it, coming on top of the religious awakening of the early seventeenth century, produced a level of participation in Easter Communion in France higher than at any time before or since; but the scenes in Saint-Médard showed clearly enough the existence of a desire for a different sort of church. For all the force which the French state commanded, continued respect for its legitimacy depended in a large measure on general acceptance of shared myths and symbols; Saint-Médard showed this consensus wearing thin, and, two generations later, the Parisian districts where this kind of Jansenism was strong were stuffed with sansculottes.

Jansenism in the Low Countries

Meanwhile Jansenism of various sorts had established itself as an opposition force outside France, and especially in the Low Countries and the United Provinces. In the former Arnauld and his friends had taken refuge, but Jansenism owed less to their influence than to the usual conflicts of jurisdiction. In the 1690s the prince-bishop of Liège, Joseph Clement, tried to replace so-called Jansenist teachers in his seminary by Jesuits, and let loose a violent pamphlet warfare. Here Canon Denys, the leading Jansenist, made no difficulties over *Unigenitus*, but preferred Austria to France. The bishop, who held four other sees by papal dispensation without ordination, acquired orders hastily in 1707 when the victories of the Duke of Marlborough were jeopardising his position;

conformity was required by both his foreign policy and his personal position. In the archdiocese of Malines, Humbert de Précipiano (1689–1711) ran a rather violent anti-Jansenist campaign, visiting convents, seizing books and generally trying to get rid of Jansenists. In the United Provinces, Archbishop Neercassel of Utrecht (1686), a rigorist theologian, had been a friend of Arnauld and an enemy of the Jesuits. His successor, Peter Codde, refused to sign the anti-Jansenist formulary, was summoned to Rome in 1699, and suspended in 1702. His chapter refused to accept the Pro-Vicar Apostolic, and the States of Holland forbade the latter to officiate in his territory. From that moment the Church of Utrecht, the Old Catholic Church which still exists, carried on independent of Rome, sympathetic bishops in Ireland and France ordaining its priests till in 1724 it was able to obtain the consecration of a new archbishop. Though it rejected *Unigenitus*, it regarded the crucial issue with Rome as one of jurisdiction. Thus once again Jansenism came to raise the question of ultimate authority in the Church. There was nothing progressive about the general Jansenist position, but having searched the Bible and Augustine to show that Christian doctrine breaks the canons of reason, they found themselves having to fight the battle of those who supported reason in another sense, against those who called for total obedience in Church and State. Thus by virtue of being in opposition they unwittingly contributed something to the great rational reappraisal of Christianity which was taking place elsewhere.

2   Christianity in southern Europe

Italy and the balance of power

The peace settlements of Westphalia, though designed to wind up a conflict in the Holy Roman Empire, also had their effect in southern Europe. Italy had been, and remained, the centre of the Counter-Reformation, and it had been one of the main bases of Spanish imperialism, the great political force behind the Counter-Reformation. That force had been intimately connected with the economic interests of the great Italian towns and ports, but it had been permanently damaged by the peace settlement. Spain remained dominant in the peninsula, could protect the route from Naples to Genoa and Milan, and overawe the Papal States. But the extension of that route through central Europe to the Netherlands had now been permanently severed, and Spain herself grievously weakened. Moreover Spain had now to face the reality of French power in the Italian peninsula. By the treaty of Cherasco France had acquired the fortress of Pinerolo and the adjacent Alpine valleys in Piedmont, and could quickly send a striking force into Italy. The minor Italian states (not to mention the College of Cardinals) lined up on one side or the other of this great-power divide, and dramatic results would have followed had not Louis XIV chosen to make his big drive eastwards rather than south-east. The Peace of the Pyrenees which wound up the conflict between France and Spain left the latter exhausted, while the Republic of Venice, unable to gain effective support from either Bourbon or Habsburg lost territory to the Turks and her Levant trade to the French, English and Dutch. A trading power which had been a thorn in the side of the papacy and the Habsburgs ended as an ally of both, transferring her capital into land. Another disruptive factor in Italian politics had been settled, and one sign of it was the readmission of the Jesuits to Venice in 1657. The Iberian and Italian peninsulas were now isolated from the main theatres of European affairs, and in any case removed from those influences which played on northern Catholicism by virtue of its proximity to Protestant faith and practice. They are therefore worth considering together, notwithstanding huge lacunae in the scholarly knowledge of each.

The church in Spain

The glory of the Spanish church, like that of the Spanish empire, was somewhat faded. Since the canonisation of saints was much assisted by powerful political backing the proportion of Spanish saints declined, while Spanish missionary achievements had diminished and the Inquisition was less active than of yore. Like most of the old religious establishments, the Spanish church had become incapable of dealing with defects in its own organisation. Four new sees were added to the existing fifty-six, but this did little for the rationality of Spain's diocesan structure. Madrid, the capital of a world empire, and Barcelona did not have archdiocesan status; the archbishoprics of Toledo, Santiago de Compostela, Valencia and Seville were enormously rich; other sees like Valladolid were run on less than one-tenth of their income, and the scale of pay for the sees in between in no way corresponded to their scale of importance. But the tenacious fight put up over two centuries by the chapter of Burgos against the creation of the new see of Santander, effectively killed off any hope of further change. This failure at the top in the towns was more important than it might otherwise have been because of the pastoral failing which the Spanish church shared with most of Catholic Europe. British visitors to Catholic Europe generally came back with the impression that Catholic countries were 'priest-ridden' not just because of Protestant prejudice, but because the big towns on the sightseeing circuit actually were priest-ridden in the sense that they attracted huge numbers of clergy who from a pastoral viewpoint would have been better employed in the country. Religious orders tended to settle in the towns where it was easier to acquire the alms and property needed for their work, and huge numbers of secular clergy battened on the possibilities of employment created by the big foundations of the towns. Barcelona, for example, had a cathedral, a collegiate church, eighty-two parish churches, 226 men's convents, eighteen women's, two oratories, a seminary, a tribunal of the Inquisition and several smaller religious houses. In Valencia there were over 2,600 priests and religious in a population of 80,000. At the end of the eighteenth century nearly 3,000 of the country's 19,000 parishes lacked incumbents, the most grievous shortages being in Galicia and Soria, and that at a time when 18,000 priests were without benefices. The censuses at the end of the eighteenth century, when it seems likely that the numbers of clergy and religious had declined only slightly, show that Spain, with a proportion of 1.5 per cent in these categories, was not 'priest-ridden' by the standards of Catholic countries generally, but that only 22,000 of the 60,000 priests were active in parish work. The bulk scraped an existence in the employ of cathedrals and charitable and pious foundations. England, with its Oxford, Cambridge, Winchester, and clergy hanging about the Fleet prison to earn fees for runaway marriages, was not without its parallels to this situation, but by comparison with Spain they were on a minuscule scale.

The career ladder in the church had the same urban bias. The key to progress was to gain admission to a university faculty or a cathedral chapter, and access to them was through a training in theology, philosophy and canon law. Bishops were mostly chosen from among the chapters, and, as everywhere, were mostly of noble birth. As in France bishops often, up to the middle of the eighteenth century, succeeded to high office, but came from the high aristocracy much less often than in France. Episcopacy in Spain provided a respectable and comfortable career for members of noble families of modest means. The bishops, as the century went on, reinforced their charitable and pastoral concerns with efforts to promote social welfare in other ways, but, of course, they could not undo the harmful social effects of the status of the church as an organisation which, as an owner of land and tithe, took large revenues out of the countryside and spent them in towns. Under the economy of the Old Regime the shorter-term fluctuations of the economy originated in agriculture, and recessions were intensified in industry by the shrinkage of the market for popular textiles and other household goods under the pressure of high food prices. The state did little for the poor in Spain; the church did much in times of need. But because the church was financially the sort of body it was, this meant that in the bad years it added the problems of the countryside to those of industry in the towns. In England in times of dearth there were often food riots to stop food leaving the producing areas; in Seville in 1709 the archbishop and chapter provided alms to nearly 20,000 peasants who came into the city in search of food, and Luis de Salcedo, who was archbishop there from 1722 to 1741, gained a great reputation for charity for coping with similar crises in 1723, 1734 and 1737. This form of relief (which was both expected and given) was bound to exacerbate the problems of the towns; but it did not result in anti-clerical riots till the nineteenth century, when an impoverished church was no longer able to give emergency relief on the old scale. For whatever reasons, the Spanish church in the eighteenth century was unable to summon up the resources of imagination and spirit which had distinguished its great days; but it was not singular in the Catholic world in its perversely intellectual attitude towards its rural responsibilities. Seminary training, much of it poor, was what the church authorities thought was needed for the rural clergy; it did not occur to them that financial resources then drained off into the towns might be better employed fixing clergy in country parishes. Not surprisingly the seminaries, down to 1766, were administered by cathedral chapters whose interest in revenues drawn from the country was much greater than their interest in scholarship.

Lacking any coherent constitutional structure and any collective means of expression, the Spanish church was dependent on royal action to solve its institutional problems, a fact implicitly recognised by the Concordat of 1753; this bestowed on the crown almost universal patronage over the most important benefices, a right hitherto shared with Rome. Charles III (1759–88), a devout king whose piety was not quite of the Spanish style, had a real vision of the church's role in a genuinely reforming state, and used his patronage to build up a caucus of enthusiastically royalist clerics in the cause. The quality of the Spanish bishops remained high, the creation of diocesan seminaries was pushed on, there were efforts to curb flagellation in penitential processions, and clergy turned their minds not only to education, but even to the development of manufactures. As we shall see, the Spanish government played a leading role in one piece of ecclesiastical rationalisation, the expulsion of the Jesuits. The practical difficulty with enlightened despotism in Spain perhaps more than anywhere else was that it could not touch a social order dominated by aristocratic and corporate privilege, a domination as evident in the church as in the state. Neither the administrative disorder, nor the lack of contact among bishops, nor the ill-coordination of the religious orders into the church as a whole, nor the maldistribution of financial resources, was touched. The predominant spiritual movements originated outside the country. Even the crisis which church and state had to face together at the end of the century, was anticipated by another age-old issue – ill relations with the papacy.

The church in Portugal

Portuguese Catholicism had never quite enjoyed the role played by Spanish Catholicism in the nationalism generated by the *reconquista*, but it had various features in common with the religion of Spain and France. At the top the episcopacy had the same social character as that in France, the aristocracy affording four-fifths of the eighteenth-century bench, some being promoted from religious orders. And at the bottom there was the same neglect of the countryside as in Spain. There were always plenty of clergy and religious in Portugal; an estimate of 1765 gave 42,200 (as compared with 4,099 parishes). But three-quarters of the secular clergy were reckoned to be without work and cadging from church to church to see if special masses were needed, notwithstanding the permanent shortage of priests in parts of the countryside. The most notorious area for this was the southern Serra, a barren land between the Alentejo and Algarve, which was already being assisted to its present dechristianised state by a shortage of priests. Numerous children died without baptism, couples cohabited for periods without marriage, and there were do-it-yourself burials without a priest, all in the first instance from necessity.

Yet as long as Portuguese commerce kept up and the gold discovered in Brazil in the 1690s continued to arrive in increasing quantities, Portugal was a wealthy country and at one level the Portuguese church enjoyed a golden age. It has been reckoned that one-third of the disposable revenues of the country were in the hands of the church, and of the other two-thirds held by the king and the nobility not a little found its way into ecclesiastical channels. John V spent lavishly to obtain privileges from the Pope. In 1716 he obtained the right to convert his court chapel into a patriarchate, and in 1739 the Pope agreed that the new patriarchate should always enjoy the rank of cardinal and should be filled by a member of the royal family. A special church was built in Lisbon, canons were created and endowed by a quarter of all the benefices in Portugal. Later Rome agreed that the canons should all be cardinals and that the patriarch should have a quite extraordinary dignity. The king himself in 1749 obtained from Rome the title of 'His Most Faithful Majesty'. Moreover, the generation from 1720 to 1750 was a splendid one for the building of churches, chapels, hermitages and convents. Most spectacular was the church-monastery of Mafra 42 kilometres from Lisbon, built between 1717 and 1730 by a labour force of 50,000. Huge sums were also spent on the importing of foreign religious articles, but there were sufficient monies over to sustain a small army of skilled native workmen producing church furnishings and decorations. A fresh period of activity which lasted for fifteen or twenty years began after the Lisbon earthquake of 1755.

The effect of all this on the towns varied from place to place. Lisbon, to the Protestant eye, was the quintessential 'priest-ridden' town, with thirty-seven parishes, thirty-two monasteries and eighteen nunneries in a mid-century population of about 270,000; in smaller towns like Braga 6.2 per cent of the population and perhaps 10 per cent of the adult population were under vows. But whereas in the big towns the surplus of unemployed clergy was a matter of resentment, in the smaller towns church spending was crucial to the local economy. The wealth of urban religious foundations was inevitably a magnet for the upper and lower classes alike. The nobility would not miss the opportunity to quarter younger sons and ineligible daughters upon the religious orders, a practice less a source of abuse than of relaxation and comfort. The eighteenth-century increase in population also brought country people into the towns, many of them non-practising. In Portugal as in Spain one of the most successful devices of the church for retaining the affections of lay people were the confraternities (*irmandades*) which were important to male sociability and also protected interest groups. Confraternities took three principal forms: there were those dedicated to the Blessed Sacrament which conveyed the Host in processions; there were professional groups, beggars, the blind, the brotherhood of carpenters from the Lisbon arsenal which was a sort of friendly society, tailors, masons and others; and there were the Misericórdia. These last were modelled on a confraternity established in Lisbon by Queen Leonora in the fifteenth century. They were under royal protection and claimed that this exempted them from church control. Many nobles and some clergy were among their leading figures. These confraternities increased *pari passu* with the religious orders, and by the middle of the eighteenth century there were towns in which a third of all funerals were escorted by confraternities, grand or humble as the case might be. But as in Spain the confraternities seemed to be losing their hold before the end of the eighteenth century, and the simplest explanation of this would seem to be that they were not able to assimilate the influx from the countryside to their ways. It was also true that the clergy were never quite happy with religious festivals and processions outside their control. The concern of the clergy was with profanities which would creep into institutions dedicated in part to sociability, but conflicts within the church provided much of the public entertainment in an eighteenth-century Portugal devoid of ordinary political life. Clergy fought over money; the seculars fought the religious; poor religious orders fought wealthy ones; the Inquisition, reinforced by lay familiars, kept watch over popular religion, sexual morality and heresy, but were often opposed by the bishops. The latter in turn collected little information about religious practice because the legal and social pressure to conform produced a result acceptable to them. There were signs in the eighteenth century that in Portugal as in Spain differences between a relatively devout north and a somewhat Laodician south which became apparent in the next century were already emerging; and the experience of Italy was to show that not all Mediterranean Catholics were as readily satisfied as the Portuguese bishops, and their experiments were to have a resonance throughout the Iberian peninsula.

Catholicism in Italy

There were two major differences between the religious situation in Italy and that in any other of the western states. There was no unified Italian state and hence no single Italian church. The fate of the Catholic church in

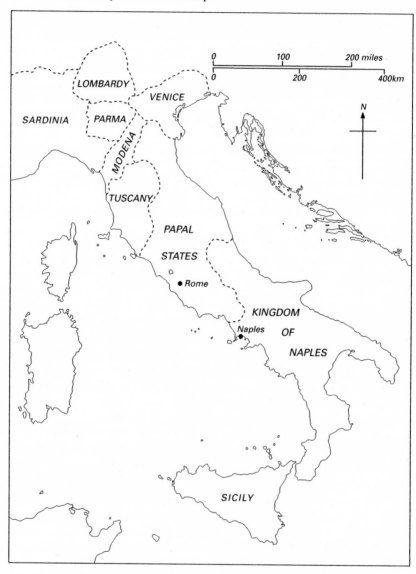

Map 2 Italy in the eighteenth century

Tuscany or Venice in the north might be very different from that of Naples in the south. Then, secondly, the papacy itself was present in Italy, and present not merely as a spiritual authority but also as a second-rank political power in the form of the Papal States. Though Italy suffered the same political decline as Spain and Portugal, she produced in the seventeenth century one pope, Innocent XI (1676–89), who was prepared to stand up to the bullying of Louis XIV, and in the eighteenth another, Benedict XIV (1740–58), whose reign marks the commencement of a distinct period in the history of the Italian churches. One common feature of the Italian churches, however, was that the episcopate was less aristocratic than in the churches of the west and north. In the Kingdom of Naples, with 131 sees, the aristocratic component of the bench remained constant at about 30 per cent, most of whom were recruited from the younger sons of noble families who served in the most learned religious orders such as the Benedictines and Theatines, and were raised to the bench through the patronage of the king himself. In the Papal States there was a social change in the episcopate, as the representation of both the aristocracy and the religious orders declined in the eighteenth century, despite the fact that there were always important sees near Rome which were governed by aristocratic bishops who were also cardinals. What was very noticeable was a great increase in the number of bishops of local origin who had made a career in the curia or in local pontifical administrative bodies. To this extent the papacy was choosing a provincial role as well as being forced into one by the great powers of northern Europe. As in Iberia there was no shortage of clergy in Italy, indeed the numbers of clergy seem to have reached their peak in the first half of the eighteenth century. There was no uniform system of parish patronage. In the south many parishes (in some parts as many as two-thirds) were in the gift of capitular clergy who appointed curates who then required only confirmation of the appointment by the bishop. In central and northern Italy some clergy were appointed by the bishops and some by lay patrons or communities. Lay patronage was most highly developed in the Republic of Venice and in Tuscany. Patronage, however, mattered less than the quality of the clergy, and the general quality of the clergy mattered less than the special insight required to grasp the particular mentality of a rural population who were often poor and still more often adherents of a mixture of magic and Christianity, itself adapted to cope with the problems of rural life.

Missions

The great difference between Italy and the Iberian powers was that Italy was and remained the centre of the Counter-Reformation, and that one of the glories of Italian Catholicism had been the missions conducted up and down the country with greater or less imagination by Jesuits, Capuchins and members of later orders, especially Redemptorists and Passionists. Matteo da Bascio, a Friar Minor Observant, who in 1525 was authorised by Pope Clement VII to preach freely all over the Papal States, launched the Capuchins and tried to go back to the rule of St Francis. Yet he was quite clear that preaching was less significant than hearing the truth; it was the work of Martha rather than Mary. The true missionary had to devote the greater part of his time to meditation, silence, retreat and privation, and then descend from the mountain to address the people under a fresh impulse of the Spirit. The preacher was thus a prophet who might legitimise his mission by miraculous cures and revelations about the future. The Capuchins did not get papal leave to go beyond Italy till 1574, and did not have permission to bring in the Forty Hours Devotion which they associated with their missions to France till 1593. In this devotion the sacrament was exposed in a church or a succession of town churches for forty hours in memory of the time between the death and resurrection of Jesus, and also of the number of days he spent in the wilderness. The faithful, attracted in crowds by the concession of a plenary indulgence to those who confessed during the ceremonies, venerated the Host and were invited to meditate on the central mysteries of Christianity by several sermons a day. As a devotion for export the Forty Hours amounted to a communal affirmation of beliefs most intensively attacked by the Protestants, especially the real presence, the eucharist and the value of indulgences. In France the Capuchins came to be regarded as the mission preachers *par excellence*, and the order grew there with astonishing rapidity, reaching a peak of almost 7,000 in the early eighteenth century. Popular with the poor because they were themselves poor, devoted to apostolic preaching on a conservative basis, and the antithesis of the traditional monk, they were liberally supported also by the Catholic elite as a militant defence against Protestantism.

The Jesuits, unlike the first Capuchins, began by regarding mission as their exclusive work. The spiritual basis of the mission was formed by Ignatius's own *Spiritual Exercises*, and the strategy was to be decided on by the head of the order with a view to the multiplier effect which accrued from the political backing of men of high rank, great nations or important cities. The tactics of the missions were also carefully prescribed. At first they consisted of catechism, preaching and assistance to the poor. But as early as 1540 a fourth theme appeared which was to become central – preparing the faithful for an examination of conscience with a view to confession and communion. This was based on the first week's discipline of the *Spiritual Exercises*.

Thus even before the Council of Trent a choice of missionary strategies was available in the Church, and before long the central machinery was adapted to exploit them. After the organs of oppression such as the Holy Office (1543) came the German College (1555) for training clergy for the regions most affected by heresy, and, above all, in 1622 the creation of the congregation for the propagation of the faith (Propaganda Fide). The purpose of the institution was to coordinate the whole missionary enterprise of the Church and to bring under the control of the curia what had been the responsibility of Catholic princes, prelates or missionary orders. In this work of centralisation, Propaganda was not entirely successful, but on the way it acquired a huge body of information and expertise. The years which followed the end of the Thirty Years War were marked by a quite stupendous missionary impulse. Groups of secular priests and religious set to work in every part of Europe, often led by men of real distinction, and employing methods which had been well tried in Italy and later in France. Nothing like this systematic effort had been seen since the early church.

The most eminent preacher of all was Fr Paul Segneri, who covered the whole of Italy between 1665 and 1692 and created a succession of revivalists who continued his work into the eighteenth century. In the same way, in the impoverished south the work begun by Cristofarini was continued in the early eighteenth century by Anthony Baldinucci, who evangelised some thirty dioceses. The missioners adapted their methods to the demands of hearers of various social levels. Fr Peter Ansalone (1653–1713) preached for forty years in Naples, aimed at a cultivated public, and employed choirs and processions, but like many revivalists he was prepared to turn the emotional screw. He subjected himself to the discipline in public, and at the end of his mission would have an *auto da fé* of bad books and personal adornments of which he disapproved. The Jesuit Francisco de Geronimo (1641–1716) who was canonised in 1839, endeavoured to repair the inability of Neapolitan clergy and monks to approach the people by creating two new congregations, the Public Congregation of the 200 which was held every morning and feast day, and alternately held meditations and exercises in prayer called *Novissime*, and a second and more advanced Secret Congregation of the 72, which met on the first and third Sundays of the month, and every Sunday in Lent. Here was another attempt to put a permanent spiritual impulse behind the emotional preaching in the streets and public places, the open scourgings. Nor did these early Italians shun the use of statistics made by their American Protestant successors. Ansalone is said to have made thousands of conversions in the course of 448 missions; Geronimo claimed an annual total of 100 to 450 over twenty years, and was further legitimated by miracles *post mortem*. Missions of this kind went on throughout the eighteenth century, and generated institutions to continue their work and develop it in new ways. They also produced a stratum of pious evangelistic laymen, one of whom, a young nobleman, Alphonsus Liguori, began his mission to the Neapolitan poor.

Alphonsus Liguori

Alphonsus seems to have been a shy youth with an almost pathological horror of corrupting his purity by contact with the opposite sex, and like Wesley was a brand plucked from the burning, or at least saved from death by the special intervention of the Virgin. 'From the altar at which he received the all-strengthening bread of angels, he went forth to preach the law and love of God to the people of the city and kingdom of Naples, producing everywhere wonderful conversions of abandoned and most notorious sinners of both sexes to the practice of the most exemplary virtue.'[1] Alphonsus's spirituality was indeed based on union with the Redeemer effected by contemplation of the Cross and the Eucharist, the love of the Virgin and prayer. In his *Visits to the Most Blessed Sacrament and to the Blessed Virgin Mary* Alphonsus offered a devotional booklet with prayers before the sacrament and prayers to the Virgin which to a Protestant eye go far towards identifying the 'law' of God with Christ and the 'love' of God with the Virgin, who is constantly praised as the source of grace, prayers to whom 'are so many links in the great chain of our predestination'; on a practical level, she is praised also for her power to heal and save, as Alphonsus himself had experienced it. Here was a direct appeal to meet the needs of the poor, and for massive acts of charity, especially in the countryside. Here a long period of economic stagnation before 1720 and the great famine of 1764–66 had intensified rural poverty. Alphonsus had indeed a perception of the needs of the poor, an eloquence of calculated simplicity based on the fear of hell and on trust in the Virgin to approach them (he circularised many bishops and heads of religious orders on this); he had also a grasp of the institutional realities needed to generate continuous effort, founding seminaries to enlarge the missionary force on which he could draw. He founded a congregation in 1732 which in 1740 took the name of the Most Holy Redeemer, discovered the advantages of what the nineteenth-century American revivalists were to call 'the protracted meeting' (fifteen to thirty days) a century before they did, enlivened the proceedings by disciplining himself three

---

[1] *Lives of St Alphonsus Liguori* [and others] *whose canonisation took place on Trinity Sunday, May 26, 1839* (London, 1839) p.9.

times with a thick rope, had the knack of getting landlords to pay for the missions, and, planting a cross at the end, began to give the Italian parish an identity it had hitherto lacked. In addition to the usual three religious vows of poverty, chastity and obedience, his Redemptorists took a further vow of perseverance; and above all devoted themselves very extensively to the countryside, that mission territory on the doorstep which had been so neglected by the church. The vision and the opportunity were not enough to sublimate difficulties within the order itself. Alphonsus met difficulties in the diocese to which he was unwillingly appointed in 1762, and was hounded from his own order when it split between Neapolitans respecting the authority of their king and Romans affirming obedience to the Pope. At the very end of the century, however, two young Germans pulled the order together, and gave it a different evangelistic mission, not of reviving the faith of backsliding Italians, but of converting to Catholicism Protestants and Eastern Orthodox in the Baltic region. Alphonsus himself received unusually early recognition by the church. Canonised in 1839, only fifty-two years after his death in 1787, and formally declared a doctor of the church in 1871, his *Glories of Mary* has appeared in 800 editions and eighty languages, while his moral theology became standard in Catholic seminaries in the nineteenth century. He also had a powerful influence upon the definition of the doctrines of the Immaculate Conception of the Virgin in 1858, and of Papal Infallibility in 1870.

The Passionists

Another evangelistic order, that of the Passionists, was founded by a northern Italian, St Paul of the Cross, in 1725. A soldier by trade, whose wish was to defend Christendom against the Turks, he lost his comrades in arms and retired into the wilderness with some fellow-penitents. Their work was to evangelise the ignorant and the poor. By 1741 he had authority to impose on his followers the three religious vows plus a fourth of devotion to the Passion, a severe rule which was eased in 1769 and (after his death) in 1785. By this time the order was established in Belgium and England, and also embraced a women's order subject to a strict rule. After the 1720s the Passionists established a network of small convents and hermitages to provide a base for their missionary work, in spite of the opposition of the traditional mendicant orders who resented competition for the alms of the faithful. Like the Redemptorists, the Passionists saw it as part of their mission to rescue the ignorant from sub-Christian beliefs and practices, and in this respect they were working with the grain of reforming governments and bishops trying to curb the excesses of popular demonstrations, and to put down penitential and nocturnal processions. The Passionists encouraged public adoration of the eucharist, especially in the evenings, to allow peasants returning from the fields to participate, and did in fact change the relation of the faithful to the Eucharist which had hitherto been little used outside the Mass (where reformers of a Jansenist style wished to keep it). Meditations on the sufferings of Christ and on the Virgin encouraged by the Passionists were designed to emphasise renunciation as a lesson of Christian virtue and to sublimate social tensions. The Jesuits encouraged the rather gentler family devotions of the Sacred Heart, and the Franciscans pushed the Stations of the Cross, but the decisive difference to popular devotions in eighteenth-century Italy, especially in the south, was made by the spread of the cult of the Virgin. In the first half of the century confraternities devoted to the Rosary and Our Lady of Mount Carmel became very popular, while the popularity of saying the rosary in public each evening as a collective devotion took very deep root. And the great impulse to these Marian devotions was given by Liguori and the Redemptorists.

The Catholicism of the people

In their various ways these late offspring of the Counter-Reformation remind British readers of the itinerant evangelism of the Methodists, and they raise the questions of what the religion of ordinary Catholics was like, and why the zealots thought the ordinary pabulum of church practice inadequate. It is reasonable to assume that, although the piety of the Catholic church as a whole was affected by the outbreak of the Reformation, in southern Europe, where Protestantism obtained very little toehold, Catholic spirituality was less subject to modification by the daily presence of alternative models, and this may be one reason why it gave birth to evangelistic orders whose main object was the conversion not of heretic or heathen but of underperforming Catholics. It was here that the threefold character of late medieval piety persisted longest. There was no very sharp distinction between the areas of the sacred and profane, which is one of the reasons why superstition is a subject difficult to treat judiciously. Nor was there much uniformity in devotional practices which varied endlessly from place to place with there being no clear preference by church authority. The upshot of this lack of direction was that the faithful could reinforce their own preferences by selecting from an ample menu of spiritual procedures which varied between world-affirming church celebrations and world-denying mystical withdrawal, between trust in God and fear of the devil. They also varied between the reliance on outright non-Christian auguries drawn from birds and animals to the abuse of sacred Christian objects such as holy water to protect men and animals, sacramental wine to cure eye diseases and holy oil as an unguent. There were similar perversions of sacred seasons and rites. On Holy Saturday those infected with leprosy or scabies would plunge into the sea to the accompaniment of church bells in the belief that a cure would follow. Flagellation rites which in Tuscany were an act of penance, became in the south a rite which replaced the remission of sins outside the sacrament of penance on the grounds that the soul was purified by an individual's own blood. There were also exaggerations of the cult of relics in which the clergy participated which De Rosa has described as 'magico-sensitive'. What was unmistakable was that in southern Europe the level of popular education was even lower than in the north, and that while the upper classes (and the bishops) might entertain their own favourite superstitions, they were distanced from those of the masses by superior education. The line taken by church authority was to build up the church as the sole fount of spiritual blessings and to make detailed liturgical provision for hazards which the flock could not escape, be they cattle-plague, flood or fire. By commonly accepted modern distinctions between Christian belief and magic, some of these provisions were as superstitious and manipulative as the magic they sought to replace, but the intention was to supplant rather than exploit credulity.

There were three great difficulties with this approach to a very intractable problem. The first was the general belief in the virtue attaching to sacred objects, places and persons. Bells had been rung as a precaution against storms since ages before there were any Christian churches, and in Spain were still rung to improve the harvest, in the belief that only rainwater, not irrigation, would do for wheat. The Archbishop of Bologna in 1735 found himself publicly arguing that the blessing of bells had no effect on the weather, but that he wished people to give more heed to the blessing of bells. Here the sacredness of calls to prayer was being confused with more immediate and tangible advantages to which the blessing of the church appeared to give access. Within seventeen years of Franklin's invention of the lightning conductor in 1752, a Protestant church in Hamburg installed one; before the end of the century German Catholic churches were putting them in. But this was a long way to the north; and church bells in southern Europe continued to enjoy a prophylactic reputation beyond their deserts. Sickness was another unavoidable trial. There were sharp limits to what medicine could be expected to accomplish; perhaps exorcism was called for, perhaps it was even a panacea. For exorcism to work, sacred places, or, still better, sacred persons, were called for. In early nineteenth-century England exorcism seems to have been an indispensable part of the equipment of Primitive Methodist preachers, than whom no one dismantled more of the conventional apparatus of the Catholic past; but the ability to convert qualified them as (superior) sacred persons, and the demand for their virtue was still lively. How much more in the Spain or Italy of the seventeenth century?

How the virtue of sacred persons worked, and how Redemptorist piety fitted, or could be adapted to fit the circumstances of the Italian rural poor, may be illustrated by the case of St Gerardo Mailla who flourished in the second half of the eighteenth century in the Kingdom of Naples, a sun-scorched region of endemic poverty. Ninety years after his death the pressure for his canonisation came predominantly from peasants, and the judges, who inquired whether the witnesses had been indoctrinated by Redemptorists hoping to increase the prestige of their order, found that the saint was the best known and most invoked in the Italian south. He was a saint of peasants and labourers; he protected animals and women in labour. The miracle with which he began his career signified what was to come; the infant Jesus descended from his mother's arms to play with him, and brought him bread of exceptional whiteness which he took to his mother. His visions were always of a useful character and involved his responding to popular request. Bread, which he distributed from his monastery without respect to the needs of the monastic community, commonly featured in his visions. Moreover the vicious cycle of poverty, dearth and epidemic, from which the local people could escape only by miracle, he could ease by destroying rats, which devoured the grain stores and brought plague, by making the sign of the cross on the ground. His frequent ecstasies sound like epilepsy, and helped to give him a reputation for curing the possessed. Of his type he was a virtuoso, taking as his model Jesus scourged, and undergoing such ferocious discipline that his bloody mortifications became sacred relics. In all these respects Gerardo Mailla was unlocking divine resources to ease the most intractable problems of the very poor. That he fitted the styles of piety promulgated by the Council of Trent, or even the Redemptorist order, is much more doubt-ful. The severity of his discipline suggests that both he and his admirers were subject to currents of eastern asceticism which the western church had tried to root out. He flirted with madness which was outside the bounds of Alphonsus's piety; he was utterly remote from the humanist culture of the Tridentine Fathers. Alphonsus had taught means of aiding neighbours by prayer; Gerardo Mailla succeeded with his particular neighbours, who were still untouched by the elite religion of the Counter-Reformation, better than Alphonsus, precisely because he worked on the frontiers of magical practices and superstition.

The second difficulty of church authority in dealing with popular superstition was that there were important areas where the upper and

lower classes stood together. Two of these were witchcraft and pilgrimages, yet both reveal the pulling apart of the upper and the lower orders.
The witch trials of the seventeenth century affected Catholic and Protestant alike and as we shall see were much more a feature of central Europe
than of the south. Yet the last judicial execution of a witch took place in
Spain as late as 1781 and during the great witch craze of the mid-
seventeenth century, judges and other men of property and learning
could be as fierce against them as any man in the street convinced that his
misfortunes were the result of a spell. Yet lawyers became harder to
convince that credible witnesses of nocturnal mayhem could be found;
one Italian, Beccaria, of the Austrian territory of Lombardy, in his treatise
On Crime and Punishment, attacked the use of torture in legal systems, and
with the decline of torture evidence became still harder to collect. Evidence against witchcraft for a great debate in the Munich Academy of
Sciences in the 1760s was supplied by the Italian historian and reformer
Ludovico Antonio Muratori (1672–1750), a zealous priest and eloquent
advocate of a rational and well-ordered devotion. Not merely did the
witch craze disappear from the courts, but the advice dispensed by the
church on the best way to protect oneself from spells seems to have
become superfluous. Pastoral handbooks which early in the eighteenth
century had commended the faithful practice of church duties, the sign of
the cross, devotion to the Virgin and other sovereign remedies in this
juncture, say less and less towards the end of the century. The presump-
tion must be that priests were less often called upon for assistance in this
area.

Pilgrimages – the seeking out of specially holy places – had various
things in common with the cult of saints, and they too in many parts of
Europe were devotions which united the faithful of all social levels. But
pilgrimages in a rather more convoluted way repeated the history of
witchcraft. On the one hand the faithful showed an endless fertility in
discovering and venerating new places of blessing, and this in itself
weakened the demand for journeys to the celebrated medieval pilgrimage
centres like Compostella. And on the other both church and state began
to discourage longer pilgrimages, and to favour those which could be
accomplished in a round trip of a day. This reduced the drain on the
labour force, took less money out of the parish, and perhaps carried less
moral danger. Governments began to ensure that these hazards were not
realised; in 1771 the government of Venice refused passports to would-be
pilgrims to Assisi, while that of Austria banned overnight pilgrimages in
1772, confiscated endowments to help pilgrims in 1773, and banned all
pilgrimages unaccompanied by a parish priest in 1784. Yet what to the
authorities in church and state was a religious custom the disadvantages

of which readily outweighed the advantages, was to the restricted women of southern Spain almost the only opportunity for a jaunt. And by no means all workmen were enamoured of pressure from above for greater productivity at the expense of holy days and pilgrimages.

Canonisation

Canonisation had a similar history. Fr Jean-Baptiste Labat, a French priest, describes jovially in his *Voyage en Espagne et en Italie* (1730) what had happened to induce Rome to get the process of canonisation into its hands. Canonisation, he maintained, had originally been a recognition of martyrdom, and when the option of martyrdom was ended by the imperial peace it seemed a pity to close the gates of heaven to those who would have accepted it, given the opportunity. So bishops would assemble clergy and people and inform them of the merits of suitable subjects, proclaim them saints without more ado and render the worship due. Abuses crept in. A saint would sometimes carry with him his father, mother, brothers and sisters and even his wet-nurse. Chapters canonised their bishops and monasteries their abbots. Rome opposed this torrent of instant sanctity, and its first weapon was that of delay. But the second was to develop principles of selection, and the nature of these is more clearly suggested in the nature of the candidates who failed to make the grade than in those who succeeded. A definitive discussion of the whole matter was provided by Benedict XIV in his work *De servorum Dei beatificatione et beatorum canonizatione* (1734–38; revised 1743). One of his principal concerns was that of false or feigned revelations and prophecies claimed by or attributed to visionaries who were commonly, if not exclusively, female. On this ground, as well as others, women tended to fall foul of a patriarchal authority, the canonisation of one at least being delayed for centuries by the hostile testimony of a Franciscan chaplain that her mystical trances were merely epileptic.

By the end of the Middle Ages a type had been established that was educated, orthodox and clerical, and, in the words of André Vauchez, 'it is clear that *vox populi* is no longer considered the *vox Dei* and that, in certain cases it tends to be identified with the *vox diaboli*'. Thus a number of claimants to sanctity from early seventeenth-century Naples were women whose case was based on alleged powers of prophecy, and they failed; in the early eighteenth century the Naples claimants were mostly men whose successful claim was based on miraculous powers of healing and who were not felt to be as subversive as the prophetic 'living saints' of the earlier generation. This shift in official opinion was not unnaturally supported by a considerable body of medical and legal literature assessing the evidence offered for sanctity, and a tightening up of the whole process on the institutional side as the Sacred Congregation of Rites and Ceremonies, founded in 1588, got into its stride. The result was a shift from a theological to a juridical definition of sanctity. The revival of the church's missionary work both abroad and at home in rural Italy, for example, brought with it a revived acceptance of the miraculous, and a willingness to use it to rekindle devotion. Since now religious practice and devotion seemed more important than knowledge and belief, the veneration of saints could be stripped of its doctrinal message and transformed to fit local ritual systems. Not quite consistently with this there was a huge output of lives of saints in Italy which responded to central policy in the church by presenting their heroes as models of virtuous action. And in this literature, by the early eighteenth century the most visible and safest mark of sanctity consisted in miraculous powers of healing. Thus of the twenty-nine candidates who came successfully through the process of canonisation in the eighteenth century, the fact that twenty-one were Italian and Spanish illustrated the political influences upon the church, while the fact that five were specially concerned with nursing, and two of them were the two most celebrated founders of nursing orders, Vincent de Paul (died 1660, canonised 1737) and Camillus de Lellis (died 1614, canonised 1746), illustrated the current trend of official policy. It was indeed a measure of the success of official policy at one level that procedures for canonisation received much aristocratic backing (and thus reinforced social solidarity) but had sufficient popular acceptance to contribute to the local rooting of church teaching.

Mariolatry

There was, however, a third and final difficulty confronting the evangelisation of the rural south and its harmonisation with official policy. The central offices of the church were offering a legalism of sanctity; the evangelists, for all their adaptation to a popular market, were offering law in a peculiarly naked form. The Jesuit missions, and those of the Redemptorists which were based on them and supplemented them with devotional instruction, did not merely seize on the fact of sin and make confession a central evidence of conversion, but made religious terror, heightened by histrionics, a device for bringing home the reality of damnation and securing a response from the flock. If, however, Christ personified the law of God under which all were by nature condemned, escape could only be found by pursuit of grace elsewhere in the Christian pantheon, and especially at the hands of the Virgin.

Legalism and triumphalism went hand in hand. The new accents of

Marian devotion in the early modern period went with the titles 'Help of Christendom' and 'Honour of the Peoples'. Officially Rome proclaimed only the first title, but the other embodied much popular feeling and inspired many papal utterances. There was indeed some tension between the doctrinal caution exercised by the Council of Trent in this matter and the popular enthusiasm expressed in pilgrimages, dedications and the habit of Christian armies and fleets after the victory over the Turks at Lepanto (1571) of carrying Marian images into battle under the shelter of the title 'Help of Christendom'. A great deal of paganism was reclothed in Marian dedications, and church authority had to defend itself against the wild concourses let loose by reports of miracles at Marian places of grace. But the Jesuits (as we shall see) sought to turn Marian enthusiasm into an engine for elevating the whole life of the church through Marian congregations; and they overcame the doctrinal reserve of Trent in a systematic development of Marian doctrine. In this they were followed by Redemptorists, Capuchins and a powerful French school. It was always possible that this technical development might blunt the edge of a popular perception of an outpouring of divine grace, but Mary remained the central figure of the piety of the later Counter-Reformation, and most especially of southern Italy. To her were dedicated 214 of the churches of Naples (to St Peter only fifteen). At the beginning of the eighteenth century the city of Naples had eleven miracle-working Madonnas. In 1708 Pope Clement XI ordered all Catholics to celebrate the feast of the Immaculate Conception and in 1716 the Marian victory festival became a rosary festival. The brakes on this process were not yet removed. A monk petitioned Clement XIII (1759–69) to define the doctrine of the Assumption of St Mary. The Pope referred it to the Inquisition, who filed it away. Nevertheless the result of enormous effort to reclaim rural Italy for Christianity had been to instil a Mariolatry powerfully adapted to very local purposes. The same parties worked across Spain and Portugal on a lesser scale, with many of the same results. What meanwhile had been happening in central and eastern Europe?

3 Catholicism in the Holy Roman Empire and the eastern Habsburg lands

Witchcraft

East of the Rhine and north of the Alps (as in Italy) the Roman Catholic Church was putting down magic and inculcating Christianity however remotely after the pattern of the Council of Trent and relying on well-tried Italian methods and missions. The problems of superstition were much the same in Protestant as in Catholic territories; in each there had been violent persecutions of witches in the first half of the seventeenth century, and belief in witches was connected with magic generally. One of the oddities about the witch trials was their geographical concentration. Beginning in Spain, they spread to Spanish Italy, north Italy and England, and there were powerful persecutions in southern France and Switzerland. But the worst was in the west of the Holy Roman Empire, where about half of all the executions, some 30,000, took place. In addition about the same number came off with lesser penalties and a similar number of suspects were not brought before the courts. (In Russia and the Balkans there were practically no witch trials.) For centuries there had been occasional trials of practitioners in magic; but since the later Middle Ages theologians had constructed a doctrine about witchcraft which led to charges not just of damage but of membership of a sect of witches pledged to annihilate Christianity. Once the belief got about that witches had concluded a pact with the devil, it was not difficult to credit that there were nocturnal dances or sabbaths of witches, gathering under the presidency of the devil for sexual orgies and for planning mischief. And the courts were able to extract confessions to this effect. There were always some, men of sense and theologians, the army of Gustavus Adolphus and Spanish Jesuits, who were against the witch trials. However, the profile of the witch obtained such clarity as to unite Church and State, Protestant and Catholic, in suppressing a form of religious deviance obnoxious to both.

The great period for witch persecution was between 1580 and 1680, and not the whole of the Empire was affected. There were virtually no witch trials in north-west Germany or Mecklenburg; there were sharp bursts in Bavaria though apparently much less in total than historians have believed; and the intense persecution was concentrated in the ecclesiastical territories of Bamberg, Bayreuth, Würzburg, Mainz and Eichstätt, in the western territories of Trier, the Saar, and Lorraine, and also in Württemberg. In large imperial cities such as Nuremberg, Frankfurt, Augsburg and Regensburg witch trials were few, and were often quickly given up; small country towns such as Wemding, Nördlingen or Ensisheim might be notorious for witch burnings. No one of the numerous theories of the witch craze seems to cover all the cases. Certainly the churches provided the theological fantasy against witchcraft, and the witch trials fit into the wider campaigns against superstition which they were waging; though it is a little odd that they should reach their peak when the churches were most violently at loggerheads with each other. It is also true that the peak of the witch craze came during the severe weather and dreadful agricultural recession of the early seventeenth century, for which there was an urgent popular demand for explanation. The churches, Catholic and Protestant, offered self-flagellation, real or metaphorical, as a means of appeasing the wrath of God; witchcraft offered an explanation by means of which responsibility could be shuffled on to third parties, and encouraged people to put pressure on the authorities. It has even been alleged that witchcraft trials were a device for intensifying male dominance over women, or of putting down the contraceptive knowledge of one special class of witches, the midwives and wise women; but there were easier ways of establishing the one without entangling so many men in the processes of law, and success with the other would have been so self-defeating as to make it impossible for villages to increase their population in the way they later did. And although some Catholic churches were clearly deeply involved in the witch hunt, others, such as the Austrian church, with its twenty-eight special liturgies for almost every conceivable agricultural hazard, provided against the popular anxieties which underlay the panic in other ways.

The imperial church

The Reichskirche by contrast was less well-equipped, being not so much an institution as an idea. It consisted of the remains of German episcopal and monastic power that had administered the west and the south of the Empire for centuries. It was now a loose federation of petty bureaucracies operating like other federations within the federation of the Empire itself. The Reichskirche supplied not only what ideology the supra-national Empire still had, but it occupied an ostensibly grand position in the

Reichstag. There were there sixty-five ruling archbishops, bishops, abbots and priors, forty-five dynastic princes, sixty dynastic lords and sixty imperial cities. But the Reichskirche was confronted by a huddle of Protestant powers organised as the Corpus Evangelicorum; its sixty-five rulers governed only fourteen per cent of the territory of the Holy Roman Empire and twelve per cent of the population, compared with eighty per cent of the land and population governed by the dynastic princes. Clearly, forward policies would be governed by the provisions of the Westphalia treaties which Protestants claimed as a fundamental law of the Empire; and here the difficulties began. For not only did the elective processes of entirely aristocratic chapters by which the great prelates came to the top give a unique opportunity to lay powers, and especially the Habsburgs, to interfere, but the lay powers had an agenda of their own. Many were looking to full royal status outside the Empire. Saxony found a foreign crown in Poland, Brandenburg in Prussia, Hanover in Britain, Hesse-Kassel in Denmark. And most serious of all from the standpoint of the Catholic cause in the Empire, the Habsburgs, who held on to the title of Holy Roman Emperor, were bent on confirming a dynastic empire in Hungary, gaining one in the Balkans and Italy, and supporting the family interest against the Bourbons in Spain. The complexity of all this was revealed in the early eighteenth century when the Emperor, the lay head of the Catholic world, had as his Imperial Vice-Chancellor Friedrich Karl Graf von Schönborn, himself bishop of Bamberg and Würzburg and a member of an outstandingly successful family of ecclesiastical magnates, with relatives (and patronage) in the sees of Speyer, Konstanz and Trier. Schönborn wanted to reinvigorate the machinery of the Reich, and pursue a forward policy. It was, however, not to be, and major conflict in the Reich was avoided, sometimes by a very narrow margin, until the cudgels were taken up by Frederick the Great in 1740.

One of the things which inhibited Catholic advance in the Reich was paradoxically the greatest Catholic triumph in the seventeenth century, by which the Habsburgs had wrested the crown of Bohemia from a Protestant claimant at the outset of the Thirty Years War. This victory they underpinned by irreversible social engineering. The lands and titles of the Protestant gentry and aristocracy were expropriated and they were replaced by a Catholic aristocracy and religious houses which would hold their lands in mortmain. This Catholic aristocracy profited enormously from the upheaval in terms of capital gains, but on current account they were very heavily taxed. They were prepared to fight to keep out the French, but they wanted no Spanish adventures, they sought to push the Habsburg enterprise into the south and the south-east, and wished to secure their northern borders by the absorption of Bavaria and by agreements with Protestant states in the Empire. Moreover, they had access to a second machine of government in Vienna, the Hofkanzlei, separate from the Reichskanzlei which Schönborn operated. Thus a Catholic victory in the Empire was indefinitely postponed by the very forces intended to seal the triumph of the Counter-Reformation in Bohemia, and their influence was paradoxically confirmed by the dynastic embarrassments of the Habsburg family. After the early death of his only son, the Emperor Charles VI had only daughters born. He provided against the possibility of the failure of male heirs in 1713 by a family statute called the Pragmatic Sanction. His possessions were to pass whole and undivided to his male heirs; failing them to his daughters, and failing them to the archduchesses, the daughters of his deceased brother. It was this arrangement which in 1740 permitted Maria Theresa to succeed him, not in the Empire, but in the various crowns and titles by which the Habsburg family lands were held. To secure international recognition of his scheme Charles had to pay a price not least to Protestant powers; and, as we shall see, at the time of the Protestant *cause célèbre* in Salzburg in the 1730s, that price included sacrificing his freedom of action in the Catholic cause.

Pietas Austriaca

The Habsburgs indeed had adopted the Counter-Reformation as a platform only at a fairly late stage, and much of what they had done in the hereditary lands amounted to reconquest, for in 1560 even Vienna had been a largely Protestant city. At the same time they had been engaged in a long-term struggle with the ancient enemy of Christendom, the Ottoman Turk. As late as 1683 Vienna was again under siege by the Turks, but in the sixteen years which followed the raising of the siege the Turks were pushed back again and Hungary was largely freed from Turkish threats. In view of these fluctuating fortunes it is not surprising either that 'Pietas Austriaca' became the emblem of the dynasty, nor that relations with Rome were often uneasy. The brutal methods used by the Habsburgs to cordon off Protestantism as a movement in their hereditary lands served less well in Hungary, which could not in any case be made a going concern without Protestant immigration. The organisation of the church in the hereditary lands would not serve, and in Hungary needed to be created from the ground up; no one of the Habsburgs thought that Rome should interfere with the superior wisdom of royal absolutism in this matter. What the Habsburgs relied on was a mixture of very importunate ideological propaganda, missions and fresh organisation; these they pursued with much consistency from the beginning of the eighteenth century, and something must be said of each.

The claim to universal empire sustained by the Habsburgs fitted well with the universal claims of Rome, whatever friction there might be between particular emperors and popes; and the Habsburgs had fought their way to glory at the expence of heretics and infidels, and had helped to bar the expansion of France which only too often had allied with both. And it was notable that in their polyglot realms no trouble arose from an alliance of Gallicanism and nationality. 'Pietas Austriaca' was the theme of a genealogical work dedicated to the dynasty by the Italian Franciscan and Innsbruck court chaplain Diego Tafuri (*De Rebus Austriacis*, 3 vols., 1655–60). This work traced the descent of the Habsburgs from the Trojans, and claimed that they had earned seven-fold their greatness, happiness and fame through their 'pietas'. In alliance with the sun and with Hercules, they had defeated the dragon which wanted to destroy their rule. The Habsburg eagle, represented in red, white and red, held in its heart the sacred host. The triumphal train of 'Pietas Austriaca' was preceded by a lion bearing the keys of St Peter in its mouth. The rock on which the church was built was actually the rock of Austria. This apotheosis of the House of Austria formed the theme of the magnificent decorations of the ceremonial rooms of the rebuilt abbey of St Florian and a hundred other baroque buildings sacred and secular. It was born of a long struggle to recatholicise the people and represented a synthesis of church policies of the ruling house, the pastoral zeal of individual reforming bishops and the spiritual commitment of old monastic foundations and new religious orders. If the new court propaganda had been simply poured down from the top it would have been less effective than it was, and might even have encountered more of the robust vulgarity familiar in modern Ulster with which it was occasionally greeted by the Protestant peasantry. But 'Pietas Austriaca' took up into itself popular elements; most notably the dynasty contested with the Protestants the religious roots of Czech nationalism by adopting the veneration of John of Nepomuk on a great scale and securing his canonisation in 1729. Nor is there any mistaking the huge sense of public relief brought about by the defeat of the Turkish menace in 1683. Among the earliest decrees to go forth from the court on that occasion were orders to restore churches, monasteries, roadside shrines and monuments. The official line was also embodied in a great wave of church building in elaborate Italianate styles right through the family lands but especially in the Vienna basin, Lower Austria, Styria, Moravia and most of all in Hungary. The alliance of church and political establishment came out in the way in which the Habsburgs and great nobles built for themselves in the same style, and monasteries built great new churches, libraries and ceremonial halls to receive visiting royalty; while the way in which native architects and craftsmen took up with the new fashion suggested a popular response. An Austrian Catholic scholar has described Austrian baroque Catholicism as 'public, demonstrative, extrovert and theatrical; its manifestations embraced all the human senses, thematically and symbolically linking artistic representation and concrete instruction'.

Baroque churches

Austria was not the first to introduce baroque architecture on a big scale north of the Alps (the Italianate cathedral in the principality of Salzburg dates from the 1620s); her military entanglements were hitherto too great. Bavaria had also suffered a good deal in the second half of the Thirty Years War, but occasional baroque building towards the end of the war became a conscious programme after the peace. Again the dynasty took the lead. The Elector Max Emmanuel, who had helped the Emperor expel the Turks from Hungary, was married to the Savoy princess Henriette Adelheid. With her came an Italianate court, a confessor from the Theatine order, Salesian women's orders in Munich, and the very latest in court festivities, theatre and opera productions, for all of which Italian artists were required. Court building, for example the Elector's summer residence at the Nymphenburg, was the first to be affected, but it was followed by striking church building. The influential example was that of Henriette Adelheid with the Theatinerkirche in Munich. This was modelled very exactly upon the mother church of the Theatines in Rome, and built to the highest standards of quality. It set a pattern in two respects. Like early baroque church building generally, it was heavily dependent on architects and craftsmen from Italy or Italian Switzerland (the Tessin or Graubünden), and its stucco work was reproduced in the monastic churches of Benediktbeuern (1680–83) and Tegernsee (1684–89). The impact of Italian missionary orders in Bavaria was profound. The churches of the Discalced Carmelites in Munich and Regensburg strictly followed the Roman classical baroque. The Jesuits were the chief patrons of the style and they built churches in Munich and Dillingen, and outside Bavaria in Innsbruck and Vienna, Lucerne and Solothurn, on the pattern of the mother church of the order, Il Gesù in Rome. Passau, the gothic cathedral of a diocese which reached deep into Austria, succumbed to fire and was rebuilt in the Italian style. But the striking thing about Bavarian baroque (especially in the eighteenth century) is that it was overwhelmingly not an urban phenomenon, but was embodied in village churches and pilgrimage chapels. It was here that the building boom came closest to the daily realities of the religion of the people; some monasteries were heavily engaged in the business of receiving pilgrims, and might justify lavish expenditure on their chapels on that ground; ordinary pilgrimage chapels were paid for by the pilgrims themselves. In Austria native architects (and especially J. B. Fischer von Erlach, who defeated an Italian competitor with his design for the Karlskirche in Vienna in 1716) supplanted Italians rather earlier than in Bavaria, but their work did not reach the villages in quite the same profusion. In Switzerland the contest between Catholic and Protestant was still being fought out on the battlefield well into the eighteenth century, and there was no royal patronage. There baroque building was the work of the great monastic foundations at Einsiedeln, St Gallen, St Urban, Rheinau and Disentis (Graubünden).

The religious message of baroque architecture made it important to the missionary orders; this was humanist to the extent that earthly order might be shown to be a reflection of the heavenly, as the authority of prince and pope might be symbols of the heavenly king. All the arts were called in to lead the worshipper to transcendent invisible realities. In a Reformed church the worshipper might be alone with the scriptures, revelation enough; in a baroque church he was always in the presence of the whole company of heaven and often of earthly majesty also. Moreover the principal weapon of the Catholic missionary orders in the struggle against popular superstition on the one side and Protestantism on the other, was the veneration of the Host; it followed that the high altar was given increasingly monumental dimensions and elevated upon steps. Pillars must not impede the view of the high altar, and side altars must lead the eye towards it. If the altar was to attain the majesty of distance but earth and heaven were to combine in the worship, then somehow a longitudinal axis must be combined with a circular togetherness; this requirement was met with a ground plan of a longitudinally set oval, and often a round arch and dome. The dome indeed could be practically useful in permitting the indirect lighting of the decorations. In many great altar compositions heaven and earth are linked in a thematic unity which extends from the altar painting to the statuary above and even to the ceiling fresco, a unity symbolic of the real presence in the sacrament. And everywhere within the church, steps, pillars, windows, were grouped to recall the symbolic numbers 3 (for the Trinity), 5 (the wounds of Christ), 7 (the words from the Cross or the sorrows of Mary), 12 (the apostles). The absence of straight lines or flat surfaces was to vitalise the building and create an ambience for joyful worship.

Less joyful was the cost of all this building and remodelling. Monasteries could supply some materials cheaply from their estates and also some *robot* labour; but vast sums were required for skilled men and artists. Some perforce were met by the sale of estates, but the great recourse was to credit, voluntary and involuntary, often up to two-thirds of the total cost. Credit or the guarantee of credit was provided by private persons of often modest standing, and here again public policy was shown to enjoy a degree of popular support, or it was granted by wealthy monasteries to parishes or institutions in which they had an interest. But by the beginning of the eighteenth century there was not enough voluntary credit to be had, and recourse to forced loans was unavoidable. In Bavaria church property was managed by the state and used almost exclusively to provide compulsory credit for church building. Monies obtained in this way were commonly interest-free and subject to very extended terms of repayment, so that they were more like grants. In 1768 there was a general mandate by which all church monies must be repaid or converted into loans at 3 per cent. But eight years later some repayments were not even begun, and large sums were still outstanding at the end of the eighteenth century. In Austria too, much of the money seems to have come from aristocratic or ecclesiastical revenues which evaded tax, though doubtless a perennially embarrassed treasury provided more than it could afford. But to take the financial brakes off church-builders, especially abbots, was, to say the least, imprudent. Many had to be dismissed by their chapter and their financial affairs put under compulsory administration. Nor was God much glorified by allowing the Electors of Bavaria to get into the way of administering church property so as to help themselves. The heavily indebted abbey of Rott am Inn was still unfinished when the abbeys were secularised at the end of the eighteenth century; but the credit needs of the modern state had in effect secularised church revenues long before.

The reform of church organisation

Whatever the case in Bavaria, in much of Austria and Hungary 'baroque Catholicism' remained something of a facade; the peasantry of Upper Hungary were apt to blame the later stages of the Turkish wars on the Counter-Reformation policies of the government, while the Protestants of Austria were not enamoured of the missions sent to convert them by the Jesuits, or by the activities of the latter as landlords; and they were always likely to become restive under influences from outside the borders, especially in Silesia and Salzburg. Recatholicisation in many areas would not become a vibrant popular fact without a more effective church structure and a good deal of missionary effort. Ferdinand III had created 300 new parishes in Bohemia, but as no parish could have a priest unless it provided him with a stipend of virtually gentry level, and as neither aristocracy, emperor nor monastic houses were willing to return confiscated property in their hands, parishes were bound to remain unfilled. If an incumbent proposed to levy surplice fees, he was soon in trouble locally. Meanwhile cathedral chapters rigorously excluded commoners, and the most notable prelates were recruited from the Thun, Auersperg, Firmian, Harrach, Wallenstein, Kollonitz, Schaffgotsch and Trautson families, all of whom belonged to government circles and the richest noble houses; it was the Catholic aristocracy which obstructed a commission of inquiry on the church in Bohemia appointed by the Estates at the end of the seventeenth century. In Austria and Bohemia together about fifty abbots and priors sat in the Estates, and they were scarcely less aristocratic than the bishops.

Because the Habsburg area was one of late conversion or recolonisation, it was for a long time subject to bishops who were suffragans of Rhenish sees and governed enormous dioceses, though there had been some recent additions. Early in the eighteenth century six bishops and one archbishop served a population of 4 million in Silesia and Bohemia. Lower Austria was dependent on the Bavarian bishopric of Passau. The see of Vienna comprised only the capital and its suburbs, and the bishopric of Wiener Neustadt was even smaller. In 1717 Vienna was raised to a metropolitan see with Wiener Neustadt as a suffragan diocese. Part of Upper Austria was subject ecclesiastically to the archbishopric of Salzburg and part to the patriarch of Aquileia – the Republic of Venice. Three more sees were added in the eighteenth century but by that time the population had increased by half. The bishops might be, and up to a point were, a force for missionary enterprise, but the parish structure was not well fitted to capitalise on the results they achieved. Vienna possessed only three parishes within the walls, though each suburb outside had its parish church. In the rest of the country things were worse, for the parochial structure had been frozen since the high Middle Ages, and now met its needs less appropriately than that of the Church of England in the early nineteenth century. In the mountains many churches which are now parish churches were then non-parochial chapels which had difficulty in finding a priest. Defects of pastoral organisation made the church more dependent than ever upon religious orders, particularly the missionary and Italian orders, which left an especial mark upon Austrian baroque piety. They also left an indelible mark upon Vienna, which might have only three parishes, but possessed also 200 religious buildings including 33 churches and 47 chapels. The number of convents there almost doubled between 1683 and 1760. The Jesuits not only played a key role in all this, supplying confessors to the emperors, and creating colleges, seminaries and residences right across Austria and Bohemia, they also trained most of the bishops and senior clergy of the country at the Collegium Germanicum in Rome. Austria was not as bereft of parish organisation as was England of the specialised religious agencies which abounded in the Habsburg lands, but the disproportion between the activity of regular and of secular clergy would be bound to be challenged if the regulars did not complete the work of defeating Protestantism begun by the sword.

The Habsburgs and the Protestants

The Habsburg desire for religious uniformity was continually whetted by political hazards. The problems created for the Protestant world by the need on one flank to salvage their co-religionists from the Habsburg Counter-Reformation in Silesia and Bohemia, and on the other from the miscalculations of the archbishop of Salzburg will be discussed in chapters 4 and 5; there were also problems for the Emperor. At the time of the Swedish incursion into Silesia, his hands were tied by his involvement in the War of the Spanish Succession; at the time of the outbreak in Salzburg, they were tied again by the need to secure recognition of the Pragmatic Sanction. Had he in the latter case contributed to a great Catholic triumph, France might have got up a great row in the Imperial Diet and destroyed his agreement with Prussia. On the other hand he had whetted the appetite of those around the king of Prussia for more settlers from his domains. And his own Protestant subjects in Carinthia were now exposed to the enthusiastic attentions of Salzburger revivalists; here unrest was a problem into 1735. In response, Charles VI established the main lines of Habsburg Protestant policy down to the time of the Patent of Toleration. An imperial resolution of 1733 proposed a combination of evangelisation and force. Not least, every effort should be made to break the international dimension of the domestic confessional difficulty. The Emperor should deny the *jus emigrandi* conferred on religious minorities by the Westphalia settlement, and rebuff the excited interventions of the Corpus Evangelicorum at Regensburg. Protestant communities which resisted conversion should be broken up by forced labour, militia service on the Hungarian frontier or transportation to Hungary or Siebenbürgen, transportations which the Habsburgs could never manage with the minimal loss of life achieved by the Prussians in getting the Salzburgers to the Baltic.

Here were exposed the dilemmas of Habsburg policy. Fidelity to the Counter-Reformation set a domestic problem, and was inimical to the development of the new empire in Hungary. If the missions did not work, the only alternative seemed to be the use of force. The Habsburg system was only capable of putting the Protestant communities under really serious pressure in time of peace, and serious pressure on people with no hope of escape by emigration had the perverse effect of evoking the signs of religious revival. Maria Theresa, having disentangled herself from the War of the Austrian Succession, began to renew the cycle of pressure in the early 1750s, and there were already signs of reconsideration. Maria Theresa (as we shall see) sent Fr Pius Manzador, the Provincial of the Austrian Barnabites, to Rome to see whether a package of reform measures could not be negotiated with papal support. His recommendations amounted to a tightening up of all existing measures to a degree which amounted to a qualitative change.

More significantly, there are signs that the *dévot* Maria Theresa believed that the Italian-style mission which had been the great staple of the crusading Counter-Reformation (and had already been condemned in Italy by Muratori as exaggerated and overdone) had come to the end of its usefulness, and needed to be replaced by a new style which had been developed in Bohemia by the Jesuit Fr Ignaz Parhamer. Austrian Jesuits were indeed sent off to Bohemia for re-education. The essence of the Bohemian scheme was that it embodied a mechanism of long-term effort and a greater appeal to the understanding. There should be two kinds of missions, long-term and itinerant (*missiones stabiles et missiones vagae*). The former should not replace ordinary pastoral care but supplement it for the special purpose of combating heresy by missionaries who remained members of their own organisation. They should cooperate with the itinerants for the main end, use extraordinary means and have an extraordinary stipend. The great object of the mission was to combat ignorance. When the mission began, first small children, then boys and girls, artisan apprentices, male and female servants were divided into groups, each including an examinator. The groups and examinators were watched over by prefects. Each group had a flag bearing the image of their patron, and one of the emotional peaks of the mission came with the dedication of the flags. These missions, it appears, had some success, thousands joining the *Christenlehrbruderschaft* and many continuing to go to catechism lectures in the longer run.

The new turn revealed the unwillingness of the bishops (so many of whom were based outside the Habsburg family lands) and the existing missionaries to change the methods to which they had been pledged for so long. Only one bishop, Leopold Ernst Count von Firmian, bishop of Seckau, was prepared to have the catechetical missions. Inevitably Maria Theresa's mind began to turn to the only remaining possibility; when this Firmian became bishop of Passau (1763–83) she called in 1771 for a plan for the redivision of parishes, a plan which would more fittingly have come from the bishop himself. Thus force of circumstances had driven Maria Theresa not merely to follow the family tradition of shaping the church to suit the circumstances, but to the starting-point of what her son Joseph II would undertake under the influence of the Enlightenment. Moreover, this plan of a revived parish system represented a turning back as well as a move forward, for it seems to have owed much to French Jansenist examples mediated by a consort and other advisers with Jansenist connections. The leap of imagination which was beyond the Counter-Reformation mind of Maria Theresa was that the straightforward way both to quieten the Protestants and even tempt home some of those who had fled abroad was by a Patent of Toleration; and this Joseph II was to grant in 1781.

Habsburg policy in Hungary

It may be argued that however defective Habsburg policies were when judged by the exclusive aims of the Counter-Reformation, they produced most of what the dynasty wanted. There was never a Protestant rebellion in the family lands; the arms of the kings of Prussia inflicted far more damage on Habsburg power in Silesia than their flirtations with Protestant minorities deeper in the system; and persistent Austrian diplomatic pressure upon Saxony prevented any major haemorrhage across the northern frontier like that suffered by the archbishop of Salzburg. This pragmatic argument serves less well in the case of Hungary, where the same policies were pursued with more brutality and less success. Seventeenth-century Hungary was divided into three parts: in the west was a Habsburg kingdom continually exposed to Turkish threats, in the centre was the area of permanent Turkish occupation, and in the east was the Principality of Siebenbürgen, strong enough to provide some protection for Protestants in the first half of the seventeenth century, but of diminishing strength thereafter. Hungary differed from the rest of the Habsburg lands in three ways. Siebenbürgen (or Transylvania) was unique in Europe in that in the sixteenth century its Diet had adopted fundamental laws granting equal status to Lutheranism, Calvinism and Unitarianism alongside Roman Catholicism. It was still substantially Protestant by the beginning of the eighteenth century, and it was so valuable as a base against the Turks that as late as 1690, Leopold I (as king of Hungary) had confirmed its peculiar legislation. The second distinctive feature of Hungary was that it possessed a vigorous system of representative local government; in the Habsburg mind Roman Catholicism and absolutism were inseparable, but in Hungary they had a system of local government to overthrow as well as the adherents of the Protestant churches. Finally military triumph had enabled the Habsburgs to get the Protestant aristocracy out of Bohemia and Austria, but in Hungary they remained and were especially strong among the Magyars. This meant that the Protestant peasantry in Hungary were never as defenceless as they were in the west. Furthermore the tactical necessities of the war against the Turks brought the Habsburgs to make repeated concessions to Protestant liberties which they had no intention of maintaining. As soon as the Thirty Years War was over they began the attempt to impose religious uniformity. It took sixteen long years of warfare after the ending of the siege of Vienna finally to get the Turks out of the country, but before the job was done the Explanatio Leopoldina (1691) subjected all Protestant parishes to the supervision of the local Roman Catholic bishop and forbade Protestant ministers to perform any religious functions outside specified places. Not surprisingly the sixteen years of war against the Turks were followed by eight more (1703–11) of rebellion led by Francis II Rákóczi (1675–1735), the Jesuit-educated scion of a long line of Protestant princes of Transylvania. Peace was eventually made by the Treaty of Szatmár in 1711, but by that time the country was in waste. This proved not to be a suitable milieu to reintroduce the Counter-Reformation.

Already the Habsburg record was notorious. Particular scandal was created in 1675 when forty-two Protestant pastors were taken off to Naples to be sold as galley slaves. Three escaped on the way, seven died of their hardships, and the remainder were eventually redeemed by Dutch merchants and given a refuge in Zurich. But the religious affairs of Hungary generally became the staple of the European press, and only where Catholic influence and censorship were strong, in Italy, Spain and in some of the ecclesiastical principalities of Germany, was the Catholic line upheld. In England, for example, Bishop Burnet and Defoe were equally critical. And in the eighteenth century things continued much as before.

When the Rákóczi rebellion was put down the Habsburgs secured their main constitutional points, that their authority in Hungary should last as long as they could produce male heirs, and that Charles III (VI) should succeed automatically. There was no total overthrow of local government in Hungary. But the Diets which met in 1714 and 1715 to confirm the settlement referred to the legal rights of Protestants as to be maintained only for the time being and in the sense imparted by the king. The king's permission was required for Protestant synods and assemblies to meet, and they might not raise taxes. The Explanatio Leopoldina was to be strictly enforced to inhibit the development of Protestant church life. All that could be said was that rebellion had bought time for the Habsburg government to feel the pressure of new influences; the Enlightenment was a long way off, but the needs of Hungary itself and the demands of western allies prevented Charles III (VI) from succumbing altogether to those

Catholic clergy who continued to demand the forcible liquidation of their rivals. But the upshot of the legislation of his reign was to try to reduce the rights of Protestants to private worship only; there were efforts to exclude them from office by oaths invoking the Virgin and saints, and this while the Emperor was having to make concessions to foreign Protestants in order to populate the military districts on the frontiers.

Charles nevertheless put a good deal of money and effort into getting a Catholic church system restored and working, and both were badly needed. Only the diocese of Nyitra had been completely free from Turkish occupation during the previous century and a half. In 1700 the bishop of Pécs complained that his diocese was short of 300 priests and that he did not have a single candidate for the priesthood. In 1556 the diocese of Nagyvárad had boasted 339 parishes served by 500 priests; in 1711 only three parishes had a priest, and when the bishop returned to his see he was too poor to re-establish his cathedral or create a suitable residence. The condition of the parish priests was of course still more wretched. Benefices were in the gift of the local landowners who were theoretically obliged to build and maintain churches, rectories and schools, but were not forward in so doing. Nor were their failures made good by the bishops. The crown must therefore take the initiative, and Charles III (VI)'s determination to enforce ecclesiastical action by virtue of his prerogative powers was a frequent cause of friction with the Pope. He drove the bishops to found new parishes and divide old ones, to give non-parochial chapels their independence, to support poor parishes, to build churches and schools, and to report their progress to him. Money was of the essence. The state fixed stole fees, and required bishops to return to the parishes one-sixteenth of the tithe. In 1734 patrons were required to provide land for the parish. Charles III (VI) set up a General Parish Fund into which bishops and prelates were required to pay; abbeys were kept vacant and their revenues paid into the fund. Future prelates must pay in, and when Joseph II reduced the number of monasteries, their wealth was also paid in. Alas! the Habsburgs also dipped into this fund, and in 1751 the disparity between episcopal wealth and parish penury was still enormous: the average annual income of a bishop was 867,776 forints, that of parish clergy 200. Charles himself put a good deal of money into school building, and in 1715 brought in the Piarists to improve the quality of the education. The largest church building programme in the nation's history was overwhelmingly devoted to baroque styles, and many churches of romanesque or gothic origin were rebuilt in the fashionable mode. With the baroque came the Jesuits, and they propagated the idea that Hungary was a Marian kingdom under the special patronage of the Virgin. This devotion never became a badge of nationalism as in Poland, for Hungarian

Catholicism could never settle its account with Protestantism on the one side, nor, on the other, its defence of the estates and counties against the dynasty, and in this way sublimate the the national differences in its ranks. Under Maria Theresa, forcible Counter-Reformation began again, and the Reformed alone lost 150 churches in the Transdanubian district. On the positive side she encouraged the settlement of more religious orders.

The ultimate religious balance-sheet in Hungary is extremely interesting. Royal direction and royal pressure got Catholicism going again as a working church system; but the misery of endless persecution did little to alter the confessional balance in the country. Catholics outnumbered Protestants by about two to one (with Orthodox and Uniats making up another quarter of the population) at the beginning of the period and at the end. On the other hand the perpetual defence of constitutional rights which were always being denied or whittled away, caused the Protestant churches to lose their sense of direction, and encouraged the real life of Protestantism to leak off into more informal communities. Finally, state action, which was the only way to secure church reform and make the church pay for a substantial part of it, set the precedents which Joseph II would exploit in the name of Enlightenment.

The ecclesiastical states

The things that were writ large in the Habsburg lands were in many ways writ small in the history of the ecclesiastical principalities in the Empire. This history is still not well-known. Yet it appears that rulers and ruled were pulling apart as they were gradually doing in the Habsburg lands. The essence of the baroque missions and the baroque styles in church-building had been that they were of Roman origin, not always, perhaps, corresponding to the Tridentine letter, but intended to add punch to Tridentine policies. The rulers of Catholic states, and especially the bishops, had struck one violent blow at popular superstition in the witch trials, and they struck another in the systematic use of the missions. One of the new features of mission history in the late seventeenth century was the commissioning of missioners by the bishop not merely to evangelise but to conduct a visitation for him. Two Jesuits visited 140 parishes in 1683 alone in the archdiocese of Mainz, and 440 parishes between 1690 and 1694 in the duchy of Jülich near Cologne.

To prosper, this policy needed political backing, though in difficult circumstances political support might not be enough. In 1685 the Catholic Neuburg branch of the Palatinate family acquired the Electorate, and, having promised toleration to all three confessions, supported the Jesuits in the effort to recover lost ground there. The most spectacular effort of this kind was the attempt to accomplish the 'reunion' of the old Lutheran city of Strasbourg, for which no effort was spared by the Church or the King of France. Its central feature was a major mission which went on throughout the winter of 1684–85, conducted by the Jesuits led by their rector Fr Jean Dez, the Dauphin's confessor. Their argument on this occasion was that the Augsburg Confession was so open to a Catholic interpretation that there was no reason for any Lutheran to oppose the king's religion. What few conversions this achieved seem to have owed most to military intimidation used by Louvois and to cash payments made to the poor and soldiers.

The Elector of Bavaria also decided in 1718 to send Jesuit missionaries into every district of his realm in order to 'rescue the people from darkness and ignorance, instruct them in pure doctrine and instil into them the proper virtues'. This 'protracted meeting' to end all protracted meetings went on for the rest of the century, and was not even interrupted by the abolition of the Society of Jesus in 1773. Similar missions were brought by the Elector Palatine into Düsseldorf. Criticism of the missions began to mount in the eighteenth century, but in the second half of the century they gained a fresh impetus from Liguori and the Redemptorists, and by this time real responsibilities were being exercised in south Germany and the Rhineland by laymen acting through confraternities of Christian doctrine. The Oberammergau Passion play, written in 1750, is an example of baroque piety still vigorously alive in the countryside.

Town and country

It is the final conclusion of Louis Chatellier, the historian of the missions, that this enormous effort changed not so much the world as the Church. In 1600 Catholicism had been a religion of the towns and the countryside had been neglected; by 1800 many of the rural areas were areas of faith and even fervour, while the towns were in need of conversion. This altered the whole church situation in two ways. In modern times, whether religious practice in towns has been relatively indifferent or worse than indifferent has depended on whether the rural hinterland has been one of good or bad religious practice, the towns only exceeding the rural level of practice where that level is very low. Then, secondly, this change of fortune enabled the religion of the countryside to become identified with Catholicism generally. It did not need the French Revolution to show that this rural religion had a strong papalist and Roman character. When Pope Pius VI (1775–99) went to Vienna to beg favours from Joseph II in 1782, he was received with veneration by ordinary people, and the same was true in France when he was finally taken to Valence to die in need.

Anti-curialism

This curialism was not characteristic of the heads of Germania Sacra or the lay Catholic states. The Catholic powers, even the spiritual powers, cared little for the diplomatic claims of the papacy, and increasingly treated it as a minor Italian power with little influence even upon the reshaping of the local political map. The same pamphlet which in 1705 assured the House of Austria that 'the promise of prophecy [to you] is to extirpate heresy and undo Islam' also urged the Emperor to 'wrest from the Popes of Rome what they have usurped over the Empire'. Anti-curial views were also characteristic of spiritual magnates. The Imperial Vice-Chancellor Friedrich Karl von Schönborn (whose portrait was painted in hunting dress with dog and gun) was prepared to talk about the grievances of the German church and to threaten schism. After acquiring great possessions in Austria he acquired the sees of Bamberg and Würzburg, and set up as a leader among the spiritual princes. This kind of magnificent pluralism was indeed one of the sore points between them and the papacy. In 1731 Pope Clement XII issued a *motu proprio* to restrain the accumulation of great German ecclesiastical foundations in a few hands; a long struggle followed which achieved little from the side of the Pope, but helps to explain why the sentiments of the ecclesiastical grandees were moving in the opposite direction to those of the ordinary faithful.

One of the anti-curial weapons of the lay Catholic states was the *Placetum*, the claim of the ruler to allow the publication of papal decrees only after examining whether they accorded with the interests of the state. The placet was nothing new, but in 1712 the Louvain Jansenist canonist Bernard van Espen argued for its extension to dogmatic decrees. The weakness of the popes in dealing with attacks of this kind was that they had extensively abdicated to Catholic governments the appointment of bishops. They had a counter-weapon in the Communion Bulls (Bulla Coenae) annually published on Maundy Thursday. These contained a series of excommunication sentences against those who attacked the papacy, the clergy and their privileged position; but church immunities were not popular with Catholic states which considered themselves short of cash. They were finally stopped by Clement XIV in 1770, and ultimately abolished altogether by Pius IX in 1869. Lastly, and long before Enlightenment became a fashionable option, there were tell-tale signs of German dignitarianism moving away from the baroque piety which had been so eagerly embraced by their subjects. If ever there had been a pillar of the old order, it had been the archdiocese of Salzburg, with its Italianate building, its Jesuit missions, and its short way with dissenters. By the end of the eighteenth century Salzburg was an eminent seat of the

Enlightenment, and already in 1737 and 1743, just after the expulsion of the Protestants, Benedictine professors and lay scholars were brought in through the Societas Muratoriana. A dent had been made in the Jesuit monopoly of higher education, and the Jesuits were now almost the last spokesmen for curialism in Germany.

4   The religion of Protestants

The Bible only?

Macaulay's schoolboy would certainly have known that in a work of 1638, which enjoyed a heyday in the later seventeenth and early eighteenth centuries, Chillingworth had magisterially pronounced that 'the Bible, I say, the Bible only, is the religion of Protestants'. As a statement of fact as distinct from an assertion about authority, this had never been true; and the seventeenth century was to explore the difficulties of embedding the Bible in cultural authorities of alien kinds, as the eighteenth began to explore the difficulties inherent in the Bible itself. This intellectual approach to the problems of Christianity as a working religion was as characteristic of the Protestant Orthodox as of the Catholics; there were other approaches which will concern us later in the chapter. In the second generation after the Reformation the Lutheran and Reformed Orthodox parties created a highly integrated systematic theology, guaranteed against Catholic polemic, and they expected that the backing of secular authority would root their formulations in popular religious life. But they had been unable to construct their systems or even expound the doctrine of the Trinity without liberal application to Aristotle. In 1697 Pierre Bayle barely exaggerated: 'Aristotle, usually called the Prince of Philosophers, or the Philosopher *par excellence*, was the founder of a sect which has surpassed and finally engulfed all the rest. It has had its ups and downs, and in this century especially has been violently shaken; but the Catholic theologians on the one side and the Protestant theologians on the other, have run to its aid as to the fire . . . Nor is it a matter of surprise that the Peripatetic philosophy . . . finds so many protectors, and that its interests are believed to be inseparable from those of theology, for it accustoms the mind to submit without evidence.'

From the beginning of the seventeenth century there were Protestants who perceived (like many Catholics) a growing gap between the church's self-understanding and the realities of parish and congregational life. It was not open to the Protestant establishments to tackle this problem by the mass evangelism which had been attempted in the Catholic world, since the religious orders had been abolished; if the parish failed there were no other weapons to hand. But party Orthodoxy, bred to battle with the Catholics, fought vigorously also against what it called 'atheism', against new developments in its own ranks of the notion of 'reason', and eventually against spiritual movements to which it had itself given birth. Whether or not there was a 'general crisis' in the seventeenth century, innumerable groups had a crisis of their own; and the crisis of the Lutheran theologians was one of internal church criticism. Never before or since has the volume of criticism from within been so great; and out of it came proposals for church reform and renewal based on the spiritual discipline of meditation.

Arndt: meditation and reform

This combination of church criticism and inwardness was classically embodied in Johann Arndt's *True Christianity* (1605–10), one of the most frequently reprinted treatises of the century. Arndt started from the perception that the Lutheran prescription of preaching to a congregation assembled by official pressure was worse than ineffective; it transformed the hearing of the Word into an *opus operatum*, and evoked, not religious assurance, but a security in respect of salvation of the most pernicious kind. Arndt's message was thus not one of comfort to those who suffered terribly in the following century from war, persecution, famine and plague; it aimed to take away the most easily available comfort, and in that sense was directed to church reform. For Arndt mysticism was a means to producing the fruits of faith without which preaching was ineffective. His book was packed with edited extracts from the Bernadine tradition, Tauler, the Theologia Deutsch, Thomas à Kempis, Angela da Foligno or Paracelsus, but was not a do-it-yourself handbook. He held that spiritual energies were released by a determined turning inwards by all the forces of the soul; meditation (of which his sources were the masters) was the means by which this was to be achieved. Arndt here aligned himself with a considerable international and supra-confessional tradition of the past century, and his own astonishing publishing history enabled this tradition to modify the Lutheran definition of faith. Faith was now the outcome of the Word of God preached, received, read and meditated upon. Between 1605 and 1740 there were ninety-five German editions of *True Christianity* as well as others in Bohemian, Dutch, Swedish and Latin (much prized by Spanish Jesuits). This market was further fed by great imports of English Puritan devotional literature, itself heavily dependent on medieval models, in the generation after 1660.

Thus Arndt spoke to a devotional movement which had taken shape far beyond the boundaries of Lutheranism or Germany. Despite the awkwardness of the materials he had thrown together, Arndt was substantially taken on board by Lutheran Orthodoxy and used to modify its inheritance from Melancthon.

In some towns and territories relations of government and the movement for piety were close. Strasbourg and its university, a lively publishing centre for the works of Arndt and the classics of English devotion, were renowned for church reform. The Strasbourg theologians were called in in 1636 by Duke Ernst the Pious of Saxe-Gotha (1601–75) for a comprehensive opinion on reform in church and society, and, like Spener later, they saw faults in every level of society springing from a piety inadequately internalised. Improvement called for reform of education and theological study, but also preaching for repentance, comprehensive catechetical instruction and house-to-house visiting. Duke Ernst responded with a far-reaching social reconstruction, the principles of which were applied to his family and the church. Tough on alchemists and witches, he was generous to Protestants persecuted by the Habsburgs, to the Lutheran church in Moscow, even to the Ethiopian church. Emphatically hostile to personal extravagance, he was yet a baroque prince of the Lutheran sort; his new residence contained a splendid theological library. Duke Ernst's relations with the movement of piety also pointed forward as well as back; his chancellor, Veit Ludwig von Seckendorff, went on to become the first chancellor of the university of Halle, and another of his councillors, Johannes Francke, was the father of the great August Hermann Francke.

The vivid response which Spener evoked in the later seventeenth century is explicable only by the broad diffusion of the movement for meditation and reform. It was still a movement operating from the top downwards, mostly through university theologians, princes and their chaplains, and this had the disadvantage that after the Thirty Years War, princes, both Catholic and Protestant, began to distance themselves from the old confessionalism. It was no accident that among those who now fulminated against 'atheism' and 'indifferentism' writers from the movement for piety were prominent. They had also acquired a new weapon in the fray. For in the same period hymns increased vastly in number and quality; they came overwhelmingly from the movement for piety, so that critics are constantly tempted to describe them as 'pietist' before there was a Pietist movement; and they influenced German hymn-books as indelibly as the evangelical writers of the eighteenth and nineteenth centuries influenced those of Britain. Thus the Dresden hymn-book of 1622 contained 276 hymns, that of 1673 had 1,505. The Lüneburg hymn-book of 1635 contained 355 hymns, that of 1694, 2,055. Even this paled before the *Wagnersche Gesangbuch* of Leipzig which presented 5,000 hymns in eight volumes. The motive of this elephantiasis (like the steady inflation of the Moody and Sankey hymn-books in the early twentieth century) was commercial, and conveyed a double warning to conservatives. It showed that the propagation of vital religion need not necessarily wait on the action of approved authorities. Moreover, this triumph of private enterprise was achieved outside the normal area of censorship and control. The conservative Orthodox still took a medieval view of what theology was, behaved like a medieval guild in defending their mysteries and training, and left extraneous matters to the lay entrepreneur. This was an opening which others would exploit.

Philipp Jakob Spener

The man who most effectively did this (and characteristically prefixed his programme for not waiting for the action of public authorities, the *Pia Desideria* (1675), to an edition of Arndt's lectionary sermons) was Philipp Jakob Spener (1635–1705). Bred on Arndtian piety and English puritanism, raised in a small court in Alsace, he might never have become a religious leader at all; for, to some head-shaking among his later followers, he acquired two other lifelong passions, genealogy and heraldry. He became the most important genealogist of his century, and put heraldry on a scientific basis. His vast unpublished correspondence in these fields helps to explain the extraordinary range of his acquaintances among the imperial counts and other aristocracy, whose patronage and political advice were of invaluable service to his religious cause. A pupil of Dannhauer, one of the stars of the Strasbourg school, he exemplified a generational drift by prizing Aristotle much less and Arndt much more than his master, and by not sharing the latter's view of the imminent end of this age. Much of what Spener acquired after his initial studies became commonplace in the Pietist movement. He met Labadie at Geneva; that ex-pupil of the Jesuits was then trying to jack up the level of devotion in the Reformed churches, and Spener translated into German his *Practice of Prayer and Christian Meditation* (1667). He attempted a biblical commentary to be put together from the works of Luther; the commentary was never finished, but, on the way, he acquired an unusual knowledge of the reformer. In particular he absorbed the message of Luther's Preface to Romans, which became almost obligatory for approved conversion in the later Pietist movement. And he made the connection between conversion and the New Birth.

Though still only thirty-one, Spener in 1666 obtained the important position of Senior of Frankfurt, one of the chief imperial cities and a major publishing centre. Among the religious minorities in this Lutheran town was an important Jewish ghetto, the very existence of which was a standing reminder of an unsolved Lutheran doctrinal problem. Late in life Luther had looked imminently to the Last Judgment, when Rome should be overcome and the Turks defeated, and this hope had revived during the Thirty Years War. It also became connected with the hope of better days for the church, one of the features of which was to be the conversion of the Jews promised in Romans 11. Lutheran exegetes differed whether this promise was already fulfilled or still outstanding, and tended to regard the end of this age as imminent. Spener's own view changed as a result of the formulation of his reform plans in 1675. The reason why the Jews were not converted (he now held) was the derelict state of the Christian church; therefore the end would not come until all God's promises to the church were fulfilled. This 'hope of better times' was a favourite theme in one of Spener's engines for reform, the *collegium pietatis* or class meeting.

The class meeting

This institution began in the summer of 1670 when a group of men approached Spener to form a meeting to discuss 'the one thing necessary'. Such a devotional gathering could not take place through any of the usual social channels, and the Lutheran church at that time permitted no other meetings than the public services. The group also desired to form a holy fellowship separated from the world. To this Spener agreed, and as a guarantee of good faith, gathered them first in his study, and then in the Barfüsserkirche. Here, in the Lutheran world at least, was the origin of those small group fellowships which were to characterise the whole Pietist movement. Originally the members were all men, mostly academics and members of professional families. But numbers increased from a handful to more than fifty by 1675, and they now included a representative cross-section of Frankfurt society, not excluding ladies, who were at first accommodated in an adjoining room with no right to speak. Spener would open with prayer, read a passage from a devotional book and expound it, and then there would be a free discussion confined to devotional and not controversial themes. By the end of 1674 the meeting had become a Bible class in which Spener deliberately enlarged the scope for lay participation. For him the meetings realised one of his precious themes, the general spiritual priesthood. If every Christian exercised his spiritual obligation to warn and comfort his fellow-believers instead of leaving everything to the clergy, church renewal would begin in earnest.

Heartfelt Desires

The big discussion, however, was launched by his programmatic tract, the *Pia Desideria* (1675). Spener took care to get the work approved by the Frankfurt theologians in advance, and sent offprints to numerous important theologians. The discussion he actually stirred up was more than he intended. No class of society was exempt from Spener's strictures. Politics had emancipated itself from the church, but the state kept a grip on the church in its own interests. Too much a churchman to take up the extreme anti-clericalism of the spiritualists, Spener nevertheless demanded that the clergy exhibit visible signs of the New Birth. The effect of the preaching as of the administration of the sacraments might be independent of the worthiness of the minister, but the reception of the preaching was not. Moreover they needed to be rid of Aristotelian subtleties; piety and a reform of theological study went hand in hand. No social disorder escaped castigation; Spener was even prepared to speak up for the early Christian notion of the community of goods. The church's barrenness in the fruits of the faith was the reason for its failure to convert the Jews, and for the Catholic prejudice that Protestants not merely despised good works but failed to produce them. The great impulse to complete the Reformation was the divine promise of better times for the church; but God would not bear the burden of this alone. The object of the pursuit of Christian perfection was to bring the Word of God more richly among the people. There should be strenuous family Bible-reading, and for families that could not manage this, there should be parish meetings for cursive Bible-reading with summaries. From this developed the Frankfurt custom by which members of the congregation took their Bibles to church and referred to the texts which were being expounded. He also cautiously contemplated the possibility that some members of the congregation might expound and admonish. The general priesthood indeed consisted not only in prayer and good works, but in the energetic study of the word of God, and in teaching, warning, converting and edifying one's fellow-men.

Opposition to Pietism

The reaction Spener had sought made the *Pia Desideria* a great commercial success. What disappointed him was not the inevitable adverse criticism, but his failure to generate a reform movement in the church based on consensus. The only route to progress would be through the devout circles of the pious and the support they might win in the *Bürgertum* of Frankfurt, Essen, Rothenburg, Nuremberg, Ulm and elsewhere. This resource, however, could not save him from perils of treading a tightrope between the suspicions of the Orthodox and the secessions of the radicals; the latter shared his criticisms of the church but did not share his basic confidence in her. The situation came to a head in 1686 when Spener was called to Dresden to be senior court chaplain to the Elector of Saxony, and thus the nearest thing to a Primate which the Lutheran churches of the Empire possessed. But a baroque court proved no place for starting *collegia pietatis*, the Saxon church and universities regarded Orthodoxy as their especial property, and when Spener as the Elector's confessor upbraided him (as his predecessor had upbraided him) for his behaviour, he was met by an explosion of wrath. The result was that in 1691 Spener accepted an invitation of the Elector of Brandenburg to move to Berlin.

Yet it was in Saxony that the Pietist movement, in the sense of a party standing in a relation of conflict to Orthodoxy, began. Partly as a concession to poor students, the Leipzig theologians concentrated heavily on dogmatics and homiletics, and economised on biblical exegesis. One of the theological professors, the formidable Johann Benedikt Carpzov, in 1686 encouraged the formation of a *Collegium philobiblicum* in which students, under the presidency of a senior man, should make up something of the deficiency themselves. The idea was energetically taken up as a modest contribution to Spener's hopes of reform of theological training by two students who were to dominate the second generation of Pietism, August Hermann Francke (1663–1727) and Paul Anton (1661–1730). They were undone by success. Francke, who, in contact with Spener, underwent a conversion experience but did not acquire the necessary degrees to lead the *collegia*, rejected the Aristotelian training given to theologians; he attracted 300 students who began to sell their philosophy books and burn their notes. Still worse, students without any degrees at all began *collegia* to study Paul, and, worse again, citizens of the very unchurched city of Leipzig, where two parish churches and five pastors had to suffice for a population of 20,000, joined the student exercises, and even opened conventicles. The spreading of the general priesthood to lay people was happening much faster than Spener intended or authority was prepared to tolerate. Carpzov determined to get all the Pietists out. His success ensured that the Leipzig troubles recurred elsewhere.

The Leipzig fiasco was indeed the signal for a ferocious campaign against Spener and the Pietists, a campaign which was renewed in each of the next two generations, the target of the first being Francke, and of the second being the eccentric nobleman, Count Nikolaus von Zinzendorf. Spener's troubles were constantly magnified by friends who would transgress the limits of strict church loyalty which he observed. Visions by ecstatic servant girls in towns in central Germany inflamed the Orthodox and evoked legislation against Pietism. There were 500 polemical pamphlets in the next decade.

Nevertheless Spener stood his ground and made the best of his protected situation. The peculiarity of Brandenburg was that its overwhelmingly Lutheran people were governed by a dynasty which in 1613 had accepted the Reformed faith. The Hohenzollerns were always interested in religious or theological movements which might circumvent the hostility between these confessions; more, their ambitions in the Baltic and Silesia set them in opposition to Sweden and Saxony, the two great players in the international game whose ideological platform was Lutheran Orthodoxy. All these factors now played into Spener's hand. There was a tolerance about the church politics of Brandenburg even at their most intolerant, as a series of edicts in the 1690s forbidding pulpit polemics against Pietists was to show; and the decision to crown the economic development of the duchy of Magdeburg, acquired in 1680, by the creation in 1694 of a new university at Halle, almost on the doorstep of Leipzig, the seat of an ancient and famous university, the home of an international trade fair, the chief business centre of Saxony, and one of the two leading German book-markets, showed clearly the anti-Saxon bent of Brandenburg policy. It also gave Spener an unrivalled opening. Throughout his Berlin years, he was steadily planting out his sympathisers in positions of influence through the patronage of lay friends, and especially the Baron von Canstein. And the new foundation at Halle enabled a whole group to be brought back, led by Francke and Paul Anton, together with sympathetic non-Pietists like Christian Thomasius. Halle became the beacon on the hill for the Pietists of the next generation.

Spener's theology

Spener was also making his peculiar contribution to theology, much of it buried in monumental volumes of sermons, correspondence, or expert opinion on particular questions, and much of it characteristic of Lutheran theologians in general. He made no secret of his aversion both to Aristotelian school-theology and metaphysics and to modern Cartesianism. The prime business of the theologian was biblical exegesis, the equipment for which consisted in philology and a pure and engaged heart. Homiletics should be revived by sacrificing rhetoric to a better exposition of the biblical content. 'Mystical theology', Arndt above all, should feed the springs of religious vitality. The three important authorities for Spener were his teacher, Dannhauer, Arndt and Luther. Dannhauer kept him within the framework of Lutheran Orthodoxy; Arndt he interpreted in an ecclesiastical sense, while constantly laying up difficulties for himself by his positive attitude towards all attempts to put new life into Christendom. But this positive attitude greatly enhanced his understanding of Luther. For Spener Luther was not the Orthodox collection of proof texts, but a practitioner of living faith and its formation. Thus Spener's doctrine of justification was Lutheran but not quite Luther's; and his systematic development of Luther's hints on the priesthood of all believers was something not found in Luther or Lutheran Orthodoxy. He did not create a theological school, but created the basis on which the next generation of Pietists could do so. Above all he helped theology to serve its generation by reducing dogmatic complications, and centring the whole study upon the saving work of God in Christ for man, his salvation and renewal. This kind of theology presupposed a living knowledge of God, but it was the only answer to the practical atheism of the day. The order of salvation began with the New Birth, which included the kindling of faith, justification understood as the imputation of the righteousness of Christ, being accepted as a child of God, and the creation of the new man. Here was the framework of an elaborate theological sequence, and, still more, a dynamic view of the Christian life against which it would be the business of class-leaders everywhere to assist the faithful to test their progress. Spener was sufficient of a Lutheran to see service in the world as a Christian vocation, and appropriately he tried to raise the standing of ethics in theological studies.

August Hermann Francke

To supply the element of system and institutional stiffening lacking in Spener was the work of his old admirer from Leipzig days, August Hermann Francke (1663–1727). Although under thirty when he came to Halle, Francke had already revealed much of what was to come. He did not graduate in theology at Leipzig, but he had been financially supported by his native town of Lübeck in a broader education than was common among theologians. This included an apprenticeship to the Hamburg Hebraist, Esdras Edzard, which equipped him in Old Testament and oriental philology. His translations of Molinos foreshadowed a long Pietist preoccupation (in their search for the springs of religious vitality) with the later Quietists, Antoinette Bourignon and Mme Guyon. Only later had he found a quiet certainty of faith, and that in a sudden breakthrough from natural life to life in God, an awakening from sleep to reality, a conversion which issued not in mystical withdrawal but in an unexampled power of work. The New Birth for Francke was less a theological concept than a vivid and painful experience which led to a far-reaching reconstitution of his personality. It guaranteed that he had more than his fair share of the clashes between authority and the Pietists, and he was expelled from both Leipzig and Erfurt.

Once again Brandenburg saved the day. That to Francke was among the early invitations to Halle, and the Hohenzollerns were not deterred by the venomous ripostes from the local Orthodox clergy and the estates of Magdeburg. Pietism did not, however, metamorphose into a state religion. In fact serious differences arose between the theologians of Halle and Frederick I (as the Elector Frederick III became after taking the title of king in Prussia) in the last years of his reign, 1709–14; but these were offset by Francke's success in winning over the crown prince, the future Frederick William I. After this relations continued close till Francke's death in 1727, and, though somewhat less intimate, till the accession of Frederick the Great in 1740.

Halle

The interests of Halle as represented by Francke were always both narrower and broader than those of the dynasty; they were narrower in the sense that Pietism never cut a great figure in Brandenburg itself, but infinitely broader as Francke showed in 1704 in his *Great Project for a Universal Improvement in all Social Orders*. This was a utopian scheme in quite the Leibnizian style, a case for Francke's institutions at Halle and for their extension. Francke proposed three different types of education for the three classes of old Prussian society, though the children of the Orphan House were to be fitted into the system according to their gifts rather than their social origin. Above all the cavalier-style objectives of upper-class education were to be displaced by practical training for the bureaucracy and the army. But what struck the ordinary observer and won the support of the crown prince was not this theory, not Francke's systematisation of the stages of the Christian life, not even the reform of theological education achieved by the theological faculty, but the charitable institutions created outside the walls of the town, the Orphan House, the dispensary, the schools, the teacher-training institutions, the Bible Institute.

Here Francke followed Dutch models, but on an unheard-of scale, and his calculated propaganda influenced charitable activity all over the Protestant world. One of the biggest buildings in Europe, it provided before Francke's death accommodation for 3,000 people to live and work. The dispensary was the first producer of standardised branded medicaments on a commercial scale, able and anxious to sell a complete public-health kit for a city or province, and marketing its wares by brochures in Latin, French, English, Dutch and Greek. For his vast enterprise, an institution of neither church nor state, had somehow to pay its way. It had modest state privileges which had a cash value, and there were charitable collections all over Europe for which Francke regularly updated his appeals, but the machine relied on commercial ventures on a grand scale. Francke's spiritual agents sounded the markets for a wide range of products from Venice to the Far East, and were particularly active in the Near East and the Russia of Peter the Great. He dealt in Hungarian oxen and wines (among the purchasers of which was the Duke of Marlborough). But the great business of Halle was the supply of medicaments and of Bibles and other religious literature. The press speedily became one of the chief in Germany, publishing not only in German and Greek and Russian Cyrillic type, but in a whole range of languages where nothing of the kind had been available before.

Francke here profited from his efforts to keep in touch with *Deutschtum* abroad from America to Russia, and from the network of personal connections, the chain of imperial counts, created by Spener. The former were, if anything, a nuisance to the Prussian state; the latter and the Slavonic publishing they encouraged, were, as we shall see, of primary importance to Prussia's long-term ambitions in Silesia. Francke was able to use the general support he received from the Prussian state for particular projects like the Tranquebar mission, which he opened in India with Danish and British support, in which Prussia had no conceivable interest, because he was prepared to be serviceable to Prussia where it mattered, and especially in Silesia and neighbouring territories. And the spread of Francke's influence was remarkable; through the chaplaincies into the army, through education everywhere, through Spener's circle of pious counts, some of whom had major interests in Silesia, and whom he turned into a sort of advisory cabinet for the management of the Halle enterprises, through clergy and civil servants trained at Halle. When Francke set out on a nine-month journey across the Empire in 1717–18, he found friends and invitations to preach in imperial cities and courts everywhere.

Francke's party

Nor was his fame confined to the Empire. A key figure in Francke's contacts, east and west, was Heinrich Wilhelm Ludolf (1655–1712), a noted traveller in Russia and the Middle East, who from 1686 to 1691 was secretary to Prince George of Denmark, the consort of the future English Queen Anne. It was through him that Francke was put in touch with the SPCK (Society for Promoting Christian Knowledge), and through him also that Anton Wilhelm Böhme (1673–1722) was appointed court chaplain to Prince George of Denmark. Böhme not only survived the Hanoverian accession, but remained an important figure in English religious life until his death. He was succeeded by Friedrich Michael Ziegenhagen (1694–1776) who exercised the concern of Halle for the huge German population in America. The Salzburgers were his especial care, shared with another old intimate of Francke in Augsburg, and former German minister in the Savoy, Samuel Urlsperger. But it was not only the Germans with whom Francke was in touch in America; he was flattered by Cotton Mather of Boston, whose son, Samuel, corresponded with Francke's son, Gotthilf August, and published a life of August Hermann, *theologus incomparabilis*, addressed to the college at Harvard.

The Reformed churches

The Reformed churches constituted a self-conscious, cohesive and independent section of the Protestant world in the seventeenth and eighteenth centuries in a deeper sense than sharing a number of related confessions and catechisms. The Swiss were amazingly generous to religious refugees from all quarters and especially from France; and they shored up financially many of the Reformed congregations left stranded by the ebbing of the Reformed tide in the Rhineland. Right through the eighteenth century the Dutch church kept a watching brief over the Dutch and German Reformed in America, as Francke's machine watched over the German Lutherans. The Dutch and the Swiss were major channels for the influence of English Puritan literature upon the German market. What the whole Reformed world lacked was the protection and leadership of a first-class military power, of the kind Cromwell had briefly provided in the seventeenth century. Moreover the Reformed world bore the weight of a tradition that if anything was wrong in Christendom, what was called for was reformation. This prescription presupposed that Christendom had an abiding if defective social reality, an assumption which was not always warranted, and was always liable to conflict with the other nostrums of renewal or revival.

The United Provinces

One of the hotly contested problems of Dutch history is whether Pietism in the real sense existed there, how far it can be equated with the movement in the Dutch church for 'further reformation' (*Nadere Reformatie*), which was also a movement for piety. The term seems to have been borrowed early in the seventeenth century by the Zeeland pastor, Willem Teelinck, from English Puritans who called for further reformation and were fertile in practical theologies for planting out the reformation they already had. There were spiritual movements outside the Dutch church as well as inside it; some of the latter bore resemblances both to English Puritanism and to Lutheran Pietism, but all were conditioned by the fact that the Dutch Reformed establishment had strategic problems unlike those of the Lutheran world. In the 1570s Holland and Zeeland had been forcibly Protestantised by the Calvinist 'Beggars', and their triumph spelt defeat for the ideal of William of Orange of religious parity between the Catholic and Reformed confessions. Established status helped the Dutch Reformed Church to build up a considerable following, but not to overcome a substantial Catholic minority. There were soon Protestant dissenters as well, a few Lutherans enjoying the protection of foreign powers, more Baptists, perhaps ten per cent of the population, and, after the Synod of Dort (1618–19), Remonstrants who sustained the traditions of Erasmus against the thunderbolts of the Reformed Church. The Dutch church thus resembled a modern government trying to manipulate a market for drugs or hard liquor which is substantially beyond its control; both hard and soft measures have their drawbacks, and in the United Provinces there were always lay magistrates who knew that they must govern the people as they found them, and put the emphasis on social peace.

Thus before the end of the seventeenth century the general atmosphere in the Netherlands was unusually tolerant by European standards and it was well known that this ethos was favourable to a nation committed to international trade and news-gathering. Never before the end of the eighteenth century did religious pluralism imply religious equality, but the fact of pluralism could not fail to mark public policy and the strategy of churchmen. The dilemma was aggravated by the general check to the European economy in the later seventeenth century and problems of poverty which affected the riotous living of that part of the Dutch population which had never taken to Reformed ways, and by the difficulties of assimilating the mass of refugees to whom the Dutch, like the Swiss, gave hospitality. Since therefore the politics of reformation now had limited relevance to the Dutch predicament, the *Nadere Reformatie* must prescribe for spiritual vitality.

Another local problem was posed by Jean de Labadie (1610–74). Thought by some to have been a bastard of Henry IV of France, and brought up by an ex-Calvinist family on the make, he had become a Jesuit before joining the Reformed Church and being hunted from the country by Louis XIV. After an uneasy pastorate in Geneva, he was called to Middelburg in the United Provinces. Here he never got properly going, and in 1670 he left the Reformed Church with a select body of disciples, including the bluestocking Anna van Schurman. For a time they migrated up and down the Rhineland until a settlement could be found for them at Altona, a port opposite Hamburg where a free market in religion was maintained by the crown of Denmark. Subsequently there were other settlements, in Surinam and Friesland, but Labadie's very elect group were not much good at the business of survival, and when their prosperous backers ceased to pay at the end of the seventeenth century, they soon died out. Labadie was in many ways an unattractive character, impressed with his own voluptuous visions, scourging a world and a church to whose problems he had no solutions, except the erroneous conviction that when he and his elite inaugurated the millennial kingdom, all the elect would join them. His movement impinged upon more substantial renewal movements elsewhere (such as that of Spener in Frankfurt); more immediately his secession suggested clearly that the Dutch church, either because of its establishment or because of its Calvinism, was no place for those aspiring to Christian perfection, and it gave a handle for conservatives to use against innovators of any kind.

The Dutch establishment had also to face a theological division which was powerfully reinforced by ethical and political differences. Gisbertius Voetius (1589–1676), a professor at Utrecht, maintained the old scholastic Orthodoxy and compensated for its intellectualism by infusions of Puritan and medieval devotional literature. As one Dutch pastor reported, 'before the Belgick churches were pester'd with the Dogmes of Cocceius,[1] the ministry of the Word was exceedingly successful, many hearers would weep at sermons, proud sinners would quake and tremble at the word preached, multitudes were converted and reformed, religious worship was strictly and reverently celebrated in congregations and families'. Here the ethical division between the Voetians and the Coccejans is emphasised; the former were Sabbatarians, the latter not. There were also social differences. The Voetians were strong in the lower middle class, affected plain dress and the 'language of Canaan'; the Coccejans were modish, their ministers wore wigs, and they were notable in the world of wealth and scholarship. The Voetians were devotees of the Orange family, a strong central power, and gained a point with the re-establishment of the Orange Stadtholdership in 1672. The up-market Coccejans stood for patriot opposition to Orange power. Yet they were not just that Puritan bugbear, 'luxury'. In Coccejus the Old Testament and the history of Israel were

---

[1] Johannes Coccejus (1603–68), a distinguished Old Testament scholar, who held chairs in Bremen and various Dutch universities, being called finally to Leiden in 1650. His distinction between the covenant of works created in Paradise and the five-stage covenant of grace founded in Christ, influenced scholars as recent as Karl Barth and Gerhard von Rad.

interpreted as images of Christ and the history of the church, and systematised as a series of covenants. His biblical scholarship was admired by Spener, and anticipated favourite themes of the Pietists, rejecting calculations of the imminent end of this present age, and talking of conversion and the New Birth. Coccejans flirted with Cartesianism; even this long-running conflict could be redeemed. Dutch traditions of tolerance, skilfully manipulated by the Orange family, ensured that neither of the great parties in the church put paid to the other, and that the Dutch church, unlike the Swiss Reformed churches, was never shackled by a recent high-Orthodox formulary. What was needed in the United Provinces was some attempt to bring the theological schools together on the positive side, and make them grapple with new elements in the theological situation. By the early eighteenth century this began to happen, especially among theologians anxious to answer pastoral requirements. What would most have helped the reconciliation would have been the disappearance of the political issue between the parties; and it was important for the development of the Reformed cause in northern Europe that there were substantial Reformed churches which never had to face it at all.

Reformed churches in the north-west of the Empire

Around the borders of the United Provinces and to a considerable distance south was a thick sprinkling of Reformed congregations and petty Reformed territories, while away to the east was the one great Reformed imperial city, Bremen. This area was deeply influenced in religious matters by the Netherlands, received its contact with English Puritanism largely through Dutch or German translations of Swiss provenance, and was not polarised by the politics of the Orange family. Bremen, indeed, was a town of strict Voetian ethos, and a stronghold of Coccejan theology. The great political issue in this region was French aggression; besides reintroducing Catholicism into old Protestant areas, and giving Catholics a hold over Protestant church buildings, this menace sapped the resilience of some, and turned the minds of others inwards towards spiritual resources more independent of outward props and guarantees.

There was certainly Pietism here. Just as the early history of Lutheran Pietism was in a good measure the extended biography of Spener, so here it was the work of Theodor Undereyck (1635–93), his pupils and colleagues. Undereyck studied under Voetius at Utrecht; his preaching in his first parish at Mülheim on the Ruhr was Voetian in style. He beat the drum about the gulf beween the kingdom of Christ and that of the world, and sought to turn every family into a house-church and worthy bride of Christ presided over by the father. Preaching of this kind appealed to those tempted by Labadism; it produced converts and it also produced suicides. When Undereyck settled as a pastor in Bremen he ran into trouble with the clergy in the town on doctrinal grounds and because he held class-meetings during service times. But with the support of the town council he successfully planted Pietism in the town, and his pupils naturalised it in the Reformed parts of East Friesland. Above all Undereyck was father-in-God to the one great name in the theology of the German Reformed in this period, Friedrich Adolf Lampe (1683–1729), whose influence was felt among the Reformed from Holland to Hungary.

Lampe wrote a great deal, and wrote much for ordinary church members; dogmatics for laymen, catechetical works, sermons and hymns gave him an influence which outlived the Enlightenment and worked with renewed power in the revival movement of the nineteenth century. Of clerical stock, Lampe was educated in Bremen in the Undereyck tradition, and went on to the Dutch universities of Franeker and Utrecht, where he studied under professors who united the exegetical expertise of Coccejus with currents of living piety like those in which he had been brought up. His first pastoral appointments were in Germany, near Cleves and in Duisburg. The pastoral problem here was that those who hungered and thirsted after righteousness had become separatists after the manner of Labadie, leaving behind a thoroughly secularised rump. By preaching in a style to satisfy the one, and energetic house-to-house visiting to keep an eye on the other, he did much to save the day. Called to Bremen in 1709, he encountered many of the same problems as Undereyck. He had now to confess that the church could not consist entirely of the elect; it must contain some of the lost for whom Christ had not died. His technique here was to address the conclusion of the sermon to the elect, who were required to stand and receive the Word. This was 'discriminating' preaching indeed, a form of moral pressure which showed how, throughout much of the Reformed world in Europe and America, the necessities of the churches were driving ministers towards revivalism. From 1720 to 1727 Lampe held a chair at Utrecht, uniting in his own ministry much of what had been divided between the Voetian and Coccejan parties, and exemplifying also the way in which the fringes of the Protestant world were beginning to act upon the centre. The same was true even in another Reformed reserve where the centre contested the process vigorously, that of Switzerland.

Switzerland

In Switzerland everything which happened in the Lutheran world seemed to happen in slow motion. Many of the churches in Reformed cantons had lost their Presbyterian features and were now simple religious establishments subject to the leadership of the urban patriciates. They were hand in glove with the senior city clergy, the Reformed equivalent of the court chaplains of the Lutheran world. Moreover, confessional warfare, the spectre of which haunted the Empire, actually continued in Switzerland; the great Catholic abbot of St Gallen and his oppressed Protestant subjects, backed by the cantons of Bern and Zurich, came to blows in 1712. The victory of the latter ensured Protestant supremacy in the confederation, but the risks of international intervention incurred on the way inflamed the touchiness of the government of Bern about religious dissidence at home. Their statement of high Reformed Orthodoxy, the Formula Consensus, coincided precisely with Spener's *Pia Desideria* in 1675. It was an elaborate attempt to block any French softening on the articles of predestination, original sin and inspiration. Bern pressed it on Zurich and other neighbours, and backed it up by a censorship which prohibited everything from Thomas à Kempis to Antoinette Bourignon, Pierre Poiret and Cartesianism. This level of Orthodoxy implied isolation, and in the generation which followed the Revocation of the Edict of Nantes the Protestant powers repeatedly urged Bern not to divide the Protestant front by it. The three great pillars of Swiss rational Orthodoxy, Turretini, Ostervald and Werenfels, who attempted a cautious concession to the modern spirit, and who were in touch with Archbishop Wake with a view to getting religious establishments to do their work together, broke its grip in Geneva, Neuchâtel and Basel, three cantons where Pietism obtained least hold. There was resistance in the French-speaking Vaud, chafing under Bernese domination, and within Bern itself there were young theologians, in touch with Francke, also seeking relief from the Orthodoxy of the Formula Consensus.

This emerged when in 1695 Samuel Schumacher, *Vikar* of the Emmental parish of Lützelflüh, sent Francke a fifty-page report on the origin and development of Pietism in Bern. The striking thing about the group of young men discussed in this report is the contrast between their cosmopolitanism and the new isolation of the church in Bern. They had become attracted to the new movements by direct contact abroad with Spener and Francke and their collaborators, with Peter Poiret the apologist of the Quietists, with the Labadists, with Undereyck. Whatever their individual routes they had a common feeling of belonging to an international movement of grace at a moment when the whole Protestant enterprise was under threat from the aggressiveness of Louis XIV. Moreover they appealed self-consciously to another crack in Bern Orthodoxy, a tract by Johannes Erb (1635–1701), *Die Reformierte Hauss-Kirch* (1677). Erb was an Orthodox pastor, thrust by circumstances almost into revivalism. Becoming pastor of Grindelwald in 1667, he had to face the plague of 1669 which carried off the ministers of Aeschi, Adelboden, Grindelwald and Lauterbrunnen. His valiant services throughout the Oberland led to his promotion. Erb too was cosmopolitan; much of his training was taken abroad, especially in England, and he was one of a new wave of Swiss translators of the later English Puritan literature. He translated Baxter and Jeremy Taylor, and the prayers and songs included in his *Hauss-Kirch* were drawn from English sources. His 'house-church' was a domestic application of Spener's *collegium pietatis* of the sort fathers were to make throughout the Protestant diaspora in the Habsburg lands. He was clearly not a man to be constricted by the Formula Consensus.

Swiss Pietism as a party (as distinct from a devotional style) had its origins in 1689, and when its adherents returned from abroad they distinguished themselves by powerful preaching of the New Birth, and a more mystical presentation of the doctrine of justification than the Reformers would have approved. They were met by another demonstration of authority. In 1699 the Bern council introduced the Association Oath to be taken by all citizens to maintain uniformity of faith and liturgy; new decrees against Pietism forbade discourse about the millennial kingdom, preaching 'in coarse and unfitting language', forming conventicles and private devotions, corresponding with suspect aliens about religious and church matters, and reading mystical writings. To ensure the orthodoxy of the German-speaking country pastors, all were to preach in turn in the Bern minster. The result was that the best of the Swiss Pietists went on their travels again, others were driven into separatism and drew inspiration from German radicals and spiritualists, and English Behmenists like Jane Leade and her friends. When Pietism returned to the Swiss churches, it returned more explosively as revivalism, and it came not in the dominant towns but in the countryside, and especially in the Bernese Oberland.

Alternatives to Pietism

Thus throughout Europe the Protestant establishments had come under considerable fire from within by those who held that the dominant systematic Orthodoxies conceded too much to Aristotle and too little to the Bible, were too remote and intellectual to meet the needs of ordinary people, and depended for their ethical urgency on assertions of the imminent end of this present age which became less plausible every day. The Pietist movements had acquired badges of their own, the New Birth, the class-meetings, the orphan houses. There were, however, three groups of people not satisfied with their attempts to ginger up the Protestant establishments. There were the 'spiritualists' who had no confidence in officially organised religion at all; there were oppressed Protestants outside the Westphalia ring-fence who for the most part possessed no church to renew, and who turned to revival; and there were the Orthodox themselves, still the party in possession over most of the Protestant world.

The spiritualists

The spiritualists are hard to pin down despite the immensity of scholarly labour expended on a sort of literary paper-chase among them. They are nevertheless important as offering another analysis of what was wrong with the official religious provision, and as showing how like-minded circles could communicate across the continent despite a heavy censorship. They gathered round the memory of the only German writer of continental importance before Leibniz, Jakob Böhme (1575–1624). He could be vividly direct in his devotional writing, and monumentally obscure in his efforts to set the drama of salvation in the context of the drama of creation. But there were other sources too; Paracelsianism, alchemy, cabbalism, Rosicrucianism, miscellaneous irreconcilables or prophets of judgment. Taking their pick individually of this ideological *embarras de richesses*, may be distinguished two main groups, the Behmenists proper, and the radical Arndtians. No modern general history of the spiritualists has been forthcoming, but they can be found together in Parts 3 and 4 of the great work of one of their spiritual descendants, the *Kirchen- und Ketzerhistorie* (1699–1700) of Gottfried Arnold.

The son of a peasant, Böhme received an early education which enabled him to write in both German and Latin, and settled in Görlitz as a master shoemaker in 1599, marrying the daughter of a well-to-do butcher. In 1613 he sold this business, and went into commerce in thread. During the hectic literary activity of his last years he was supported in part by his followers. Böhme spoke to laymen, including many doctors, who felt alien to Protestant Orthodoxies and sought a philosophical setting for their skills in Paracelsianism. Like the movement for piety he was intensely concerned with problems of good and evil, and he also venerated Sophia, the divine principle of wisdom, which in the Catholic world had been altogether overlaid by the growth of Mariolatry. 'God [he declared] has given me knowledge. Not the I who am the I knows it, but God knows it in me. Wisdom is his bride, and the children of Christ are in Christ, in the Wisdom, also his bride.' Böhme struggled to a comprehensive interpretation of God and the world (incorporating nature) employing the theosophy, Christosophy and cosmosophy of his day. In the divine *Ungrund* (or abyss) wrath and love are at first unseparated in

God. From the mutual relation of these two principles spirit is born, and in these three principles subsists the 'eternal nature' which brings forth the creation. The harmony of creation which corresponds to the Trinity was already destroyed when the angel Lucifer sinned and fell out of relation with God. He became the enemy of further creation. Adam, made in the image of God, was to have existed in the unity of the Trinity in androgynous form with the divine Sophia as his partner. This, however, does not satisfy him, so Sophia withdraws, and Eve is created for him. Eve occasions the Fall, and destiny becomes darker. But to Adam and Eve is already promised the incarnate Word, as redeemer, restorer and head of the body of Christ. But in the world the church of Abel is always confronted by the anti-church of Cain. This offers a peg for criticism of the world and the church, and especially the ungodly Babel through which the confusion of speech and warfare among theologians comes about. Böhme's followers made the most of this occasion for criticism of the church. In Christ there follows the New Birth out of Adamic man, which is conceived as a radical new creation, and a turning away from the old form of life.

Böhme was clearly heavily exposed to the objections of the Lutheran Orthodox that he speculated where scripture was silent, and blurred the distinction between God and creation, between God and the creature. But he retained an enduring interest for those thinking synthetically about God, man and the world. In the Pietist tradition Friedrich Christoph Oetinger (1702–82) used him in constructing a new map of knowledge of formidable complexity. *Aufklärer* in pursuit of natural religion took him up; philosophers like Hegel, Schelling and the romantics went back to him, as did the celebrated Russian Orthodox theologian Berdyaev (1874–1948). And in the eighteenth century a Böhme renaissance was assisted by the systematic publication of his work. This was begun by one of his Silesian admirers and his biographer, Abraham von Franckenberg, who got hold of his work posthumously and took it to the United Provinces .

The atmosphere there was right for little groups of Behmenists, and the same was true of Interregnum England where Ranterism, Quakerism and other new religious options were given a run. A short biography of Böhme appeared in England in 1644 followed by an English translation of his works (1647–62). This collection was the source of his influence over a wide area from Independent sects to Cambridge Platonists and Newton. Behmenism also took institutional shape in a group of adherents gathered round an Anglican clergyman, John Pordage (1607–81), who was purged from his living on account of his theosophical interests, and two fellows of All Souls, Thomas Bromley and Edmund Brice. Pordage's small group in London was later joined by Jane Leade (1624–1704), who after the death of her husband in 1670 received a great vision of the Virgin Wisdom, devoted herself to the virginal life and moved into Pordage's house in 1674. It was she who in 1694 founded the Philadelphian Society which aimed to gather a pure congregation out of all denominations; it was her tracts which created for her a reputation in German religious history greatly in excess of anything she ever enjoyed at home. And it was her German agent, Johann Dittmar, who moulded the Philadelphian Society into a compact missionary body. The strength of the British Behmenist tracts was that they greatly simplified and systematised Böhme's original scheme. This gave them an influence on the fringes of the Pietist movements and also upon the radical separatists of the Wetterau, whose Berleburg Bible (1728–43) contained special prefaces and notes to guide readers to the mystical implications of the text.

The radical Arndtians who are reckoned among the spiritualists must here be summarily dealt with. The dreadful events of the Thirty Years War, followed by the aggressions of Louis XIV, were bound to provoke some far-reaching reassessments of the status quo, and in this sense the radical Arndtians are related to the anti-war prophets of the Thirty Years War. One of them John Georg Gichtel (1638–1710) produced an estrangement between August Hermann Francke and his wife. For the radicals the Franckean institutions were a characteristic lapse into 'outwardness', their complaint against the church. The common factor among the spiritualists was the urge to realise an inward Christian existence through the New Birth and sanctification, and to turn away from the Orthodox doctrines of justification, from church institutions and the secular authorities which used them. Policy for them meant a return to ascetic, world-denying traditions through a rigorous theology of the Cross, and their chief constructive achievement was the creation of house-fellowships and a correspondence network over much of Germany and the Netherlands. Thus the spiritualists tapped a market which was broad if not deep. But the large-scale exploitation of what could be achieved by domestic fellowship and informal links came a little later among those who could not afford to wait for the results of ascetic discipline; they were the revivalists of the Protestant diaspora.

Silesia and revival

Of all the partially Protestant areas unprotected by the Westphalia settlements, Silesia (as explained in chapter 1) was in one sense the most fortunate; it had been granted a few religious rights (though they consisted mostly of the right to attend services in Saxony) and Brandenburg/ Prussia had long-term ambitions in that quarter which Protestants

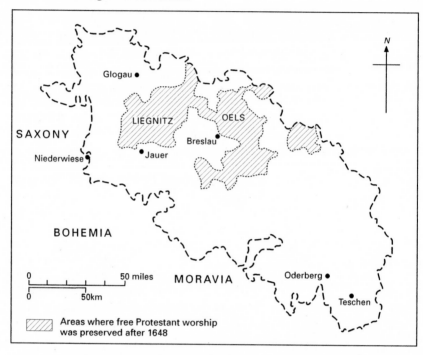

Map 3 Silesia after the Thirty Years War

welcomed. Silesia's troubles did not come singly. During the Thirty Years War the towns lost population and were slow to recover; the mining industry in Upper Silesia suffered from the exhaustion of seams as well as the emigration of Protestant miners. There was continuous ethnic conflict between Pole and German. By the seventeenth century the German towns of Upper Silesia had been steadily Polonised, and in that part 'Silesian' came to mean the mixture of old Polish inhabitants and denationalised Germans who regarded the new Poles as adherents of the Polish state. There was a steady crescendo of rural conflict, a response to intensified serfdom and eviction; this conflict between peasant and lord was very largely a conflict between Pole and German. The ethnic and rural conflicts were complicated by bitter religious conflict between Catholic and Protestant. The Reformation had strengthened the German element in Silesia, particularly in the duchy of Teschen in Upper Silesia, where thousands of the old Polish inhabitants were now Protestant. But in the second half of the seventeenth century the driving force behind German supremacy in Silesia was ruthless recatholicisation by the Habsburgs. The German Protestant cause in Silesia was thus ground between the upper millstone of Habsburg determination to assert confessional supremacy quickly, and the nether millstone of Polish immigration which proved ultimately the most potent force of all. Protestant despair was attested by the rash of new Silesian villages created in Brandenburg, Saxony and Poland, and the growth of the places on the Saxon frontier where there were churches for Silesian use. And no sooner had the Westphalia agreements been signed than the Habsburgs (aided by the chances of mortality in Protestant ruling families) set about undermining them. Hundreds of Protestant churches were confiscated and the clergy and schoolmasters expelled. What brute force could not achieve was to be made good by an impressive array of Jesuit colleges, residences and missions, Capuchin settlements, baroque monasteries and pilgrimage places. Protestant Silesians must now face a crisis for which Spener and Francke had not prescribed, the total collapse of a church system and prospective assimilation into an alien nationality or religion.

Even now the Silesians were not helpless. There was the remnant of a Protestant aristocracy, including great names such as the Promnitzes and Henckels; there was a privileged inheritance in Breslau; and there was a circle of correspondents early built up by Francke and maintained by his son. But the familiar Protestant techniques of securing reformation from above were unusable, and in the second half of the seventeenth century Silesian Protestantism seemed to be facing the same kind of annihilation as that in Bohemia and Moravia after the White Mountain. Working Protestantism (as in Austria) began to be concentrated in the hills and in the farm kitchens of miners and shepherds. With ever more severe measures being taken against the *Wald-* or *Busch-prediger* (the Silesian equivalent of the later Methodist field-preachers) who had brought encouragement from Hungary, these informal *collegia pietatis*, conceived by Spener as a supplement to the regular devotions of the church, came to bear the entire burden of Christianising successive generations. What began in Upper Silesia extended gradually everywhere; only the city of Breslau and the duchy of Oels-Bernstadt escaped forcible catholicisation.

Breslau

In Breslau the Westphalia guarantees had confined confessional rivalry to an educational level. In 1702 the Jesuits had created a university there, clearly with a view to creaming off the Protestant upper crust. But the Breslau Protestants maintained two gymnasia which were equal to Jesuit competition, and compensated for their lack of a university by founding scientific societies earlier than any of the great societies of the west. And the town's theological adviser, Caspar Neumann, was not merely of international repute in practical theology, but was himself a member of the scientific elite, concerned to apply empirical methods to theological studies. Neumann in short embodied an empiricism not characteristic of the Orthodox with a Silesian inwardness of faith, a tenderness of piety, which became one of the hall-marks of revival.

Swedish intervention

To restore a Protestant system in Silesia required outside intervention; when it came in 1707 it was not the expected Prussian intervention, but a great attempt to break the mould of international politics by Charles XII of Sweden. With the Emperor involved with the War of the Spanish Succession in the west and in the east with a revolt in Hungary Charles was able to wrest the Convention of Altranstädt. By it 120 churches were to be returned to the Protestants in the indirectly governed principalities, six new 'Grace' churches were to be built in the Habsburg family lands, and to these and some other churches schools were to be attached. The city of Breslau got back four churches in the neighbouring countryside. Silesian Protestants were still second-class citizens, but the threat of imminent disaster was removed.

Peace proved to be more than the restoration of the *status quo ante*. Since almost all the Protestant churches had been confiscated, the Swedish troops held their church parades in the open air, introducing what later became a familiar Methodist word, camp-meetings (*Feldgottesdienste*). When the troops moved on, the children of the principality of Glogau in Lower Silesia astonished everyone by holding their own camp-meetings, gathering round their elected leaders in prayer and singing, often several times a day, and often against parental opposition. Despite the onset of winter, these prayer-meetings, 'the uprising of the children' as they were called, spread across the country, reaching Breslau in 1708. The Silesian children were taking their cue from the child-prophets of the Cévennes, and were acutely embarrassing because the objects of their intercessions, the return of Protestant churches and schools, were in the last degree politically sensitive.

Halle made the best of the story in the European press, and its English friends in the SPCK immediately brought it out as a pamphlet. Moreover the *Buschprediger* who had been put down by the Habsburgs now reappeared, and the mass awakenings they evoked qualify as primitive revival meetings. The children's camp-meetings, miraculously orderly as long as the adults were hostile, looked like getting out of hand when sympathetic wild men began to exploit them. Their meetings, however, were the one part of the movement which Neumann could get hold of; he set aside some of the newly returned churches for their use where they now acted under clerical oversight. Later, when Protestant revivalists became self-conscious about what they were doing, the theory of their work was that at the bottom of every man's heart there were fragments of faith and conscience still unblunted, which could be revived and made effective. Silesia had been almost without a Protestant church system for half a century, but had lively memories of what it had inculcated; it had a generation of young zealots anxious to make good the failures of their parents; and it perfectly fitted the theory before it had been created. Silesians also enriched the revivalist tradition; denied the opportunity of ecclesial action, they made their way empirically, and did so so successfully that even Francke's agents found themselves drawn into the revival business.

The Grace churches: Teschen

Among the diplomats in the camp at Altranstädt was Francke himself; he helped to get the most important of the Grace churches for Teschen in Upper Silesia. Teschen was strategically crucial, the natural meeting-ground of Poles, Czechs and Slovaks, just below the Jablunka pass, the best commercial route into Hungary. Francke was deeply concerned about the fate of Protestantism among the Czechs and Slovaks; and though Teschen had been a Protestant duchy, Lutheranism had gone to pieces in and about the town. There was still a Protestant flock in the hills, and when the Jesus church opened it claimed a congregation of 40,000. The man Francke commissioned to get the Teschen institutions going was his (and the Prussian government's) agent in Hungary, Anhard Adelung; and what he built first was not the Jesus church, but a large house, with cellars for the wine trade, a ground floor for a bookshop and stock-room, a first floor with accommodation for three preachers, and a second floor with a seminary for nobles. What was envisaged was a miniature Halle, uniting propaganda and commerce at a point where the question of confessional survival was most acute. The first staff appointed were the tutors to the children of Francke and his brother; they did not last long, because they did not satisfy the requirement of the Altranstädt convention that the clergy of the Grace church should be Silesians, and they did not possess the Slavonic tongues essential in a congregation three-quarters of which was Polish. Nevertheless the work went on, and in 1730, though still unfinished, the Jesus church could accommodate 5,000 or more. For seventy years it remained the only Protestant church and school in Upper Silesia, the centre of a remarkable ministry.

The key figure was Johann Adam Steinmetz (1689–1762). He had already proved himself a successful revivalist at a parish in Münsterberg, reinforcing his preaching with fruitful but politically hazardous class-meetings and prayer-meetings, developing his own skills by carefully recording what he learned in confession and visiting, and discouraging the more extravagant phenomena, such as ecstacies and visions. At Teschen he collected an extraordinarily strong team, with special assistants for the Czech and Polish preaching. The theological assistants at the school were still more fiery, all young and active and trained at Halle in Slavonic languages. The most famous of them, Liberda, in whom the preacher and political agitator were almost indistinguishable, was not only one of the most capable theologians Teschen ever produced, but one of the most effective revivalists of all time, with a long-term future among the Czechs.

Circumstances, indeed, pushed the Teschen Pietists into revivalism. German confessions began at six on a Sunday morning, and communions, confessions and preaching in various languages went on all day. The great crowds arriving from a distance would spend the time until it was their turn in enthusiastic hymn-singing of the sort that later became a revivalistic prescription. Revival spread to Bielitz in 1725, and, finding themselves not far from the church after a Whitsunday service, the Bielitz people prayed together and ended by renewing their covenant with God, New England-style. There was an enthusiastic character about their new piety which was certainly not derived from Saxon Orthodoxy. And the Teschen staff were less like ordinary parish pastors than circuit riders, dividing up their duties by rota: one week public prayer-meetings and ministerial duties, the second week travelling out to the sick, the third week rest, and the fourth week riding out to support the travelling preachers. Once again the Jesuits got them out fairly speedily, but they could not stop the Jesus church funnelling religious propaganda from Halle into Bohemia and Moravia to the tune of scores of thousands of volumes. Nor could they prevent the staff destabilising the situation there by their preaching. Francke was bringing the Protestants of Silesia, Bohemia and Moravia under his own pastoral oversight.

Bohemia

The victory of the White Mountain had given the Habsburgs the opportunity for irreversible social engineering in the lands of the Bohemian crown. The Protestant nobility and much of the professional and commercial class were got out of the country before the end of the Thirty Years War, and the peasantry were left to the tender mercies of a new aristocracy and of an alien church which salted away into mortmain huge quantities of former Protestant property. Over most of eastern Europe serfdom was being intensified, and in Bohemia the process could not be separated from recatholicisation; for if the only defence of Protestantism now lay in flight, the new Catholic order could hardly avoid shackling its labour force to the soil more firmly by law. Right through the Habsburg lands the Reformation had been a relatively late arrival, and had been a defence of older social customs against innovation as much as a theological or religious programme. And in Hussitism Bohemia had at least the memory of its own form of religious deviance to add an element of nationalism to peasant hostility towards the new order and its expensive baroque monuments. However, a desperate peasant revolt in 1679–80 was savagely put down, and the last barriers to recatholicisation seemed to collapse. So great was the emigration as to leave the population on the Lusatian side of the Bohemian border permanently greater than on the other side; and among those who were left were all the signs of religious as well as ecclesiastical collapse.

Nevertheless a long-running contest began which involved not only force, but rival appeals to the religious roots of Czech nationalism. The Habsburgs took up the veneration of a fourteenth-century Bohemian, John of Nepomuk, obtained his canonisation in 1729, and, at the crisis of Habsburg survival in 1742, with Silesia lost and French and Bavarian troops in Prague, pressed it on a great scale at court. In Vienna churches, chapels, and statues by the score at every bridge and river bank testified to the new standing of the only Boheman saint of international significance. Czech Protestants could hardly avoid their own attempt to appropriate their country's religious past; they generated a religious revival at Hernhut which beat the canonisation of John of Nepomuk by a short head, and considerably outdid him in international significance.

One solution to the Protestant dilemma was ruled out for a generation. When Charles XII invaded Silesia 7,000 peasants applied to him for religious freedom, a boon not in his gift. But very early there had been a tentative revival in Bohemia in response to the movements in Silesia. Protestants found their way out to Teschen and some were converted by Steinmetz's preaching; the preachers and the Pietist literature found their way in to Bohemia and restored a sense of direction to the Protestantism which remained. By 1720 the Teschen preachers were generating revival among the German-speaking remnants of the old Bohemian Brethren round Fulneck and Zauchtental; revivals broke out independently in other parts, and even Catholics were drawn in. In Bohemia as in Silesia revival offered among other things a great relief from the accumulated guilt at the compromises of a century, at public conformity and secret practice. But public profession of any kind of Protestantism implied a clash with authority, whether those who made it proposed to stand their ground or to emigrate. There was one obvious goal for emigration; the king of Prussia was advertising publicly every year to fill the 3,000 vacant peasant lots he had in Brandenburg alone. Religious refugees would be particularly welcome; they might abscond to Russia, but they could not go home. Already German-speakers were trickling out to Zinzendorf's estate, Czechs were getting to his aunt's adjacent estate at Gross Hennersdorf, and were being organised into a congregation by a colleague of Francke. By the 1720s it was reckoned that there were 20,000 secret Lutherans in Bohemia, anxious to escape, while the Czechs at Hennersdorf put it at 30,000 and radical Pietists would go to 100,000. As we shall see, in 1732 Prussia agreed to accept 6,000 immigrants from Salzburg, and finally acquired 20,000. It seemed likely that Bohemia could be milked on an even bigger scale. The awkward thing was that the old Teschen hands were pressing immediate action on both the king of Prussia and the restless peasants of Bohemia. In September 1732 Liberda dashed off into Bohemia armed with supplies of his own inflammatory works to head a peasant revolt brewing there, and to be utterly crushed by superior force. Meanwhile the bulk of the Hennersdorf Czechs made off to Prussia and were eventually settled to industrial tasks in Berlin. Of course the emissaries of Halle and Prussia still went to and fro, and in the winter of 1737–38 another peasant uprising began. No great train of refugees set out for Prussia, but a steady trickle escaped, and it was disquieting for the Habsburgs that Protestant minorities much nearer home in Lower Austria, Styria and Carinthia were also restless. And the old firebrands from the Teschen school, Macher and Liberda, fetched up quietly as preachers to the new Czech congregation in Berlin.

Halle and Russia

Silesia's importance as the catalyst of revival was ended by the conquest by Frederick the Great in 1740, which froze the religious situation there. But it had a connection with two other revivals which showed the capacity of this kind of movement to flow through unlikely channels. There was little love lost between Prussia and Sweden, and even less between the Swedish church, recently and publicly anchored to Lutheran Orthodoxy, and Halle Pietism. Nevertheless the crushing defeat of Charles XII at Poltava (1709) created a pastoral responsibility for Francke which despite warnings from the king of Prussia, he would not forswear. In addition to prisoners taken early in the war, another 20,000 troops and 10,000 camp-followers were taken at Poltava, who were mostly pushed off beyond the Urals to Tobolsk, the capital of central Asian Russia, and starting point for the China trade. The Swedish church made remarkable efforts to keep this lost flock under pastoral oversight, and Francke also cared more about them than any of his enterprises other than the Tranquebar mission; they offered a means to extend his influence in Russia.

Francke had friends, including two pastors, in the German community in Moscow who cared for the early Swedish prisoners, and sent them literature when they went east. In this circle Curt Friedrich von Wreech began to read sermons and underwent a spiritual crisis when he was lent an old German Bible with Luther's prefaces and marginal glosses; this crisis was brought to a head in best Hallesian style by Luther's Preface to the Romans. One of his fellow-prisoners was deepening his religious experience by reading Arndt and Francke, and when they met up with the main body of the Swedish prisoners at Tobolsk, their preaching caused a great revival. Francke assisted the process with pastoral care and encouragement, with hymn-books, tracts and medicaments transmitted through the German community in Moscow. Revivals began to break out among the Swedish prisoners elsewhere in Russia. Francke characteristically sought to consolidate the results of the revival by education, enabling Wreech and his friends to begin excellent schools on the Halle pattern at Tobolsk, which attracted even the Russian aristocracy. No protracted meeting of the nineteenth century ever presented its promoters with the opportunities created by the Swedes' fifteen-year incarceration in Russia. By the time they came home in 1722–24 the effect had gone deep, and they came back in such force as to make an impact upon a Sweden itself much changed. Legislation against conventicles, followed by the deaths of Francke and leading Swedish Pietists, disappointed the wider hopes. Nevertheless the Pietist cause opened the way to revival movements often led by quite humble people. (Von Wreech retied the knot with Silesia by obtaining employment under the Promnitzes and writing the history of his revival.)

Schwedler and revival

The Prussian conquest of Silesia in 1740 outdated the long chain of Saxon frontier churches built to accommodate Silesians bereft of the ordinances at home. To these churches they had toiled their way, some having to leave home on Fridays to be in time for the Sunday services. These gatherings offered the same kind of opportunities for fellowship and revival as the later camp-meetings of the American Old South, or the great communion-days of the Scottish Highlands, or the services at Teschen. But the opportunities needed to be taken, and the main concession of Saxon Orthodoxy was to hold services, especially in the summer, in the Bohemian language. One pastor, however, was prepared to do much more. Johann Christian Schwedler (1672–1730), minister at Niederwiesa in Upper Lusatia from 1698, was of Silesian peasant stock, and understood his people. He managed to combine a parish of seven towns and eighty-seven villages with a great Silesian following from over the frontier. He reinforced evangelistic preaching – nine hours at a time on occasion – with charitable effort including an Orphan House, Halle style. He also created an ideal escape route for Silesians and Czechs, and had recruited labour for Zinzendorf's grandmother long before the foundation of Herrnhut. It was he who converted Zinzendorf's turbulent henchman, Christian David, and David who used the route via the Silesian villages where Steinmetz and his friends had stimulated revivals to get refugees to Herrnhut. Long before this, however, Schwedler had created a network for moving part of the Bohemian and Silesian revival into Upper Lusatia. Here under the intolerant but mercifully inefficient rule of Saxony it took root and expanded in every direction. Schwedler contributed two things to the history of revival; he helped to transform it from a covert to an open religious phenomenon, and he helped to move it westwards, its principal direction thereafter.

The persistence of Orthodoxy

Whatever its problems Orthodoxy could still make a fight, and this chapter may be rounded off by some examples of its political resistance, and its efforts to sustain itself intellectually. In most states Orthodoxy was emphatically the party in possession, and in none more so than Hanover. The house of Hanover was conspicuously on the make, flirting with popery to attain the electoral dignity in 1692, assuring the Protestant succession to the British crown in 1714, and acquiring part of the Swedish patrimony in Germany in 1719. The strength and weakness of Orthodoxy in Hanover was the complete Machiavellianism of the dynasty in matters of religion. Pietism was strongly represented at their English court in one of the king's mistresses, the Duchess of Kendal, in the Countess of Schaumburg-Lippe, and in a succession of court chaplains; but it was put down in the Electorate by savage legislation, and kept down by the policy of the first two Georges (of England) to employ no clergy in the Hanoverian church except natives. Even so, when the university of Göttingen was founded in 1734, it was shaped by a mixture of Pietist and Enlightenment principles, given unlimited freedom to teach, and exempted from church censorship. As in the days of Leibniz and syncretism, the Welfs were not going to be bound by Lutheran Orthodoxy any further than it suited them.

There were territories such as Waldeck and Hesse-Darmstadt where the Pietist cause went into retreat; and in the imperial cities, at least in the west, Orthodoxy staged a remarkable comeback. Spener's cause had begun well in the cities, especially in the south, but ultimately his 'Second Reformation' had lacked the impetus which Luther's Reformation had obtained from the towns. Space here does not permit an account of what went wrong in so many cities, but it is worth noting the most dramatic and violent case of all, that of Hamburg. The growth of Hamburg had altogether outstripped the capacity of the city clergy to provide pastoral oversight and had aggravated its constitutional and diplomatic ambiguity. Hamburg claimed to be a free imperial city, but was always subject to Danish claims; its trade was menaced by French and allied depredations in turn, and provided arguments for seeking Danish protection. There was no consistory to regulate the relations of the council with the church. The final ingredient of trouble was that Hamburg was one of the points of entry of English Enlightenment. In contrast with the big towns of Switzerland, Hamburg Pietism found its support in the upper crust, while Orthodoxy was strong among the craft trades. The outcome was a civic uprising in 1708 led by what Tholuck called 'the last of the Orthodox pulpit demagogues, Krumbholtz', and put down by an imperial commission led by the troops of Prussia, Hanover and Wolfenbüttel. In Erdmann Neumeister, who died in 1756 aged eighty-five, Hamburg appointed a chief pastor of the St Jacobi church who associated with the gallant poets in his youth, came unstuck at the Pietist court of Sorau in Lower Lusatia, and later became the most violent of the Orthodox polemicists.

Yet no town showed more clearly how fragile the Orthodox position had become. The last schools of Orthodox clergy were Rostock and Wittenberg, neither of them academic pacemakers. In 1735 Hamburg called Provost Johann Gustav Reinbeck of Berlin (1683–1743), a disciple of Christian Wolff, the uncrowned king of the early German Enlightenment, to one of the town parishes. Required by the king of Prussia to refuse, he substituted Friedrich Wagner, another Wolffian. Orthodoxy had gone straight over to rationalism, as it did in so many German towns in the nineteenth century.

Löscher and Orthodox intellect

The capacity of Orthodoxy to survive politically away from the main centres of power supplies a necessary corrective to the rather dismal history of its last great exponent in the Lutheran world, Valentin Ernst Löscher (1673–1749). The son of a high-powered clerical family, Löscher was promoted young, and in 1709 became superintendent in

Dresden and *Oberkonsistorialrat*. He was thus already isolated, for the Elector, Augustus the Strong, had turned Catholic, and Löscher himself had a temperamental distaste for the baroque magnificence of his court. Löscher's great achievement was to launch and edit the first Lutheran theological journal, the *Unschuldige Nachrichten* (1701). This journal, originally a defensive publication, evolved into a review organ in which the whole theological output of the age was subjected to the test of Lutheran Orthodoxy, and it remains a most valuable source for the period. But the defence of the Reformation did not suit the Elector, and Löscher was forced out of the editorship in 1720, and did not get it back till 1732. Nor could he flee to the Hohenzollerns next door, for they were Reformed by conviction, and hand in glove with the Halle Pietists against whom he delivered two fat volumes of polemic. Still worse, Löscher early spotted a far-reaching change in the European intellectual atmosphere, and developed the long-running struggle of the Orthodox with atheism into a ferocious assault upon 'naturalists' and fanatics who had no respect at all for traditional ordinances; this[2] was the most successful thing he ever wrote, but not only was he backing a losing cause, he could not get to the root of the controversy. For the claim of the old-Protestant Orthodoxy to give valid answers to all questions of truth depended on its Aristotelian metaphysics. All being in knowable reality pointed beyond itself to an ultimate and absolute being, to God. True knowledge was based on the coordination of faith and reason; to faith was revealed the decisive thing, the essence and will of God; reason had the subordinate function of demonstrating the necessity of such a revelation, and logically ordering its content. Thus the relation of philosophy to theology was that of maid-servant to mistress; if philosophy overstepped these limits its results must be uncertain, for the probabilities of inference could not yield the certainties of demonstrative truths. Yet Orthodoxy seemed trapped on every side. What it understood by reason so far determined that structure of revelation, that the content of the latter appeared only as a piece of additional knowledge which had to fulfil the usual canons of being unequivocal, reasonable and hence demonstrable. And if philosophy made bold to ask for demonstrative answers to its own questions, theology seemed not to have much additional knowledge to offer. Likewise on the scientific side, the claim of Orthodoxy to disclose the meaning of creation generally became impossible to sustain, leaving Orthodoxy simply as the domestic language of the church usable for its own business. In much the same way, the old-Protestant system was losing its ability to hold together rationally stated doctrine and mystically experienced piety.

---

[2] *Praenotiones Theologicae contra Naturalistarum et Fanaticorum omne genus* (Wittenberg, 1708; 5th edn. 1752).

For Löscher this was a matter of cause and effect, of pure life dependent on the doctrine of justification forensically understood. For Pietists and others to claim that conversion was the indispensable qualification for the theologian and for sound theology was to Löscher nonsense, but he could neither show why, nor overcome the growing opposition between *Aufklärung* and Pietism.

Swiss high-Orthodoxy

Orthodoxy in Reformed Switzerland also survived in many places throughout the eighteenth century, though much more in German-speaking Switzerland (with the notable exception of Zurich) than in French. Bern, which had been the driving force behind the Formula Consensus, and St Gallen were the centres where it hung on longest, with Schaffhausen and Graubünden not far behind. But the deep roots which rational Orthodoxy quickly struck in the French cantons showed a clear desire to avoid the isolation created by the Formula, and the exposure of Bern to Pietist and revival movements in the eighteenth century suggested that there were existential as well as intellectual difficulties with Reformed Orthodoxy. The Reformed had the same difficulties as Löscher in holding the mystical side of religion together with Aristotelian intellect, and when the former took wing with Tersteegen in the Lower Rhine, it left all the church structures behind. Failure on this front was reinforced by a general pessimism about the world as a vale of tears. This pessimism about nature was indeed balanced (at least for the elect) by an optimism about grace, and it was certainly warranted by the rough passage which most of the Reformed churches had had since their foundation; but it was inappropriate to the long economic upswing of the eighteenth century and the decline of plague, which brought with them a vast improvement in the circumstances of some, and some new opportunities for many. And there were two final respects in which Reformed Orthodoxy did not do well, particularly as a state religion. Orthodoxy was as hostile to popular superstition as were the Catholic missions, yet it was hazy as to a strategy for dealing with it. The basis of popular superstition was that it was safer to believe in too much (and take precautions accordingly) than to believe in too little, and it was this central conviction which needed attack. The Reformers had greatly simplified the understanding of the cosmos; the Orthodox had, on the intellectual side, set this process in reverse, and now tended, at their own level, to believe (like the peasants) too much rather than too little. The Moravians were to show, in the Baltic area, that it was possible to blot out a pagan culture altogether, and that the way to do it was to press on a narrow front for an imaginative identification with the sufferings of the Saviour. To the Orthodox, burdened with Christian (or Aristotelian) baggage, this was fanaticism. Finally, high Reformed Orthodoxy possessed special difficulties as a state religion. Half the object of the Formula Consensus had been to block any Huguenot retreat from the doctrine of a limited atonement, the view that Christ died not for the world but for the elect. It goes without saying that whatever virtue there was in this doctrine was much reduced when it was compulsorily enjoined on a whole population. In practice all the baptised tended to be regarded as regenerate and in due course admitted to communion; and the funeral liturgies of Zurich, Schaffhausen and St Gallen had no scruple in regarding all the deceased as regenerate. This was indeed to transform a miracle of grace into that curse of conventional Christianity, the belief that to do what was compulsorily enjoined was an *opus operatum*.

5   Revival moves to the west

Salzburg (1) Schaitberger

Two local dramas played out contemporaneously not in the Habsburg lands, but within their sphere of influence, further unsettled the Protestant world and signalled a shift westwards in the driving forces in it. The Salzburg emigration caused a shock everywhere, from Oxford common rooms normally devoted to port and politics to those attempting to complete Sweden's unfinished work in Christianising the Baltic provinces, and from the transatlantic colony of Georgia to Augsburg. The Moravian revival created a new kind of missionary force which carried the gospel to the ends of the earth, and with it a legend about the sorrows of central Europe and a vigorous feud with Halle. Revivalists like Wesley and Whitefield found that the fields white to the harvest were hazardously mined.

Unforeseen as the great emigration from Salzburg in the winter of 1731–32 was, it was not unprecedented. Salzburg was both an archdiocese and a principality, though the boundaries of the two jurisdictions did not coincide, and they were not always harmoniously administered by the same person. Consistency indeed became a hazard when in the later seventeenth century the archbishops, hungry for money to finance their building schemes, set out to produce a loyal public by exterminating magicians, witches and Protestants. In 1683 this policy produced outbreaks of revival at the Dürrnberg and in the remote Defereggental. Many of the miners in Gastein and the Dürrnberg bei Hallein were Protestants and enjoyed an unofficial toleration in return for their services, but there was now an apparently trivial clash at the latter place between the Austin friar who ran the parish and some of the miners there. There was from the beginning an international reference to this dispute. The ringleaders at the Dürrnberg were related not only to each other but to other miners across the hill at Berchtesgaden where the authorities were alerted. In April 1686 expulsion orders were issued and over the next five years some fifty to sixty miners and their wives were turned out (going mostly to jobs

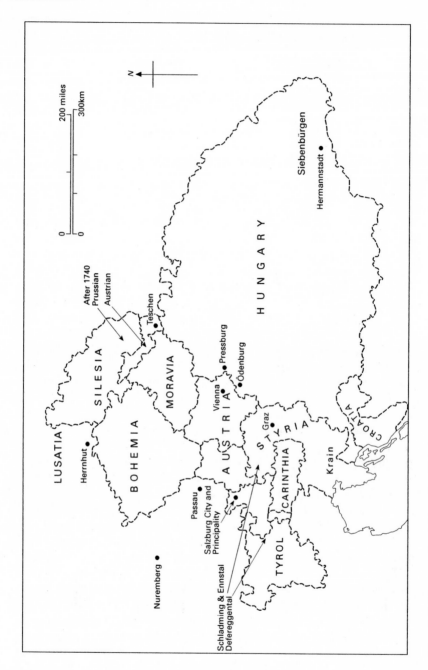

Map 4 Salzburg and neighbouring Habsburg territories

in the mines in Saxony), their property being retained ostensibly to provide for the Catholic rearing of their children, who were kept behind. This action called down the inevitable protests of the Protestant powers, but these would have been entirely ineffective but for an accident. One of the miners Josef Schaitberger (1658–1733), took humble manual employment in Nuremberg, and, developing unsuspected literary gifts, became the most notable Protestant propagandist and evangelist over the whole area of Salzburg, Styria and Carinthia. The son of a Protestant peasant and miner, at the age of eighteen Schaitberger inherited on the death of his father property worth about 1,000 thaler. By the age of twenty-five he was married and had accumulated a theological library of some 300 volumes. He and his friends 'frequently met, prayed, sang, read the scriptures, the catechism and other good books together'; like the Silesians they had stumbled upon the Spenerite *collegium pietatis* and used it not to supplement the devotions of a church now out of reach, but as a substitute for them. And like so many in these years he came to find the secret practice of the faith unbearably equivocal. Exile meant the sacrifice of all these assets; worst of all it meant that he and his wife had to abandon their daughters. Soon after arriving in Nuremberg Schaitberger's wife died of consumption and a broken heart, on her death-bed constantly begging him to get their children out. Three times he returned to do so over the next twenty years, but they had been raised as Catholics and regarded their father as a stranger, and at least one was married. It was while he was hoping to recover his children that Schaitberger began to write the printed letters which made him famous and spread through the Protestant communities from Salzburg to the eastern end of Hungary. The letters were designed to comfort, but also to stiffen faith and mark out a Protestant hard line to which oppressed minorities should stick. In this mission Schaitberger could not offer polemic alone; he had to be, in the words of one of his sermon titles, a 'preacher of penitence and awakening', one who sweetened his message by the 'delight of God's word'. His works were the first thing the Salzburg exiles asked for, and, still banned from Austria after Joseph II's Patent of Toleration in 1781, continued to be smuggled in.

Salzburg (2) The Defereggental

How Protestantism first got into the remote Defereggental is not known, but, like the impoverished inhabitants of other mountain valleys in that region, the Defereggers eked out a living as pedlars and itinerant musicians in Germany, and probably themselves brought in Protestant ideas and books. In 1683 they were reported as religious deviationists, and the archbishop brought on a clash by sending in a Capuchin mission. The Catholic accounts of this conflict contain two details which link it with later events in Silesia and in Salzburg itself: the children were a principal agent in the spreading of Protestantism, and 'the number of Protestants grew daily'. In short some of the common elements of revival were already present; so were the standard responses of the archbishop's government. They maintained that the Defereggers were a new sect with no rights under the Westphalia settlement, and turned out 1,000 of them, without their children, over the winter of 1684–85. Most fetched up in Augsburg and Ulm, though a few went into Switzerland and conformed to the Reformed faith. This act of violence did its work, and Protestantism died out in the Defereggental. But the cause of helping the Defereggers brought to prominence a man who made it his life's work to aid the remaining Protestants in the principality: Samuel Urlsperger. Himself the descendant of a Protestant emigrant from Styria, and a pupil of Francke in Halle, he had been pastor of the German congregation in the Savoy in 1710–12, and, when he left England, became a corresponding member of the SPCK. In 1728 he ended up as Senior of Augsburg; that town was to be the great base for his work for the Salzburgers.

Salzburg (3) The great emigration

The crisis in Salzburg began in 1727 with the election to the see of the Baron von Firmian, a member of one of the great prelatical families of the Habsburg circle of influence. He had already shown himself to be a reforming bishop in the sees of Lavant and Seckau, and he now set the Jesuits upon the hill country of his new see, where there were Protestants believed to number about 5,000. What everyone knew was that the Corpus Evangelicorum, the Protestant caucus in the Imperial Diet, had supported the Defereggers who had fetched up in exile; what no one could foresee was the organisation which enabled the first two peasants expelled to make straight for the Diet, to be followed rapidly by a petition for the free practice of the Protestant faith bearing no fewer than 18,000 signatures. The Catholic authorities claimed that this petition had been got up by Protestant agents from the Diet; this was not credible since the last thing the Protestant estates of the Empire wanted was a demand for toleration which would destroy the basis of the Westphalia settlements. Moreover it was internationally noted not only that the scale of the Salzburg problem was much greater than had been supposed, but that the Protestant cause was being boosted by what would now be called revival, a coarser version of what had happened in Silesia, and was to happen again in America. The Catholic sources show most clearly that styles of piety were being put to the service of the Augsburg Confession which did not characterise the churches of that tradition. There were night meetings at Goldegg where they sang hymns and wept so that the whole countryside could hear; the signs of the day of the Lord were fulfilled by women preaching. The Mosegger family attracted congregations from far and near, and could reduce a congregation to tears. There were active attempts to proselytise the Catholic population.

In November 1731 the archbishop finally expelled all Protestants over the age of twelve at eight days' notice with no other opportunity to clear up their affairs. Protestant Salzburgers left in huge numbers to be picked up by Prussian agents at different points in Swabia, and marched in columns by different routes to the north-east, some to be settled in Berlin, some in Pomerania, some in East Prussia, the bulk in Livonia. The whole operation, in which Salzburgers were paid a daily subsistence allowance on the way and rapidly settled at the other end in peasant lots or domestic service was one of the outstanding achievements of eighteenth-century government, the more remarkable as no one could foresee the scale on which it had to be carried through. It cost the Prussian government half a million thalers, but they got 20,000 settlers, the largest group to be displaced in Germany since the Reformation. All the Protestant powers subscribed and took their share. The English received a first instalment of 200 who were settled by the Georgia trustees near Savannah with two ministers from Halle, and put under the general spiritual oversight of the Wesley brothers. The Dürrnberger miners failed to get the mines shut down, but tempted away half the Protestant population of Berchtesgaden, who mostly settled in Hanover.

Salzburg (4) The consequences

The Salzburg crisis had both a diplomatic and a moral resonance. The archbishop was in financial toils and in ill odour with the Holy See for allowing heresy to become so rife in his diocese. Catholic as well as Protestant powers looked increasingly to the secularisation of ecclesiastical principalities as a way out of diplomatic difficulties. The Emperor had got much of what he wanted. By blocking the Alpine passes he had prevented his Catholic subjects leaking off to profit from the flooded land-market in Salzburg. His need to protect Protestant guarantees of the Pragmatic Sanction, a family settlement which would enable his daughter to succeed him in at any rate the family lands, had allowed the Salzburgers a better outcome than the Defereggers, at the cost of encouraging all their sympathisers among his own subjects to think that the miracle might be repeated; nothing was further from his mind. Equally, a tremendous press campaign had ventilated the advantages of religious toleration. The immediate beneficiary of the great shock, however, was religious revival. The Salzburgers' march across Germany created a tremendous impression; even the news that they were coming inspired 'moving awakenings'; enthusiasts believed that similar outbreaks could be expected anywhere, and even the Lutheran Orthodox wondered that so many thousands could become Protestants without a teaching church. Certainly revival in the Baltic lands was brought nearer by the unsettlement created by the arrival of so large an army of religious refugees.

The Austrian Protestants: their options

There was also domestic anxiety in the Habsburg lands. The Protestant hotheads in Bohemia and Moravia took heart for emigration or even rebellion, and the governments became fearful in Carinthia, Styria and the Tyrol, and even in Austria itself. This anxiety lasted till 1735, and out of it were born not merely the main lines of Habsburg Protestant policy down to the Patent of Toleration of 1781, but also the strategy of Protestant survival. As a young man the future Joseph II was educated upon documents insisting that Archbishop Firmian had ruined his principality by depopulating it, and considered how to strengthen his own army and population. His principal solution was to be the Patent of Toleration, but even under Maria Theresa, a government was persecuting Protestants which knew that a 'final solution' to its problem of confessional minorities was not among the options open to it. For in time of war Habsburg confessional strictness fell victim to the uncooperativeness of provincial authorities. The Austrian authorities soon learned that the only way to finish Protestantism was to break up the communities which sustained it, but they could never extricate themselves from other embarrassments for long enough to finish the job. Protestant revival was a response to the exigency of government, especially in the years immediately before and after the War of the Austrian Succession. This intermittent unrest was fanned partly by home-grown propagandists, but quite largely by Salzburgers from the west. From the beginning they were active in Styria and Carinthia; special measures were taken to keep them out in the early 1750s, but they were back again in the 1770s, always liable to generate an enthusiastic piety. The lessons taught in Silesia, Upper Lusatia, Bohemia and Salzburg, that Protestant communities could overcome their fears and pull themselves up by their own bootstraps, lessons which had already been absorbed in the British Isles and the northern and middle colonies of America, were embraced in Styria and Carinthia.

Revival was the reason why Austrian secret Protestantism issued not in the Lutheran Orthodoxy of even a Schaitberger, and certainly not in the Pietism of Halle or Württemberg, but in what one of their own bishops has called 'an awakened Christianity' rather unconfessional in character, but strong enough eventually to create a church system and provide the substance of its life till the end of the nineteenth century.

There were four ways in which Austrian Protestants might respond to their predicament – they might accept assimilation, they might attempt flight to a less adverse environment, they might draw courage from apocalyptic fantasies, or they might fan the embers of religious conviction in revival. Each of these courses was accepted by some Austrian Protestants, some accepting more than one. But when the Habsburgs pursued the same intolerant policies in Hungary with a desperate violence, they achieved a different result, and the reaction of the Hungarian Protestants was also different.

Hungarian Protestants

Under extreme pressure the Hungarians retained their church system, and kept a foothold in those social strata with traditional access to power. Hungary, therefore, had a full-blooded age of Orthodoxy as the Austrians did not. The difference was not total; the growth point among the Hungarians was the so-called 'widowed' congregations without a pastor which appeared to the tune of about a thousand under the Toleration Patent, and had been kept going by the informal means which were all the Austrians had. The Hungarians also put Philip Doddridge into Magyar dress, and under the Toleration Patent made a remarkable missionary effort; despite all the language difficulties, they got Bohemian and Moravian Protestantism organised again by supplying sixty ministers. Where the Hungarians differed from the Austrians was in their addiction to apocalyptic. When organised Protestantism collapsed in Bohemia in the Thirty Years War, Bohemians took refuge in Hungary and got a hearing for their pipedreams of revenge upon the Habsburgs. One of the least rational, Nikolaus Drabik, identified the papacy and the house of Habsburg as Antichrist and Babylon, and forecast their downfall at the hands of Sweden and the princes of Siebenbürgen. When the Hungarians finally got over these delusions, they began, like the Reformed elsewhere, a long slide into rationalism. The Austrians also were addicted to the Book of Revelation, and when, after the Toleration Patent, they built their churches, the highest figure above the altar was commonly the lamb with the flag of victory and the book of the seven seals. That Austrian

Protestantism survived to build its altars, however, owed much to the fact that under persecution its energies went not into rebellion, but into revival on this side of the apocalypse.

Zinzendorf

This lesson was not lost on Protestants elsewhere; and the Emperor also drew the lesson that he would do well to contain the various phenomena of religious dissidence within his own frontiers. One small revival which did get away was used by the eccentric Count Nikolaus von Zinzendorf to stamp the history of Protestantism indelibly, and to link the disparate revivals of Silesia and Salzburg. Zinzendorf (1700–1760) came from an Austrian noble family which had grown great in the Habsburg struggle against the Turks, but had ultimately made Protestant confessional solidarity its choice. His grandfather joined the flight of the Protestant aristocracy from Austria in 1661; his father became a privy councillor in Saxony, but died immediately after his son's birth. Four years later his mother married the Prussian Field-Marshal Dubislav Gneomar von Natzmer, like herself a supporter of the Francke foundations, and left the boy to be brought up by her own mother, Henriette Katherina von Gersdorf, née baroness of Friesen. Zinzendorf was thus raised almost exclusively in the company of women, the chief of whom was two generations older than himself, a remarkable bluestocking possessed of all manner of languages, and a shrewd and strenuous politician. Her estate at Gross Hennersdorf was in Upper Lusatia, Saxony's most recently acquired and restless province. She was in the thick of its resistance to the centralising policies of the Electors of Saxony, and held the family view that the enserfed Slavonic populations of the province, the Wends and Sorbs, needed reconstruction through the propaganda and literature of Halle.

Zinzendorf absorbed and modified this heritage. Like his grandmother, but unlike his mother, he was never a slavish adherent of Halle. He never went into politics as his grandmother wished, and found his own way of dealing with the Wends who proved to be good material for religious revival. Very importantly, a man who, but for the untimely deaths of his father and grandfather, would have been brought up in court society at Dresden, became an adopted Lusatian, with the ingrained Lusatian love of independence. As late as 1753 a German tourist in London was surprised to hear him preaching in the Fetter Lane chapel in 'a quite simple and common Upper Lusatian dialect'. He took his formal education at the Pietist school of Halle and the Orthodox school of Wittenberg and spun many legends about both. His informal education revealed clear signs of the future. A visit to Holland convinced him of the virtues of religious toleration, and in Paris he became a friend of Cardinal de Noailles who later stood godfather to two of his daughters. These two strands in the count's make-up, toleration and interconfessionalism, were different, and each helped to confuse his contemporaries.

Between 1721 and 1727 the count acquired an independent position, and, very importantly, in 1722 married Erdmuthe Dorothea, Countess Reuss of Ebersdorf. Very much his second choice as a wife,[1] she emancipated him from his grandmother, brought valuable financial resources, and a head for business much better than his own. In the 1740s Zinzendorf turned against her, and let it be known that after her death he was going to marry one of the Moravians, Anna Nitschmann; in this period of neglect her capacity for business affairs was sorely missed. The one thing she could not do was to raise any of her six sons to adult years. This first marriage appeared to tie Zinzendorf to the network of pious counts which supported the Halle institutions; in fact it set him on an independent course. For Ebersdorf, the court of what was supposed to be the tiniest principality in the Empire, offered Zinzendorf a pattern of Christian existence for which he was looking. The congregation of the court separated from the parish, and invited whatever preachers they chose, including noted revivalists; the court offices were filled by Christians without respect to sect or party, who held together harmoniously on the basis of common love of the Saviour. This ideal, 'Philadelphian love', Zinzendorf hoped to realise when he built a house at Herrnhut, on the Berthelsdorf property purchased from his grandmother; in the event estate development launched him on a career which was not quite Philadelphian.

The Moravians

The first Moravian settlers were brought to Berthelsdorf in 1722 by Christian David, a remarkable but difficult man. A Moravian carpenter, the son of poor and strict Catholic parents, he encountered Protestant ideas in the course of his trade travels to the north, and was eventually converted to them in the circle of Scheffer, the minister of Görlitz, and Schwedler, both of them evangelists who were skilled in getting Protestants out of Silesia. Partly under local influences and partly under the stimulus of Steinmetz's preaching at Teschen, revivals were breaking out

---

[1] In 1721 Zinzendorf intended to become engaged to his cousin Sophia Theodora of Castell-Remlingen. On the journey to Castell he accidentally discovered that his friend, Count Henry XXIX of Reuss-Ebersdorf, also had her in view. The two went together to Castell, resolved to accept the lady's wishes as the will of God. Her preference was for Henry. The following year, however, Zinzendorf married Henry's sister, in the presence of the Castell, Ebersdorf and other families.

in Moravia, and David's new friends put him in touch with them. Steinmetz, however, warned David not to start bringing out Protestant refugees till he had somewhere religiously wholesome to take them. That condition was satisfied by Zinzendorf's Philadelphian establishment at Bethelsdorf and his appointment of Richard Rothe to the parish living. David could now comfort secret believers in his homeland with the news that toleration was to be had much nearer than Poland or Siebenbürgen. His contacts were limited to three villages, Sehlen, Zauchtental and Kunwald; these were peculiar in that before the Thirty Years War they had been strong centres of the generally weak German branch of the mainly Czech church of the Brethren. Nevertheless the handful of refugees he now brought out via Schwedler and Scheffer, were to impress the history of Protestantism indelibly.

The original Moravians – German-speakers as distinct from the Czechs who went to Gross Hennersdorf next door – formed only half of the first 300 settlers at Herrnhut, for the threats of the Emperor to the Saxon government effectively checked the haemorrhage of his subjects and jeopardised the future of those who had already escaped. The difficulties of the Moravians in creating a completely new settlement were aggravated by the distaste of the Saxon church for the toleration prevailing at Berthelsdorf, and the genuine fears of the neighbouring clergy. Apart from the old suppressed Slavonic minorities, the area was full of footloose immigrants from Silesia, Bohemia, Moravia and Hungary, and when Schwedler and other revivalist preachers were abroad they would assemble in their thousands from every quarter. Public order and the parish system were at stake. Moreover the Herrnhuters themselves were much divided. Well-known figures among them were tradesmen (like David), but the bulk were peasants who had to forsake everything to escape. The majority of the non-Moravian settlers were artisans, shoemakers, potters, tailors, turners and the like. They were also divided by religion. The old Unity of the Brethren had been nearer to the Reformed than to the Lutheran churches. Christian David now took up with Reformed doctrines. So the Moravians now divided into a Lutheran party led by the Neisser family supporting Zinzendorf and the parish minister Rothe, and a separatist group led by David. The political risks created by the emergence of separatism were obvious. Zinzendorf came home to reside and imposed a village constitution and a religious constitution which should be coordinated into the church structure of the province. Christian David moved out of the village, built a new hut, dug his own well, and asked what use it had been for him to risk his life bringing souls out of popery, if, by being entangled in Lutheranism and kept from conversion, they were to be made doubly children of hell. The community at Herrnhut would fall apart, unless its divisions could be sublimated in revival.

The revival at Herrnhut

Revival, however, was in the air, originating in Silesia, spreading in Upper Lusatia among Germans, Wends and Czechs, concentrated in Berthelsdorf by the increasing resonance of the preaching of Richard Rothe. The temperature was raised by visits of inflammatory preachers like Liberda and Schwedler. Signs and wonders began to appear in Herrnhut. Christian David began to hold men's Bible classes. There were all-night meetings on the Hutberg. It needed only one more sign of the recent revivalist past, an intense spirit of prayer among the children, to precipitate one of the most remarkable of all religious revivals.

It began with the personal crisis of an eleven-year-old girl, Susanne Kühnel. Her mother had died shortly before, and the girl's distress was compounded by the perception that her mother had a religious grace which she lacked. For three days and nights her distress and prayers lay upon the whole community. Then she and three other girls received a conversion experience in the same night. There was a dramatic first communion to which the whole community turned out with much weeping and singing, and the movement spread to the adults. The entry in the Herrnhut diary describing the girls and boys praying in their separate gatherings carries self-conscious echoes of the 'revolt of the children' in Silesia, 'so powerful a spirit prevailed among the children as is beyond words to express'. In this tidal wave of emotion the community at Herrnhut overcame the forces of disintegration in their midst, accepted Zinzendorf's plans for pastoral oversight, and discovered a usable past from which the count himself was not allowed to escape. Finding a copy of Comenius's history of the Brethren in Zittau town library, the Moravians concluded that they had stumbled on the essence of their old church discipline and 'resolved to stick by it'. If the kings of Prussia met their match with the Czech emigrants, Zinzendorf met his with the Germans. He would have to pursue his Philadelphian ideals through their objectives, and it was his genius to divert them into a mission to the universal church.

This change of direction was furthered by the crises in Salzburg and Bohemia, for the Emperor knew that a staging-post was being prepared for Czech emigration at Gross Hennersdorf. His constant pressure upon a Saxon government which was itself exasperated by Moravian evangelism in Upper Lusatia, told. Two commissions of inquiry were sent down to Herrnhut in the 1730s, and Zinzendorf was banished while he was out of the country, so that he could not return. Special legislation destroyed the diaspora work of the Moravians and put the whole community on notice that without conformity to the Augsburg Confession they would follow the count.

Moravian migration

Zinzendorf's response to all this was to get the Moravians proper off to the Wetterau, leaving Herrnhut to be peopled by Lutherans, and to negotiate other refuges in the United Provinces, Prussia, Sweden and Britain, where an act was obtained in 1748–49 for a grant of privileges to the Unitas Fratrum as 'an antient, apostolical and episcopal church'. In all these cases Moravianism was never anything but independent of the local established churches. The problem between Zinzendorf and his Moravians was that they were not prepared to forgo what they believed to be their traditions, while he would not surrender his original Philadelphian ideal. Both needed toleration, and practical toleration was only possible in Germany on the count's principle of a movement within confessions; to establish a fourth tolerated religion in the Empire would breach the Westphalia settlements. But the result of constant pressure from the count's enemies was that with every year the Moravian church seemed to become a more distinct body, and to put down roots not within the bosom of the historic Reformation confessions, but in those lands where the state was prepared to tolerate dissenters. There was, of course, a sense in which Zinzendorf no longer wished at any rate the 'Pilgrim Congregation' of original Moravians to put down roots; their readiness to move, first born of political necessity, could be put to the service of the gospel. Preselected in Moravia on the basis of religious determination, welded together by revival, permanently uprooted and possessing the life-style and economic skills of humble people, they were poles apart from the style of the Catholic missions, but were no less effective at the ends of the earth – the Baltic, Greenland, Pennsylvania, the West Indies, eventually South Africa and Tibet.

Zinzendorf and Halle

Paradoxical in everything, while the count's motley army was opening distant doors to the gospel, it found doors in the Lutheran world barred to it by a long-running feud with Halle, and this notwithstanding that the most successful Moravian missions, in the Baltic lands, were built directly upon the labours of Francke's pupils. In January 1734 Zinzendorf concluded that a party had been got up against him by Halle, that they were determined to destroy his movement, and that they had the backing of the pious counts. The evidence of this was afforded by two public disappointments. In 1731 August Gottlieb Spangenberg, who later became Zinzendorf's right-hand man, received an academic appointment at Halle as a pledge of the unity of 'all the children of God'; correctly perceiving him as standing close to the separatists, and having no means of foreseeing that after the count's death Spangenberg would push the Moravians back towards Lutheran Orthodoxy, the younger Francke had him summarily expelled in 1733. Worse things followed in Denmark. In the 1720s Denmark possessed the most important Pietist court in Europe, and when Christian VI was crowned in 1731 (the queen being a friend of one of Zinzendorf's elder sisters) the count's hour seemed to have struck. He received all manner of honours, and was alive to the prospect of safe bases for the Moravians and access to colonial missions. By 1734, however, he was banished from the kingdom, his settlement at Pilgerruh was on the way to dissolution, and anti-Moravian legislation was in prospect. This fiasco was due partly to Zinzendorf's tactlessness and to the fact that Moravian evangelism was too successful for the taste of the Danish church, but it was also due to Halle pressure, brought to bear through the Count of Stolberg-Wernigerode, a first cousin of Christian VI.

Part of the difficulty was that since the death of the elder Francke in 1727 the Halle foundations had been directed by his son, Gotthilf August, a man of much less ability, whose very anxiety to preserve his father's work created a legalism in the Halle mentality from which it had once been free. This legalism was bound to irk Zinzendorf, and to be particularly irksome on the matter of conversion. Protestant pastoral theology was perennially exercised by anxious souls who found no difficulty in believing in justification by faith alone, but were tortured by the existential question whether they actually had the saving faith. Both the Reformed and the Lutherans had given heed to the morphology of the Christian life, and in the eighteenth century a vogue of collected biographical studies of the regenerate aimed to assist the believer to determine where he stood in the Christian pilgrimage. One of the most influential models was that of August Hermann Francke, clearly based on his own conversion experience. Zinzendorf, nothing if not a cheerful Christian, provocatively admitted that according to the Franckean scheme he was an unconverted person; temperamentally averse to the *Busskampf* or penitential struggle which was central to Francke, he abused it as 'a chimera, an imaginary illness, a self-induced sickness', Christ himself having suffered the *Busskampf* for all mankind. This conviction could only be strengthened by the priorities of revivalism. Revivalism in the Habsburg lands was a response of those who must achieve results quickly or go under, who not only had no time for programmes of church renewal to succeed, but for the most part had no institutional church to renew. Zinzendorf held that the highly structured Hallesian pattern of conversion actually delayed the conversion of many; it fixed men's gaze on psychological thresholds they could not detect in themselves. Something quicker was needed, and his quicker method was that of imaginative identification with the Saviour. A man was a child of God as soon as he received forgiveness of sins and showed evidence of the fact in heart and life. To Pietists this 'quick' method was simply frivolous, and an unwillingness to cheapen the Christian vocation was one of the things which enabled Pietist and Orthodox to join in a combined assault on Moravianism in the 1740s.

Zinzendorf and money

Disputes over the 'quick' method of conversion were compounded by a different matter which in the public eye was related to it. Zinzendorf had spent more than all his modest resources in purchasing the Herrnhut estate, and developed it on the Halle joint-stock principle. But he had an aristocratic disdain for money and for the labour required to accumulate it. His financial education took a giant leap forward when he was banished in 1736, and many of his original Saxon creditors called in their 6 per cent loans. Bailed out in the United Provinces by pious merchant circles including Mennonites, Labadists and others alarmed at the progress of rationalism, Zinzendorf survived buoyantly by borrowing at 3 and 4 per cent. The same supporters continued to supply the capital needed to establish settlements and mission stations world-wide. Eventually Zinzendorf bought his way home by lending to the Saxon government at rates better than they could obtain for themselves; and in the 1750s his profligacy bankrupted his community. Meanwhile though cheap Dutch credit had nothing to do with the 'quick' method of conversion, the remarkably quick results of other kinds which it made possible gave the count's religious position a peculiar resonance. The contrast between ebullient Moravianism and the low morale of the Protestant establishments, not to mention the doldrums of the Halle foundations, sharpened the edge of their protests against superficial conversion.

Halle and Herrnhut in the Baltic region

Despite this feud, Moravian successes in the Baltic lands were clearly built on foundations laid by Halle. In 1701 Frederick I had taken the title of king in Prussia because only in the duchy was he sovereign and not subject to the Emperor. But Prussian forward policy in the next two reigns guaranteed protection for Pietism in the university, the schools, and the Orphan House founded in Königsberg, and enabled it to take advantage of the vacancies created by the calamitous plagues which ravaged the Baltic area between 1709 and 1711. In 1724 a boy theologian from Halle, Georg Friedrich Rogall (1701–33) came back to a chair at Königsberg with the warm support of the king and Francke. The Orthodox frustrated his hopes of going on a mission to Livonia, but he trained a whole new generation of Pietist clergy, and got some 30,000 devotional tracts into circulation. Men trained in the Halle style were well fitted to deal with the linguistic Babel created by the labour recruiting of the kings of Prussia, who brought in families from all over Germany, and from Lithuania, Poland and French Switzerland as well. The result of their efforts, abetted by old hands like Steinmetz, was that a series of revivals of limited scope set in which, like those of English Methodism, had considerable cumulative force. The biggest single blow to old rigidities was given in 1732 by the arrival of some 14,000 of the Prussian contingent of Salzburgers. Those who came by Halle brought five preachers with them, and gradually the Prussians provided them with the barn-like churches they also built in Silesia; the sensation, however, was the Salzburgers' own revivalistic ways, and the Silesian-style camp-meetings put on by the children. Even Lithuanians who could not understand a word of the language came to admire the devotion and hear the songs.

Zinzendorf had long dabbled in Salzburger affairs, on the whole unsuccessfully, and before the breach with Halle he was sending preachers to the Baltic to them. The social situation was in many ways ideally adapted for them. The German nobility of the area had managed to swing much of the cost of the Russo-Swedish war which ended in 1721 on to the indigenous population, and serfdom steadily intensified. They did not repair the ravages of war as resolutely as the Hohenzollerns in East Prussia, but they did keep importing Hallesian clergy who kept the pagan culture of the native population under pressure. By the 1740s the bulk of the clergy in the area were of the Halle stamp, and Livonia and Estonia had together become one of the great bastions of Pietism in the Russian empire.

It was a Pietist pastor who first invited Moravian assistance in 1729 and Christian David and a colleague were sent for a year to the Reval area, supporting themselves by manual labour and organising prayer and Bible-study groups. Trouble with church authority made it clear that the Moravians needed the aristocratic protection which had so often been the salvation of Pietism, and by the mid-1730s Zinzendorf had organised this on the Campenhausen estate at Brinkenhof in Estonia, and especially at

Wolmershof, north-east of Riga, the estate of the widow of General von Hallert, a former German general in the Russian imperial service. She was a Saxon, a von Bülow, a friend of August Hermann Francke (with the Hallesian enthusiasm for dealing with serf races in a new way), and is said to have been acquainted as a young woman with the future countess of Zinzendorf. The result was that in a few years some fifty Moravians, a force numerically equal to the entire clergy of the area, came, by invitation, to assist them. They kept themselves by lay labours, and speedily acquired an influence which no one, least of all the clergy, ever expected. The attraction which the long-suffering Salzburgers had held for the Lithuanians was exercised in Livonia and Estonia by the long-suffering Moravians.

The implication of subsequent events is that two generations of public battering had weakened the old heathen culture of fire and nature to the point where its adherents were susceptible to a new religious appeal. Even before the Moravians arrived the occasional Hallesian pastor encountered a revival in his parish. Johann Christian Quandt, for example, minister of the Estonian parish of Urbs, was faced with very high-pressure revival in 1736, with the usual features of children's work spreading to the adults. What distinguished Urbs from revivals in central Europe was that it was in the front line of the struggle against paganism. Previous pastors had made assaults on holy places and groves, but had not destroyed their sanctity to the people who used to pray and sacrifice there in cases of sickness and other need. Quandt reported:

Sixty to eighty such places remained in the parish of Urbs entirely without the knowledge of the pastor. With his schoolmaster the pastor destroyed such places, twenty-four with his own hand within two weeks, the sexton and other young people supported them, and the holy places were ploughed up and sown, and thus even their memory was expunged. Also the other superstitious customs of the people at work, sowing, ploughing, haymaking, baptisms, marriages and burials, the playing of bagpipes and jumping, fell away without compulsion.

This revival was on the ebb before the Herrnhuters arrived in 1738, but it shared one characteristic with the revivals which they promoted; the voluntary repudiation of old ways was so vehement that when, a century later, the folklore specialists came hunting for folk-songs, the area south of Dorpat was completely barren. Even among the Letts the folk-songs were described as 'good for nothing'.

The 'year of revival' among the Letts began in 1739 when that old campaigner Christian David and a colleague held their first meeting in the Latvian tongue. That summer the movement seized the whole of northern Livonia and by 1742 the Moravians had gathered into their own fold some 14,000 members in this part of the Baltic, of whom 3,000 were in Latvian Livonia, 2,000 in Estonian Livonia, and the rest in Estonia and Oesel. Oesel, the Baltic island which suffered the worst from the rise and overthrow of Swedish absolutism, had a unique place in the history of the Baltic revival. In 1738 Gutsleff, one of the Pietist clergy of Reval, and an acquaintance of Zinzendorf, was appointed superintendent, and began to set up peasant schools; on the count's initiative he translated the Bible and hymn-books into native tongues. When revival broke out at Uppa bei Arensburg in 1740 there were dramatic results including conversions in a number of noble families. There was now high-pressure revival among the mainland Estonians and a Moravian preaching force able to take advantage of the opportunity when it came. Drunkenness and crime were replaced by intense devotion, and there was a voluntary repudiation of the old culture:

They put aside all worldly delights: bagpipes, harps, bugles, they burned and totally destroyed. The women put away their headbeads and their pinafores, which were gracefully embroidered with all kinds of ribbons and silver and gold braid, and all their pearls, corals and necklaces, and went into modest and honourable clothing.

The excitement ended suddenly in 1743. Not all the Moravians were equal to the opportunities which came their way, and the clergy who had invited them in turned against a great movement of lay Christianity which seemed to be escaping from their hands. Still worse, the Tsarina Elizabeth issued a ukase in 1743, forbidding the Brethren's meetings and looking to the confiscation of their meeting-houses and literature. Three of the leaders of the revival, including Gutsleff, were brutally hauled off in chains to imprisonment in Russia.

The vineyard of the Lord seemed to have been destroyed in full flower, yet appearances were deceptive. The ukase was not strictly enforced. The revival of 1738–43 left a working capital which continued to yield dividends. The Brethren continued to breed men able to work under persecution, and their hymns, translations of devotional classics and music continued to provide a culture to replace the one they had destroyed. There were new revivals in the 1770s and 1780s, and, when the Unity of the Brethren was again legalised by Alexander I in 1817, they had 144 congregations in Estonia and Livonia with some 30,000 members, and were poised to take advantage of the social stresses occasioned by the abolition of serfdom, to reach the peak of their influence in the next generation.

Internal difficulties of the Moravians

Yet all was not well with the main centres of the Brethren. In the early 1740s Zinzendorf was in America, partly with a view to Indian missions, partly to offer his movement as a solution to religious chaos among the Pennsylvania Germans. Both these missions were very unsuccessful, and he returned to Europe in 1743 with a romantic vision of the noble savage and the life of nature, and an increasing reluctance to face either the political or the financial problems of his movement. From 1747 the interest charge on his debts exceeded his income, and disaster was only staved off till 1753 by discreditable shifts. He nevertheless involved himself in new extravagances at his settlement at Herrnhaag in the Wetterau in 1745–50, the period known in the history of the Brethren as 'the time of sifting'. The period was the most productive of the count's literary life, but it was also one in which he encouraged an enthusiastic piety to run riot, an in-language of sentimental diminutives to grow around the adoration of the wounds, an anti-modernism apparently to please his conservative Dutch backers, and a joyous existence of feasting and fireworks which could only hasten the day of financial reckoning. In 1750 the settlement at Herrnhaag was in effect expelled at the cost of the capital investment there, and had to be relocated. The count's attempts to sublimate the troubles of his community in a display of child-like innocence, as in 1727 they had been sublimated in revival, failed disastrously. The in-language he encouraged, at once Christocentric and esoteric, inflamed the opposition to his movement and was directly contrary to the main Moravian mission strategy; this was to preach Christ from the outset, to realise the Christian profession within the cultures they encountered, and, above all, to avoid language unknown or incomprehensible to their hearers.

What was to be done? Spangenberg had a remedy and it involved the suspension of Zinzendorf from his offices. Firm control was to be applied to every department of the Brethren's life. Spangenberg pushed the Brethren back steadily towards Lutheran Orthodoxy in language and systematic theology. The count's eccentric language was purged from their devotions, and with it went the lighthearted cheerfulness which had been his redeeming feature. On the economic side the Brethren were to be subjected to the discipline of the market. In Herrnhut Abraham Dürninger, a successful linen merchant, opened a factory to make profits for the community; the firm still trades. These devices secured a modest future for the Brethren, and the count's debts were paid off in fifty years. But the days when the Brethren could excite the world of revival by a quick method of conversion, and astonish the world of religious establishment by the speed with which things could be done on Dutch credit were over. The religion of the Unity had acquired the burdensome features which had irked Zinzendorf in Pietism and Orthodoxy. The lead in revival passed to others.

Zinzendorf and the Inspired

Zinzendorf and the Dutch money which sustained him for so long were among the forces moving the axis of revival westwards, to the Rhineland, the United Provinces and Britain. In all of these places, however, he was to find revival already in being or in preparation, and in the south-west of the Empire a shape was given to his action by conflict, not with Halle, but with another revival, that of the Inspired. As we saw in chapter 1 they had found refuge from anti-Pietist legislation in the Wetterau, where a number of tiny Reformed principalities had raised cash by selling toleration; and they had been invigorated by contact with the inspired French Prophets. The first separatists to encounter the Inspired, Gottfried Neumann and his unmarried sister-in-law Melchior were each suffering from the spiritual blues. They were impressed by the conversation, the prophecy and the physical contortions of the Inspired, and were finally given a prophecy: 'Your sighs have not mounted unheard, I have heard and sworn to help you, and your petition shall be granted.' Both of them fell into convulsions, and, while the Inspired prayed, Melchior came through her distress, and herself began to prophesy. The Inspired went on to Wittgenstein where they were 'as voices of God – there were sounds of trumpets, thunder and explosions . . . They roared like lions and spoke in foreign tongues and mostly explained what it all meant'. In the end E. L. Gruber (1665–1728), the leader of the separatists, after long resistance, was converted to the new ways, finding a deeper sense of the forgiveness of sins, of health and wellbeing, and the moral bonus of greater personal generosity and patience. His henchman, J. F. Rock (1678–1749) was even more reluctant. But he searched the scriptures and found that the Inspired proposed no false doctrine, that they pressed on to personal sanctification, that they had sublimated many of the conflicts in the district, and revived the prayer meetings as no one else could. When the moment came Rock was seized with violent convulsions at a prayer meeting, and then by powerful laughter. Some weeks later, the contortions were followed by prophecy, and prophecy by peace of heart. This seemed indubitably the work of the Lord: the separatists were won for Inspiration.

Inspiration came in the company of others, often in the prayer meeting. The subject fell into a half-conscious sleepwalking state. Eyes and ears were mostly closed, but the sense of smell and taste were enormously enhanced, and the subject could perform his movements and even go upstairs in this condition. Utterances were usually preceded by a warm feeling of the heart of the kind Wesley experienced in his conversion; but with the Inspired this gradually spread over the whole body and the face glowed. First there were movements, then utterances. The gentler the company, the more gentle the movements; the more hostile the company, the more violent and noisy. There was also a heightened sense of community; indeed in general the effect of the Inspiration revival was to counter the isolation and individualism of the separatists, to bring about the formation of prayer fellowships with public and proselytising functions, to encourage hymn-singing and -writing, and love-feasts, and most important of all to carry out strenuous itinerant evangelism with a view to gathering in all the children of the prophets from among all sects and peoples. In this respect they were the successors of the itinerant Anabaptists, Quakers and Labadists of the seventeenth century, and the forerunners of Zinzendorf's Moravians. Their preaching tours led to the formation of great numbers of prayer fellowships across Swabia and in the cantons of Bern, Zurich and Schaffhausen, which were kept in personal fellowship with the congregations in the Wetterau. Religious revival was in being.

The radicals of the Wetterau believed that the church was in a fallen state and derived from the Reformed federal theology the idea that church history could be divided into stages yielding an interpretation of the present. The present moment was the time when the true seed scattered among all nations and confessions was to be gathered and the true word hidden in the letter of scripture mystically revealed. What gave the tiny events in the Wetterau their resonance was not historical perspective, but two apparently damaging developments. Rock could not stop his brethren joining the national flood to Germantown in Pennsylvania, nor could he avoid conflict with Zinzendorf. The need for toleration had driven the count, as it had driven the Inspired, to the Wetterau; and having arrived he tried to establish his movement as a ground for unity there, exactly as he did in Pennsylvania, and with as little reason. The negotiations were peculiarly exciting and uncertain, for each side had an unpredictable weapon, Zinzendorf the casting of lots, Rock prophecy in Inspiration, which he used to inflict the maximum embarrassment. Zinzendorf made the mistake of trying to patronise Rock, and attempting sheep-stealing behind his back. When Rock died in 1749 the game seemed up for the Inspired. Yet within a year the Moravians had been expelled from Herrnhaag and their buildings taken over by the separatists and Inspired, whose numbers grew steadily in the next two generations.

In the 1840s the movement fell out with the government of Hesse over the control of their schools, and in 1843 took off for America to the number of 1,000, as stately a train as the Moravians had mustered a century before. Meanwhile the conflict left its mark on religious revival in Switzerland and Württemberg.

Revival in Switzerland

Pietism made more progress in the canton of Bern than in any other canton and the stiffness of the official line transformed it in two important ways: it pushed Pietism increasingly in the direction of revivalism, and it drove it from the towns into the country and especially into the Oberland. The great name in the church Pietism of the next generation was that of Samuel Lutz (1674–1750), who fittingly became a hero with Steinmetz's circle in Germany. Pushed out of the way into the French-speaking Vaud, he made his base the Pietist centre for the whole area. In 1726 he moved to Amsoldingen bei Thun and thrust himself into the leadership of a great revival taking place in the Oberland. He held evening class-meetings and despite government warnings dashed about the whole area preaching as a 'general apostle'. In this work Lutz had special gifts; he could write acceptably for peasants, and use the resources of forest communities in an innovative way. But the crucial thing was his elemental religious spirit, his vivid sense of being always in the hand of the Saviour; he republished Luther's commentary on Galatians, and helped to spread piety of a Lutheran kind in the Swiss Reformed world. He impressed Christian David and kept his finger on the pulse of experimental religion internationally. He entertained Rock, the leader of the Inspired, but tempted his followers back to church. He had worked revival; how had others fared?

That opportunities were there is shown by the familiar reports in the 1730s and 1740s of revivals among children; indeed those at Gutannen in the Haslital (Bern) were internationally reported. In that valley expectations had been raised by another religious original, Christen Huber. A former chamois-hunter, he was said to owe his conversion in 1723 to having pursued his quarry so deep into the Gelmerfluh that he could extract himself neither forwards nor back, and seemed to face certain death. In fact after an appalling night he escaped, and escaped radically changed in character, though recognisably unchanged in temperament. Still a solitary, he contemplated the work of grace as a hermit, pouring out a stream of devotional prose and verse. And still he needed his prey; his unauthorised preaching brought a clash with church authority, but he was not a separatist and he was finally left in peace on condition that he did not compete with church times. In a microcosm of the revival as a whole, Huber's evangelism put the Haslital on the map. George Schmid, a Herrnhuter and subsequently a missionary among the Hottentots, extended a Swiss tour to take it in; and in 1738 that old Inspired warhorse, Rock, came to deliver an oracle in person.

Prophecy of this kind was not new in Switzerland. The Swiss had been exposed direct to the Cévennes prophets and highly exposed to the hybrid variety, Inspiration. Numerous Swiss religious refugees had fled to the Wetterau; great numbers had emigrated under economic pressure to Swabia and the Rhine valley across the routes of the Inspired into Württemberg; many who stayed at home still hankered after an absolutely contemporary Word of God and made off to the Wetterau for longer or shorter visits. The result was that Switzerland was drawn into the Inspired mission-field, and by the time they were in competition with the Moravians in the 1730s a good deal of manpower was at work. Their main response was in the Bernese Oberland and the Oberaargau, the more deferential low country remaining closed to them. They created a network of conventicles in which the key figure was often an artisan or a woman. A bizarre example of the latter was the blind Christine Kratzer, the prophetess and 'tool' of Aeschi, who claimed at one stage to have taken no solid food for four years and no liquid for two. In the end warfare on three fronts against the Orthodox, the Pietists and the Moravians broke the expansiveness of the Inspired, but the community in the Wetterau continued to exercise some pastoral oversight over the Swiss brethren for the rest of the century.

Quite apart from the struggle with the Inspired, and the need for safe havens in the Reformed world, Zinzendorf was drawn to Switzerland by Swiss colleagues, and from an early stage was in touch with Samuel Lutz. The wife of Friedrich von Watteville, one of his right-hand men, was heiress to Montmirail, an estate which proved a splendid setting for Moravian jamborees of all kinds. The result was a long series of Moravian missions, full-scale negotiations with the church of Geneva, and much personal animosity towards the count himself. It was not difficult for most of the Protestant cantons to legislate against 'foreign' teachers, but Moravianism managed to establish itself in west and north Switzerland and in places in Graubünden.

Revival in Württemberg

Württemberg was another region in which the Inspired and the Moravians clashed. Most of the separatists who took refuge in Ysenburg were from Swabia, and from exile maintained close relations with home. Rock with twenty-seven visits spent much of his time in Württemberg.

The duchy had a long tradition of *Konventikel* or private gatherings for religious purposes, and it was not difficult to win some of these by very sharp prophecies against church and state. Like the Saxon church, the church of Württemberg was confronted by a dynasty turned Catholic; unlike it, it was enabled by the constitution of the duchy to become a powerful vehicle of opposition, or, in English parlance, 'country' politics. The bad years in the church, when many despaired of it and separated, came in the War of the Spanish Succession; but that corner was turned, the class meetings began to die out, and fresh comfort came with Bengel's confident location of the Second Coming in 1836. This implied that the saints would not have to wait for ever to be vindicated, but need take no drastic action yet. Thus Rock's philippics against the 'mad priests, the so-called shepherds and teachers' came either ten years too late or 120 years too early.

Württemberg was almost uniquely exposed not only to French invasion, but to the charitable claims of every group of suffering Protestants from the Defereggers onward. A church harrowed so regularly by the sufferings of others, and mindful of its own, responded in the 1730s to the forces of revival all round it; there was 'a great awakening in Tübingen and throughout Württemberg' and a considerable group of clergy, with the leave of their consistories, made for Herrnhut. This was an opening for Zinzendorf to recover some lost ground in the Lutheran world by getting a favourable opinion from the Tübingen theological faculty on the status of the Moravians within the Lutheran church. He also encountered one of the rising names in the religious life of the duchy, Johann Albrecht Bengel (1687–1752). This meeting was a disaster. The count had no intention of sitting at the feet of a still little-known Swabian schoolmaster; Bengel was hurt at his failure to turn Zinzendorf into a sounding board for his eschatalogical calculations, and pursued him relentlessly in the press thereafter. In truth there was no way in which minds as different as those of Bengel and Zinzendorf could be made to meet. Bengel was not only a philologist whose grammar went on being reprinted until recent times, he was a theologian who contributed massively to every branch of his discipline. Zinzendorf was kin to all those who wished to escape the age of Orthodoxy, while Bengel was recognisably Orthodox. He held that it was necessary to believe the basic truths, that the Bible was a system of basic truths, and that theology was a science logically constructed on indestructible biblical foundations. In particular the scripture contained the elements of God's chronological plan for mankind, some knowledge of which was indispensable as the end-time was approaching. This system spoke to neither the hopes nor the fears of the anti-systematic Zinzendorf, neither the prospect of world-wide mission, nor the menace of deism.

The influence of Bengel struck a blow to the hopes of the Brethren in the duchy from which they did not recover till the nineteenth century. And though Bengel was received in the world of revival, it was outside the Lutheran sphere, and through the influence of Wesley.

Tersteegen

In the north-west of the Empire the Moravians travelled busily but never became the mainspring of revival. An indication of the changing temperature is given, however, by the most distinguished Protestant mystic of all, Gerhard Tersteegen (1697–1769). That such a man became a revivalist requires explanation, but also explains a good deal about the milieu in which he worked. Born at Moers (still an Orange principality though taken by Prussia in 1712), Tersteegen grew up with fluent Dutch in a tiny Reformed territory surrounded by Catholic lands belonging to the see of Cologne, and always liable to French invasion. Nearby was the dependent lordship of Krefeld. This was active in the history of religious revival and emigration, partly because its Mennonite congregation, protected by both the Orange and the Hohenzollern families, attracted Quakers, Baptists, Labadists, revivalists, visionaries and sectaries of every kind; it formed a permanent opposition to the official order in church and state, and one capable of setting all the towns of the Ruhr area in a state of excitement. There was also the popular mysticism of the Lower Rhine area immortalised by Jung-Stilling, who describes the charcoal-burners, away from home in the forest six days in the week, cultivating an inner ecstasy, absorbed by intellectual problems like perpetual motion or squaring the circle. Jung-Stilling's own father 'read all sorts of mystical books and pursued a middle course between a mystic and a member of the Reformed church', as indeed did Tersteegen. The industrial towns of the Lower Rhine collected innumerable artisans of this bent, and were also full of class meetings. Some of these were part of the old Reformed church apparatus, some had been begun by the Labadists in competition with the church, and some by ministers of the church in competition with the Labadists. It was this religious public (in his case outside the church) among which Tersteegen was converted, for which he wrote, and which eventually drew him out of seclusion into a public ministry of revival.

Bred to commerce, Tersteegen found it impossible to serve God and mammon, and eked out a solitary existence by ribbon-weaving. A conversion experience in 1724 led him to sign a covenant with God in his own blood and prefaced a return to society. He began to create *Pilgerhütten* (pilgrim-houses) and to be so actively involved in the religious societies that by 1728 he had given up his trade and was supported by members of the societies and other friends. The man through whose agency he was converted introduced him to a mystical diet of Poiret, Bernières-Louvigny and Mme Guyon. This mysticism spoke to his personal need and was also apt for local policy. Tersteegen's life-work was to realise the presence of God in a universe from which cosmologists and atheists seemed to be excluding him, and to which the physico-theologians could restore him only at the end of a long argument. The mystical apprehension of God became the vivid mainstay of his life, but it was also politic. Fine souls had attained to the vision of God in all confessions and none, and Protestants who did so need not surrender to apocalyptic fantasies if their milieu succumbed to one more French aggression. Moreover Protestants generally, and not just the artisan mystics of the Lower Rhine, had sustained themselves during a terrible century not by Orthodoxy but by pre-Reformation spiritual writing. Some of this they imbibed direct through classics like Thomas à Kempis, some indirectly through Puritan writings or the endlessly popular Johann Arndt. It was Arndt who supplied the name ('true Christianity') of the living tradition to which Tersteegen appealed. The other ingredient was supplied by Gottfried Arnold, whose *Impartial History of Churches and Heretics* (1699–1700) attempted to demonstrate the historical basis of 'true Christianity' in the churches and the heretics they purged. Tersteegen adopted this 'impartial' or unconfessional standpoint, and lived it out by abstaining from the sacraments of the church. As we have seen his understanding of the mystical tradition was enormously enriched by his inheriting the library of Peter Poiret, and his editorial labours on his three huge volumes of *Select Lives of Holy Souls* (1733–54).

This work might be thought enough for one pledged to withdrawal into the interior life, and committed to a life-style so straitened that there was always something left for those who came to beg, or for the intelligent medical treatment of the sick. In fact the public would not let him go. His poems (the *Blumengärtlein*) have gone through at least thirty editions; he took over the *Big Neander* hymn-book, trebled its size (with, among others, 100 hymns of his own) and became one of the most numerously represented hymn-writers in the books of the Lutheran churches with which he had never had any connection. Then in the 1720s, 1730s, 1740s and in 1750 there was a series of revivals in the whole area of the Lower Rhine, Ruhr and Wupper, fuelled by the old conventicles; they hauled Tersteegen out of his seclusion and made him the representative, pastor and finally revivalist to the whole movement. The recent publication of his addresses has made clear that as a Bible expositor in the context of a class-meeting or revival gathering, he has probably never had an equal.

The addresses also define Tersteegen's special position among the revivalists. He needed to distinguish himself from Zinzendorf, who spared no pains to recruit him. However, the quick method of Moravian conversion, not to mention the feasting and fireworks, left Tersteegen cold. Most of the Anglo-Saxon revivalists had sought a result by compressing the decisive stage in the spiritual life into the period known as the New Birth, and, following Francke, Halle Pietists had insisted on the *Busskampf* or penitential struggle. But Tersteegen made Wesley's call for Christian perfection without Wesley's abrasiveness. He was a great admirer of Bunyan, insisting (in the Reformed style) that what commenced with conversion was a long pilgrimage, characterised on the one side by denial of the world and of self, and on the other by taking the fruits of the spirit out of the conventicle and prayer-chamber into the kitchen and field. And this doctrine was apt for his public. His core-congregation, the members of the religious societies, enjoyed a measure of religious experience and theological knowledge. To revive *their* faith it was crucial to destroy the illusion that there was no more to spiritual life than they knew already. And to charm his call for self-denial Tersteegen deployed all his eloquence to describe the 'grace-reward', the companionship of the living Christ mediated by the Holy Spirit.

Revival in the United Provinces

Tersteegen had a personal following in the United Provinces, but to revive the Dutch churches required pressure from the Reformed churches first from outside the Dutch borders, and subsequently from New England and Scotland. In this instance revival strengthened rather than undermined confessional solidarity. Wilhelmus Schortinghuis (1700–50), an orthodox Voetian, educated at Groningen, received his first pastoral charge as second preacher at Weener in East Friesland (1723–34). The pastor of Weener was a Pietist of the German stamp moving towards revivalism, the sort described as a Boanerges in the pulpit and a Barnabas in pastoral care. His most important convert was Schortinghuis himself, who thundered his way to major influence in East Friesland and across the Netherlands frontier. In 1734 he returned to the Netherlands as pastor of Midwolda, and, though his congregations were no less, things began to go wrong. He had always pleaded for inward Christianity, against the tendency of men to put their trust in institutional conformity. This call to repentance he poured into a book, *Christianity Resting on Inward Experience* (1740), which landed him in trouble with the authorities in church and state. This contretemps was, however, less significant than the fact that he was defended in print by the Reformed pastors of Emden. To the charge that he had put forward doctrine which had never been heard in the church before, they answered that his teaching was to be found in scripture, and, with varying degrees of force, in the early fathers, the Reformers, and the churches of England and Scotland as well as the United Provinces. In short, the Reformed churches generally were called in to make the point which Friesland could not make on its own. And the fact that religious revival was promoted by many of the best ministers of the Reformed churches of New England, and was eminently represented by George Whitefield among the few remaining Calvinist clergy of the Church of England, showed that revival was not necessarily a foible of separatists or neo-Labadists.

In 1745 (a dangerous year for internationally guaranteed Protestantism) the lesson was drawn when Amsterdam was shaken by the preaching of a candidate for the ministry, Gerardus Kuypers (1722–98). Cries of distress from anxious souls interrupted his preaching, and enormously mutiplied his congregations as people came to see what was going on. When in 1749 he obtained a living near Amersfoort, and informed an admittedly moribund congregation that it was under the unrestrained domination of Satan, there were more than cries and groans. Many members of the congregation collapsed; others became incapable of leaving their seats at the end of the service, and had to be carried out. The kirk sessions forbade the interruption of services, and required the elders to instruct the people that physical excitements were not of the essence of conversion. As in New England the movement sharply divided opinion, and spread rapidly into every province. The movement also showed how far the old party lines in the United Provinces had become confused in the previous half-century. For Kuypers was a pupil of the moderate Orthodox van den Honert, a powerful opponent of Schortinghuis. But van den Honert's work had been entitled *The Church in the Netherlands Considered and Admonished to Conversion* (1746), and this was what, in their different ways, Schortinghuis and Kuypers were calling for. Again church discipline was brought into play and by the beginning of 1752 all seemed over (though in fact much more was to come in East Friesland). In 1759 Kuypers moved to Schortinghuis's old parish at Midwolda, before, like so many Reformed revivalists, accepting a university appointment.

Revival in Britain

The peculiar shape of the revival in Britain was created by the conjunction of continental and American influences with the domestic problems of establishment in various parts of the Union; something must be said of each. It was not for nothing that the Protestant succession in Britain was saved by a brace of foreign monarchs at the heavy price of continental entanglements which high Tories like the Wesley family loathed. England also felt the modest impact of the European migrations caused by religious persecution. The French Prophets had raised all the questions about spirit-possession which were to be posed again by the revival, they drove the point home by disturbing the early outdoor meetings of the Wesleys, and they reinvigorated the anti-enthusiasm lobby. There were religious leaders like Philip Doddridge, whose maternal grandfather, John Bauman, had been a Protestant refugee from Bohemia, who had been raised on German theological literature, and repaid the debt by corresponding with Steinmetz, who had his *Family Expositor* put into German. There were the unassimilated religious minorities like the Huguenots who tended to gather round Wesley. He was still more successful with the Palatines who had been settled on a group of estates in the south of Ireland early in the eighteenth century. Wesley found them in an almost Silesian situation – a German population, deprived of their church, but clinging to their Luther Bible. Detecting echoes of Reformation preaching in Wesley, they responded vividly, and made their own contribution by taking Methodism to America.

John Wesley

Britain like most European states attempted actively to assimilate linguistic and racial minorities, especially in Scotland, Wales and Ireland, and like other states, depended heavily on church establishments to do the work. That Wesley and the other revivalists should themselves be agents in the task itself illustrates the slow but relentless pressure on the elite of one of the institutions binding England to the continent which they liked least, the court. Wesley's parents, ex-dissenters both, were equally high Tories, and almost equally high royalists. Samuel, however, accepted William III as king; Susanna did not. The difference of opinion bore practically on the obligation to pray for the king, and led to a breach of conjugal relations which was not healed by the death of William III. The fruit of the ultimate reconciliation was the birth of John Wesley himself, and, as if to make good any defect in his Toryism, old Samuel, if his son may be believed, helped to write the defence speech in the trial of Dr Sacheverell in 1710. Wesley, in short, was born of the Jacobite issue, and born into a rabidly Tory circle which damned foreigners, foreign religions and foreign entanglements; it kept up Jacobite sentiment far down the eighteenth century, and united it with country-party principles to form a wide-ranging critique of British society and government. These prejudices were confirmed in Wesley by his Oxford education, and, in the shape of a hostility to the memory of Walpole, survived into later life; on this point at least Wesley preserved the radicalism of a party which had been totally defeated by the court in its hopes of controlling the church establishment. The Little-Englandism of Wesley's high-churchmanship was, however, substantially changed by his Georgia experience and the action of the hated foreign court.

The Church of England had adapted to the new conditions under which the establishment must operate by applying the principle of contract to the work of the kingdom of God. Societies for every social and charitable purpose multiplied, with the SPCK and the Society for the Propagation of the Gospel (SPG) at the top. The SPCK was originally intended to put down Quakerism at home and dissent generally in America. It also gave its mind to the assimilation of Welsh Wales and the promotion of the church cause in England by largely educational means. From the beginning the Society recognised that there were others in Europe with similar objectives. Francke was elected the first of the Society's European corresponding members, which warmly endorsed his fund-raising tract, *Pietas Hallensis*. The translator of the tract, Anton Wilhelm Böhme, became through the patronage of Prince George of Denmark, Queen Anne's consort, a leading figure in the SPCK and English religious life; he was perhaps the only survivor of the gigantic purge which befell the English court at the accession of George I. Wesley prescribed the reading of his sermons to his preachers at the Conference of 1746, and commenced his Christian Library with a two-volume abridgement of his translation from Arndt. Böhme's translations from Francke were formative reading of all the early evangelicals. This work of spiritual mediation between Germany and England was the less unpalatable face of the Hanoverian court; the king's mistress, the Duchess of Kendal, was a Pietist devoted to Spener's penitential sermons; the Countess of Schaumburg-Lippe was a supporter of the Tranquebar mission patronised by the SPCK. When Böhme died, George replaced him by another Hallesian chaplain, Friedrich Michael Ziegenhagen, who became even more significant as a go-between between the Franckes father and son with their plans to meet the Protestant crisis in central Europe, and to assist the rocketing German population in America. To the Franckes, Ziegenhagen was indispensable at the point where their ambitions diverged most widely from the ambitions of the Prussian monarchy. To the early Hanoverians he gave some substance to transitory ambitions to head the Protestant interest in the Empire, and he was invaluable in the long haul of recruiting the population on which the future of the American colonies depended. And he helped to change the outlook of a disaffected section of the church.

The great moment for Ziegenhagen and the SPCK came with the

Protestant crisis in Salzburg over the winter of 1731–32. They created the organisation which shipped the British share of the refugees to Georgia and found themselves committed in the long run to paying their pastors, reporting their progress, and rendering spiritual and administrative assistance to everyone who went out to them. They had to work hand in glove with the Georgia trustees and to involve many more people in the rescue operation. Oglethorpe, the governor of Georgia, wrote to old Samuel Wesley for help in finding a missionary, and eventually his two sons John and Charles went. The extraordinary feature of the whole operation was that it was a Jacobite affair. Oglethorpe had been christened James Edward for the Old Pretender, and his sisters devoted themselves to Jacobite conspiracy; Sir John Philipps, the principal lay member of the SPCK, though a cousin of Walpole, had gravitated at Oxford into very high Tory circles, and had been immersed in the charity school movement, the political loyalty of which was very suspect; the Wesleys were sons of non-juring parents, and younger brothers of a protégé of the Jacobite Bishop Atterbury. Those who during the 1745 Jacobite rebellion persistently accused the Methodists of Jacobitism understood quite accurately the hole of the pit out of which they were digged.

By that time, however, there had been important changes in Wesley's outlook and the general situation. His Oxford reading had been confined to English, French and the biblical and classical languages; now he had access 'to the writings of the holy men in the German, Spanish and Italian tongues'. Indeed the work he did in translating thirty-four German hymns of every school, from confessional Orthodoxy to the radical spiritualism of Gottfried Arnold and the mysticism of Tersteegen, was supplemented by extensive prose reading in German spirituality, from the Luther Bible and Tauler to Arndt and Jakob Böhme. He had been versed in the great feud between Halle and Herrnhut by the Salzburgers on the one side and Spangenberg on the other and was familiar with their shared addiction to heathen and children's missions. Wesley in short took on board the practical theology of most of the central European Protestant schools without making a choice among them. When these religious burdens were added to those he already carried, flight from Georgia did not offer a way out; a conversion experience was the only hope. And were he to be converted it would probably be in Moravian company and 'where one was reading Luther's Preface to the Epistle to the Romans', as was now nearly obligatory in the Pietist world.

Equally significantly, Wesley's misery on his return seemed to mirror the plight of the church establishment at large. Edmund Gibson, bishop of London, had staked everything on support for the Whigs as committed defenders of the Protestant succession in return for political backing and legislative support for church reform. In 1736, while Wesley was in Georgia, Gibson bitterly concluded that Walpole had reneged on his side of the implied contract, broke with him, and in the following year was passed over for the succession to Wake at Canterbury. Of all the church-policy failures of the eighteenth century Gibson's was the most public, and it came at a time when there was a deep and genuine revulsion against what Walpole had done with British politics. On the political side there was no alternative to merging Tory and country traditions in a policy of reform and rolling back the powers of the state; on the side of the church, the state was clearly a broken reed, and there was now no alternative but to turn to private enterprise. The revival was one of the ways in which private enterprise was applied. And the revulsion against Walpole which also enabled dissenters like Philip Doddridge, who had earlier been bound politically to the Whig chariot, to support the Methodist coalition as it emerged in the 1740s was a programme of reform in church and state.

One of the oddities of the revival lay in the continued relations of the principals with the movements abroad. Wesley was converted among Moravians, and on his deeply impressive visit to Herrnhut in 1738 looked as though he might join them. But like every other man of independent mind, he could not endure Zinzendorf for long, and his spiritual odyssey ended not only with Wesley's coming down on the Hallesian side of the European conflict, but in his imagining that Francke had been engaged in the revivalism which was now his life's work. Fortunately the financial crisis into which the Moravians fell in the 1750s put an end to the competition between the two bodies. Whitefield reached the same conclusion by a different route. A less bookish man than Wesley with a better idea how to survive, Whitefield had been rescued in 1735 from emaciation and exhaustion by a joyful conversion experience which was a New Birth in an almost physical sense. He acquired a working knowledge of modern Calvinism from his reading and from correspondence with the Erskine brothers before he went to America. The practical concerns of the Orphan House which Whitefield resolved to create on the Franckean pattern in Georgia in 1738–39 kept him in closer touch with Halle than Wesley ever was. He corresponded with the younger Francke, usually directly, but sometimes through Ziegenhagen, sometimes in English but more often in Latin, frequently down to 1750 and then occasionally until 1760. He was on much kinder terms with the Moravians than the pricklier Wesley, but he turned against their doctrine during the time of sifting and still more against their finances thereafter. Halle had held its unlikely English allies against its inveterate Moravian enemies.

Revival in Wales

Halle propaganda also made a mark upon Wales, where the British revival began. Here the English church played a role like that of the Swedish church south of the Baltic. There were two great paradoxes in Wales. A sustained campaign to assimilate Wales to the English language, culture and religious establishment generated by way of reaction a religious revival which ended by being Welsh, evangelical and dissenting; though the elite which launched it was almost as anglicising as the official policy. And the successes of a movement which was launched by men with powerful English ties and a strong international awareness of what was happening in the Protestant world as a whole were deeply marked by the tribal structure of Welsh society. This was to be the special Welsh contribution to the almost universal history of revival as resistance to assimilation.

Griffith Jones (1683–1761) in 1738 launched the general propaganda for his 'circulating schools' in a publication justly bearing the Hallesian title of *Welch Piety*. By origin a Carmarthenshire shepherd, Jones had been taken up by that pillar of the SPCK, Sir John Philipps. Philipps got him the mastership of a school, and in 1716 the living of Llandowror, Carmarthenshire A thunderous preacher in the Voetian style, Jones also beat the Pietist drum of the New Birth, and, had he converted no one else he would have left a mark on the Welsh revival by converting the celebrated preacher, Daniel Rowland. In fact his special contribution sprang from harrowing experiences in catechising people before sacrament Sundays, which taught him the folly of requiring the monoglot Welsh to drag through devotional exercises by rote in English. So in 1731 he sought SPCK support for a 'Welch School' at Llandowror, and over the next six years created thirty-seven circulating schools, through which in that period 2,400 scholars passed, the masters being trained by him at Llandowror. Like the great communion seasons in Scotland, these schools were adapted to rural underemployment. They met for three months at a time, generally in winter, with evening classes for those at work in the day. Pupils were taught to read the Welsh Bible and to learn the Church catechism. After Philipps's death Jones had to appeal to the successful London Welsh to support his movement, and did so with such effect that by the time of his death in 1761, 3,495 of his schools had been set up and more than 158,000 pupils had passed through them.

The SPCK campaign to civilise, Christianise and assimilate Wales also incorporated an important holding operation. There was an enormous crescendo of Welsh-language publishing to save the souls of the monoglot Welsh until such time as the schools raised up a generation whose heavenly pilgrimage should follow the broader and safer path of English. Almost half this flood of Welsh books were translations from the English; the bulk were devotional prose or verse; and most of both the religious and the secular works (including the inevitable almanacs) were directed towards the family, and especially the head of the family. Unlike the Protestant family head in the Habsburg lands, the Welsh *paterfamilias* was not church-less, though the Welsh church was poor and ill-organised; but as the head of a natural community forty-four per cent of whose members were supposed in 1695 to be under sixteen, he had a prospectively priestly position of great significance. The revival began by strengthening the centrifugal forces of Welsh life by adding public worship to the functions of the farm kitchen; it grew rapidly by recruiting the family rather than the individual; and it later contributed to the curious distribution of Welsh rural chapels. What appears as gaunt isolation was often the intersection of routes linking the farms and avoiding the nuclear village with the church at the parish centre. On the negative side the literary pounding was directed mainly at the magic, astrology and witchcraft which constituted much of the popular mores; more positively (and at first to reservations among the evangelicals) the Welsh spirit thrived on the mass of religious verse which poured in. In Carmarthenshire it was much used by the revivalists, William Williams especially adding notably to the fund of Welsh culture.

Neither at the time nor since has there been any agreement as to who was the father of the Welsh revival. One claimant might even be Philip Pugh (1679–1760), the Independent of Cilgwyn; he advised Daniel Rowland, who had mastered Griffith Jones's denunciatory method only too well, to stop driving people mad and 'apply the balm of Gilead, the blood of Christ, to their spiritual wounds'. This advice, well taken, certainly marked one fountain-head of the revival. The claim, however, would have been contested by another revivalist, Howel Harris (1714–73). He began itinerant preaching immediately after his conversion in 1735, repeatedly sought ordination and was refused it, but himself refused openings for ordination when they came his way. He was indeed an enthusiast, convinced of his calling to the New Testament office of exhorter, enjoying nothing better than the 'power' of exhortation which was evidence of spirit possession. He had a universal dimension. He sustained a huge correspondence, almost all in English. He was for ever in London preaching for the religious societies; he brought into Wales the whole English evangelical circus as it took shape, and helped to make Whitefield the leader of Welsh Methodism. His settlement at Trevecca derived from Halle, his knowledge of the place coming not only from Griffith Jones, but from Anton Wilhelm Böhme, and the latter's biographer, Jacobi. He was in touch with Zinzendorf and his own biography was written by the Moravian La Trobe. He read Jonathan Edwards's *Surprising Work of God* (1737) at an early stage and perceived its relevance to Wales. He helped get works of the Erskine brothers in Scotland put into Welsh. He had the same country view of English politics in the mid-1740s as the other evangelicals. He was on his way to joining that 'Grand Table' of opposition politicians which in the later 1740s gathered round Lady Huntingdon and the outskirts of Leicester House, and entertained pipe dreams of having Whitefield made a bishop.

Like some other men of irenical views, Harris could be an irascible curmudgeon, his temper unnecessarily shortened by a lack of worldly wisdom and by a failure to pace himself as effectively as Wesley. But he and Rowland made a powerful combination and Whitefield supplied a leadership they could both accept. They quickly secured the conversion of other young lads who made admirable lieutenants, and obtained a public response greater than they could organise, many converts drifting off to the dissenters because they could not find an evangelical message in the Church. Nor could they contain the protest against assimilation; the Welsh Calvinistic Methodists soon cut their ties with their English brethren and went their own way. Moreover doctrinal differences divided the religious societies more sharply than the leadership; so Wesley, who was prepared to preach and travel in Wales, but not to organise societies against those who invited him in, was left with a tiny handful of exclusively English-speaking and anti-Calvinist societies. But by the time Rowland and his friends parted company from Harris on doctrinal and personal issues in 1750, there were 433 religious societies in Wales and the borders. Rowland held this flock together until a fresh tide of revival set in with the war crisis in 1762, and Harris could be brought back into the work.

Even then many features of Welsh religious life as it emerged in the nineteenth century were apparent. The Calvinistic Methodist movement was much the largest of the religious movements of the Principality. The Welsh sees could no more absorb this movement than the English sees could absorb any variety of English Methodism. But the Calvinistic Methodists bore the marks of their origins in the establishment: an allegiance to the Thirty-Nine Articles, men in holy orders at the helm, the enduring contempt of the more fastidious dissenters for their 'eagerness of zeal, devoid of the light of knowledge'. The movement also reflected the tribal structure of Welsh society. Pembrokeshire was the stamping-ground of Howel Davies, an unbeneficed clergyman, but with its substantial English population it also attracted Wesley, Whitefield and the Moravians. Cardiganshire and Carmarthenshire were preemi-

nently the territories of Daniel Rowland and William Williams of Pan-
tycelyn. Radnorshire, Montgomeryshire and Brecknock were the original mission fields of Howel Harris, the work in the last proving more
permanent than the others because the Welsh language was more deeply
rooted there. Glamorgan and Monmouth were the most densely popu-
lated, and felt the power of the revival more deeply than anywhere
except Carmarthenshire. This was partly because English penetration
encouraged the attention of Wesley and Whitefield, and partly because
the relatively numerous dissenters of that area were unusually receptive
to the Methodist appeal.

Revival in Scotland

The history of the Church of Scotland was full of ambiguity in the first
half of the eighteenth century. A national establishment, it retained a
proud sense of belonging to an international Reformed fellowship, which
had indeed recently provided many ministers with a refuge from persecution. Moreover although the Kirk was among the vested interests on
which the sun shone at the Revolution, and received every conceivable
guarantee at the Union of 1707, it had a tremendous struggle to give
substance to its privilege. There were episcopal ministers to get out of
parishes, the power of the chiefs of the Catholic clans, and the chivalry
and Gaelic culture which propped them up, to break, and the patronage
question, that is, the authority to appoint ministers to parishes, to sort
out. And the Kirk was caught between the threat of armed Jacobitism in
the Highlands, and, after the Union, the long arm of the London government. Scotland had its high Orthodoxy in the Westminster Confession
and associated documents, but was unique among European Orthodoxies in preserving the vivid memory of mass revival in seventeenth-
century Ulster and in parishes in the West of Scotland. All Orthodox
bewailed the degeneracy of the times; Scots Orthodox measured the
decline by the falling off of communion conversions, and the disappearance of the extraordinary scenes which gave rise to them. The patronage
question was especially vexatious, because it was easy to assume that if the
church was in decline this was because the wrong kind of ministers were
being appointed under the Patronage Act of 1712; this act was passed by
a Tory government in England in defiance of the promises of ecclesiastical autonomy made at the Union, and it left church patronage in the
hands of the crown and the aristocracy. This patronage was among the
resources exploited by Walpole to create a following for English political
purposes, and it raised the spectre not merely of ecclesiastical incorrect-
ness, but of assimilation. Mercifully for the Kirk, these issues which led in

the Lowlands to a steady growth of Presbyterian dissent, counted for little in the Highlands, where the Kirk itself was an agent of assimilation in the interests of Lowland religion and the English Bible.

The problems of the Highlands were more acute than those which confronted the Church in Wales; but the Kirk succeeded where the Church failed. Economic as well as religious and political changes created a hostile atmosphere in which ministers were often rabbled. It took till 1730 before they could gain access to the lands lately dominated by the Seaforth family. There was, however, no doubt as to the identity of the enemy, and the Kirk sharpened the definition of the enemy. Sabbath discipline created a public benchmark distinguishing the loyal from the disloyal, and preaching, in the north German Reformed manner, to address the regenerate and unregenerate separately, created another. The General Assembly treated the area north of the Tay as a mission area, and reinforced the efforts of ministers by catechists, and by schools which, though bad, were good enough to produce pupils able to give current translation from the English Bible into spoken Gaelic. This artificial exercise was indispensable at a time when ministers were often not literate in Gaelic, but it drove home the need to penetrate Highland society from the inside.

The means for this were developed in Sutherland and Easter Ross, where there had been bitter recent struggles between episcopacy and Presbyterianism. John Balfour became minister of Nigg and began systematically to develop the eldership. A fellowship meeting of the elders and a few others gave an impulse to all the other local prayer meetings, and enabled the elders, 'the Men', to acquire a real expertise in prayer, scripture exposition and experimental religion. Moreover, 'the Men' came to apply the public benchmarks of Highland religion in the communion seasons to determine who might communicate and who might not. This contentious practice, eventually upheld by the General Assembly, not only proved effective in planting the distinctive features of Highland Presbyterianism in the Gaelic community, but issued quickly in deep and genuine revival. The revival among the Ross-shire 'Fathers' provided the power for the evangelical conquest of the Highlands as nothing else could have done. It was not limited or local; they sent out David Brainerd as missionary to the Red Indians, and influenced the revival in the United Provinces. The revival in the Highlands had the usual Reformed characteristic of being mostly managed by the ministry; but whereas Protestant revival usually offered some relief from the niceties of confessional Orthodoxy, in the Highlands it helped to root them in a popular milieu.

Though the Highlands comprised one-third of the population of Scotland of that day, the drama there could not decide the destinies of church and nation. In the strategically decisive Lowlands, the patronage question, and especially the use of it made by Cameronians who wanted ministers to be chosen by heads of families in the congregation, was crucial. It was this spirit, kept alive since the seventeenth century by the Praying Societies, to which Ebenezer and Ralph Erskine appealed when they seceded on a patronage issue in 1733. They rapidly created a new denomination, the Associate Presbytery, fifteen congregations in 1737, thirty-six in 1740, forty-five in 1746, ninety-nine in 1766, and more in Ireland and England. Was this a revival or was it not? Revivalists on both sides of the Atlantic seemed to think it was; and the Erskines themselves compounded the delusion by inviting Whitefield to Scotland. They seem to have thought that Whitefield's conscientiously professed vocation as universal evangelist in Anglican orders could be mitigated if they got hold of him. The result was instant disaster. When Whitefield arrived he was condemned by a meeting bent on exercising Presbyterian discipline, control of which was seized by Cameronian hardliners. He went on to great triumphs under the aegis of the establishment accompanied by torrents of abuse from the Associate Presbytery; that body had made its choice – its metier was secession and reform, not revival.

Yet the Erskines' movement contributed to revival in Scotland in three ways. The fact of secession increased the anxieties of the establishment; by turning in upon itself the secession encouraged the search for a different way to combine the forces to which it appealed – a way actually discovered at Cambuslang; and there were fresh appeals to bring outside forces to bear in the shape not only of Whitefield and the Leicester House circle of alternative religion, but even (unsuccessfully) of the Moravians.

In 1742, Cambuslang, a parish south-east of Glasgow, which encapsulated all the problems of the Scots church, actually recapitulated the revival memories of Kirk o' Shotts in the previous century. Cameronian activities led to the suspension of the greater part of the kirk sessions, and there had been considerable vacancies in the living owing to delays by the patron in presenting. The final choice, however, William McCulloch, was of Galloway covenanting stock, and also the editor of a Whitefieldite newspaper reporting revival on the Atlantic rim. This propaganda had an instant effect in Cambuslang; high-pressure revival began in February 1742, and when Whitefield, the greatest awakener of them all, arrived in mid-July there were scenes without parallel. Many had heard him preach in Glasgow the previous year, and the day before communion 20,000 appeared. The sacrament was perforce celebrated in the fields, evoking nostalgic memories of the days of persecution. The kirk session decided to hold another communion the following month, and this time 30,000 turned up. Enthusiasts thought it was a prelude to the end-time, and

Whitefield took good care to report it at length in papers on both sides of the Atlantic. Events in Cambuslang had the usual contagious effect upon all the parishes within a dozen miles, and by means scarcely indirect on parishes at a distance, and especially at Kilsyth, where the minister, James Robe, had long organised a system of praying societies. From there the movement spread to Perthshire and the north-east.

Yet in Scotland the convulsive excitements of the summer of 1742 did not herald the glories of the last days. The evangelical party remained a minority in the Kirk, and could neither stem the tide of secessions nor dim the lustre of the Scottish Enlightenment. The patronage question remained painfully divisive, and the next vacancies in the parishes of Cambuslang, Kilsyth and Nigg were the signal for dreadful conflicts. Without the elemental simplicities of the struggle in the Highlands, the Lowland church could neither sublimate its policy disagreements in revival, nor sustain revival itself. And in so far as it responded to fears of assimilation, the revival assimilated its adherents into a broad fellowship not of confessional solidarity, but of unconfessional revival. The Erskines had cast a fly over Wesley, and so did James Robe. Wesley's arrival in 1751 brought with it both a theology and a movement which had no obvious place in the Scots establishment or indigenous religious societies; it could hardly develop except into a form of non-Presbyterian dissent. On this point the Associate Presbytery spoke more truly than they knew.

The Methodist movement

The fact crucial to the comprehension of the origins of the revival in England is understanding that there was a British Methodism which was a movement, not a denomination, and which never became a denomination. The pioneering elites of establishment men were not quite interlocking directorates; but the roles played in succession by Sir John Philipps, Harris, Whitefield, and the Scots evangelicals, with their international networks and their common 'myth' about the regenerating work of Halle, have something of this character about them; and Wesley, the most tetchy among them, kept his differences with the others within bounds. In England they were all establishment men, so there was no question of organising a denomination. Just as the revivalists of Germany and Switzerland tended to make for known cells of religious virtuosi, so in England they began work mostly on the basis of the religious societies, especially in places like London, Bristol and Newcastle, where anti-court sentiments were strong.

The London religious societies with their Church of England membership and their few favourite churches where they arranged themselves communions and heard their favourite preachers were becoming a con-solidated market in the 1730s, even before Whitefield, newly in deacon's orders, got to them and speeded the whole process up. It was into this milieu a year later that the Wesley brothers came and were converted, a milieu already delighted by news of the revival in Wales, and of Ingham's missions in Yorkshire. Thus the London societies provided not only a model but a springboard for revival.

They also showed a capacity to absorb things other than their own disaffected Anglicanism, not least Moravianism. The Moravian presence in England sprang not from missionary intent, but from Zinzendorf's diplomatic need to negotiate with the Georgia trustees about settlements in America, with the Primate about the recognition of Moravian orders, and with a number of important clergy in the country including the old Oxford Methodist circle; they would come in useful should the count try to mount a university mission as he had done in Jena. Thus although no one intended that the Fetter Lane Society (where Wesley was converted) would be a virtual Moravian society from the beginning, or that through it the Moravians would be drawn into the world of English and Welsh revival, this was always a possibility. For the Moravians were where they were in England because of the political milieu out of which that revival had sprung, and which continued to give them parliamentary support in the 1740s when they came back for legislation which would give the Moravians special privileges in the colonies. Wesley became furious with them, but proposed union in 1744–45; Benjamin Ingham, the Oxford Methodist, who married the sister-in-law of the Countess of Huntingdon, handed over his societies in Yorkshire and Lancashire to the Moravians, and set them up at Fulneck. Despite all the rubs Moravianism was sufficiently part of the Methodist movement for its headquarters to be established in England from 1749 to 1755.

It was on the whole harder for dissenters to become Methodists than for Moravians. Political loyalty to the Whigs, even for many years to Walpole, was one barrier. Moreover, English dissenters, like the Reformed world as a whole, were rebalancing the claims of orthodoxy, reason and life, and from Watts's relatively conservative position in this process, Whitefield appeared an enthusiastic fideist. Moreover the middle way which Baxter had proposed between Calvinism and Arminianism became harder to hold. The hyper-Calvinists clung to sovereign grace with increased ferocity and republished the works of Tobias Crisp. The men of reason found difficulties with the doctrine of the Trinity, and could be passed off on both sides of the Atlantic as Arminians. What changed Watts's view was the outbreak of revival in New England, abetted by many of his oldest friends there. It was he who had Jonathan Edwards's *Faithful Narrative of the*

Surprising Work of God at Northampton, Mass. (1737) published first in London, and in his preface commended Edwards's preaching as embodying 'the common plain protestant doctrine of the Reformation, without stretching to the antinomians on the one side or the Arminians on the other', that is, the Edwardsian revival actually was the Baxterian middle way. Philip Doddridge, the next in this succession, combined a stronger impulse to Enlightenment and a more pronounced inclination to affective religion than Watts. In the 1730s and 1740s, however, he became more evangelical and Calvinist, he itinerated round Northampton, and could find sympathy even for Zinzendorf. Above all he deserted Walpole before the end, and pinned his faith on Frederick Prince of Wales. He was drawn into the web of the Countess of Huntingdon, and, impossible as it had seemed in the early 1730s, he was in the 1740s a Methodist in the sense of an adherent of the movement for revival and reform. In this he was not typical of dissent as a whole, though there were others like him. In the early 1750s, the British Methodist coalition had overcome its worst dangers from mob violence, and had created some very durable mechanisms. Yet like the revival in Europe and America, its course was almost run. Doddridge died in 1751; much more importantly, so did Frederick Prince of Wales. His untimely end broke the normal cycle of British politics, and ensured that the revival movements would never be more than movements in the country. Had Wesley died in 1753 when he was seriously ill and wrote his own epitaph, most of the evangelical legends about the revival would never have been written. The open breach between Howel Harris and Daniel Rowland removed the former from the fray for a dozen years, and with him the most important force keeping the Welsh revival within the establishment. And as we have seen, financial collapse changed the whole nature of the Moravian movement.

Wesley too had made mistakes which came home to roost. Like all the evangelical leaders, he made the necessary anti-Jacobite demonstrations in 1745, but in 1747 he urged his followers to prove their loyalty by voting for government candidates. This was more than the country party would stomach, and the peculiarly sour tone of the references to the Moravians in Wesley's *Journal* over the next three years reflects his chagrin that they were much more able than he to secure favours from his old political friends. The bishops, with Jacobitism now defeated, began to push disagreements with the Methodist coalition towards the schism they purported to deplore. Wesley's preachers, fearing that life in the Church was to be denied them, began to look to the advantages of nonconformity. By 1755 Wesley himself seemed to have lost hope: 'My conclusion (which I cannot give up) that it is lawful to continue in the Church stands, I know not how, almost without any premises that are able to bear its weight.'

Circumstances came to his rescue. The Seven Years War broke out in 1756, the initial line-up of the powers creating the impression that the long-delayed day of reckoning between Catholic and Protestant had at last arrived, evoking new revivals in England and Wales. The national rally induced by the victories of Pitt began the process by which old irreconcilables came back to court; more came with the accession of George III, and still more (including Wesley himself) came back with the outbreak of colonial revolt in America and associated troubles in Ireland. Relations between Wesley's followers and Church authority remained easier, until the time, after his death and in the shadow of bitter differences about the French Revolution, when they mostly decided to separate.

One thing at which Wesley was highly talented, was taking over and managing evangelistic work initiated by others. The small connections created in the Midlands and the north by John Bennet, David Taylor, William Darney and Benjamin Ingham were at various dates absorbed into his machine. Along with the work the Wesleys themselves opened in the Newcastle region, they got the Wesleys off the unadventurous London-Bristol axis, and, like the coalescence of the London religious societies at the very beginning, provided the impetus for expansion into every part of the Union. The outcome of expansion, however, was not the original Methodist hope of reform of church and nation, but a new kind of nonconformity, and one which ran the constant risk of becoming a holiness sect. Likewise Whitefield's achievement was the conversion of many who subsequently served as Independent ministers, helping to transform the size, ethos and administrative assumptions of the community to which they gravitated. Lady Huntingdon's connexion too, had to become dissenters to secure the protection of the Toleration Act for their buildings. The original meaning of the word 'Methodist' was most accurately preserved in Wales, where the Calvinistic Methodist Association came much nearer producing a national revival than any of their English counterparts. But this triumph of 'colonial' resistance could only be achieved on an antichurch basis, and even the honourable name of CMA was ultimately dropped in favour of the misleading designation of Presbyterian. In short the historical propaganda which dissolved the Methodist revival into the founding myths of a number of accidentally created denominations has been unable to preserve even the names let alone the substance of the original movement.

Achievements and limitations of revival

This equivocal result was paralleled by the history of the revival movements on the continent. They had little success against the New Leviathan of the modern state, but Joseph II's Toleration Patent (1781) shows that Leviathan had learned from them to proceed more carefully. Equally what had begun as an effort to revive the embers of faith in the absence of ordinary ecclesiastical mechanisms, and demonstrated the real force of the doctrine of the priesthood of all believers, became as it moved westward a device of the clergy for solving intractable pastoral problems, and in America led to the creation of denominations far more bureaucratic than those left behind in Europe. If revival was nowhere able to rout Orthodoxy, it ensured that theological pluralism would be the future condition of the Protestant churches. The final paradox was that the xenophobia which was a usual ingredient of the new religious movements convinced them that the modernisms launched under the patronage of the French Revolution were worse even than Orthodoxy. Yet the massive blows dealt by the Revolution at institutional stability gave evangelical religion the best opportunity it ever had, and opened the way to another revival movement even on the continent of Europe.

6   The Enlightenment and its precursors

Public and private anxieties

The Catholic missions and even Protestant revival touched very considerable numbers of people; elite movements, dependent on literacy or even scholarship, were mostly confined to universities, towns, and religious orders. Even in 1750 the Enlightenment is said to have affected less than ten per cent of the population. Nevertheless, the anxieties which underlay the great atheism controversy which kept dons and clergy scribbling furiously in the late seventeenth and early eighteenth centuries were visible also in a newly swelling genre of private literary creation, the journals and diaries, the family books and autobiographies, of a much wider circle of the literate. The fact that these were mostly written with no view to publication (and the bulk did not see the light of day till the present century) adds to their interest. Published work tended to be much influenced by established exemplars like Plutarch's *Lives*; unpublished diaries did not much influence each other. At all events the seventeenth century gave birth to a great quantity of such material, more Protestant than Catholic, though including plenty of both, earlier in Germany than England, though less city-based in England than in Germany. The whole corpus was deeply marked by painful anxieties as writers sought to impose some order on their perceptions of a disordered world.

The key to the enigma, it appeared, was to relate events to the end-time and to show their providential significance to individuals and social groups. There was a general belief in the seventeenth century in both Providence and special providences, and the latter encouraged a sort of 'scientific attitude' of their own as men planned comprehensive collections of their evidences with a view to delivering a knockout blow against the advocates of witchcraft and magic, atheism and sin. There ought, it seemed, to be not only a history of Providence but also a science of Providence in which irrefragable evidence would compel reasonable beings to acknowledge the hand of God. This view of Providence also helped in the Reformed world to counter the mystery involved in the less

147

Christologically-based doctrines of predestination by showing God's presence in the everyday life of both the individual and society. Before the end of the seventeenth century, however, the consensus about Providence began to break up. Those who had emphasised a general providence as distinct from special providences were attracted by the idea of a nature governed by immanent laws, and this shift in intellectual taste helped to take the psychological substance out of the doctrine of election. But it was the middle of the eighteenth century before history could be regarded as a seamless robe of immanent relationships rather than a set of episodes rendered meaningful by reference to a transcendent *Heilsgeschichte*. The attempts made (and finally given up) by John Wesley in his *Journal* to reduce his experiences in field preaching to an ordered sociology of religion, show how hard it was to break away from the old ways. And as long as they lasted scholars would need to calculate from whatever biblical evidence was available the date of the Last Judgment, when the just judgments of God would be made plain. Not till then would 'atheism' be put down by the ultimate and unmistakable demonstration of the divine Providence.

Meanwhile there was some comfort in the fact that if Providence seemed to need a little salvaging, things were rather worse with its traditional rivals, magic and witchcraft. And the professional theologians' controversy over atheism, like the diarists' treatment of Providence, began with a backward reference to the literature of the ancient world and ended in a new modernism, the Enlightenment.

Atheism

Men of the seventeenth century might shed blood liberally to secure one or other Orthodoxy from its rivals, but scores upon scores of the titles of their works of scholarship incorporated the word 'atheism'; indeed a treatise of 1701 declared that although the word was derived from a Greek root, it had become so familiar among Germans that even 'many simple and unlettered people know what is meant by it'. The defence of the doctrine of Creation against the Aristotelian notion of the eternity of the world, the defence of the idea of the immortality of the soul or the resurrection of the body against 'atheists', had begun in the sixteenth century. However, the seventeenth century was not far gone before a general defence against atheism had been produced from the Catholic side in the form of a commentary on Genesis by Marin Mersenne (1623),[1] and in 1648 the Dutch Reformed theologian Voetius produced

---

[1] Mersenne was the pseudonym of the Sieur de Sermes (1588–1648).

the first Protestant monograph in the field in the shape of four *Disputations on Atheism*. The works of both these authors were part of the regular stock-in-trade of their successors, and Spener's friend, Gottlieb Spizel of Augsburg (1639–91), introduced with his *Root of Atheism* (1666) a veritable avalanche of anti-atheist literature which lasted for over half a century before petering out into routine polemics and the attempts of the unenterprising to obtain notice and preferment.

There are a number of very odd things about this literary onslaught. It is not clear why it was so prominent in an age committed to precision and Orthodoxy, though it is quite plain that the Orthodox themselves put the concept and literature of atheism before the reading public. Often they did this in pursuit of feuds of their own, Aristotelians rubbishing the Cartesian proofs of the existence of God, with the greater enthusiasm as their opponents were often anti-scholastics of Jansenist, Augustinian, Benedictine or Oratorian provenance looking for a return to Neoplatonist traditions of apologetic. Again Catholic writers were as prominent as Protestant in the early stages of the controversy; but their interest was in a good measure political. In the glory days of Louis XIV they left the fray to Lutheran and Reformed, and in the later stages to English, writers. And in the Protestant world the Swedes and the Swiss notably abstained from the controversy. Even in Germany not all the Lutheran faculties participated. The conspicuous presence of religious dissidence may have fuelled the fear of atheism; certainly, in their worst moments, both Catholics and Protestants were apt to regard the other as an invincible step on the downward path.

From the outset there was clearly more than one form of atheism. Had not the Psalmist twice affirmed that the fool had said in his heart that there was no God (and hence no ultimate sanction against wrong-doing)? And in the prolonged recession which followed the Thirty Years War the church courts everywhere were filled with cases of this kind of practical atheism. The polemicists, however, rarely ascribed their problem to that war, and the new vogue of histories of atheism was based on the fact that it went back to the ancient world, and had afflicted Christendom again since the Renaissance.

Moreover atheism had an alarming future. Mersenne referred to a prophecy that the Catholic church together with some mighty kingdoms would come to an end in 1661, and there were Lutherans convinced that after Luther's death the prophecy had been found in his study that it was no longer the Pope who was anti-Christ, but atheism. Voetius gave a comprehensive eleven-point specification of the atheist which carried conviction to his successors. The atheist was a man who (1) denied the supernatural, (2) suspected scripture and looked for contradictions in it,

(3) investigated it by the 'light of human history' and understanding, (4) dismissed theologians as other-worldly and partisan phantasists, (5) praised other atheists' utterances to the skies, however mediocre, (6) lived fearlessly by the principle 'Let us eat, drink and be merry, for tomorrow we die', (7) had nothing to do with the clergy, (8) zealously circulated the opinions of sympathisers, (9) simulated orthodoxy when necessary, (10) practised his religion sparingly, and (11) behaved badly to all who wrote against atheism. For the moment the big guns were turned backward upon the classical heathen culture which the churches had so often used for Christian purposes. But to the end of the atheist controversy it remained an unsettled question whether the 'atheist' philosophers of the ancient world simply made light of the superstition they knew or whether they really acknowledged no divinity at all.

Opponents of atheism

The worst problem was posed by Aristotle, on whom the church had leaned so heavily. He had taught the eternity of the world, so disposing in advance of the Christian notion of Creation. Desperate straits called for desperate defence. Mersenne tried to convince the disciples of Campanella, Giordano Bruno and Galileo that Catholic theologians did not depend on Aristotle alone; Protestants held that he had been misinterpreted by a caucus of atheists, Arabs and Italians, or that he was a singular exception to the main body of ancient philosophy. But right into the eighteenth century there remained uncertainty whether Aristotle was the 'divine philosopher' or an atheist. 'The Italians', those Renaissance scholars who had brought unpalatable aspects of Greek thought back into circulation, men like Poliziano, Aretino and Pomponazzi, now found themselves on lists of 'guilty men' compiled by assailants of atheism, who had not always read their works, but who claimed to know which way the wind was blowing. Philosophy itself became suspect, and the chief comfort which spokesmen from the old German heartlands of Protestantism could draw from such equivocal characters as Descartes, Hobbes and Spinoza, was that they were all foreigners. The one clear atheist produced at home, Mathias Knutzen, who in 1674 had set Jena alight by two works in which he maintained that there was neither God nor Devil, that the Bible was as fictitious as the Koran, and that men should be led by their conscience alone, was effectively put down, and was not in any case of the calibre of the foreign prophets.

The anti-atheists felt absolutely secure because atheism seemed irrevocably excluded by their natural theology; what actually happened was that atheism was excluded from its premises. If, as the anti-atheists assumed, there was a general divine revelation imparted at least in its rudiments to everyone, there could not concurrently be any possibility of atheism. To this natural theology, atheism must appear as unnatural, even impossible, and an irresponsible menace to church, state and morality. As there evidently were atheists against whom to write, then either atheism must be defined so that it was conceivable within the framework of this natural theology, or else normal humanity, including the use of reason, must be denied to the atheist. Both these lines of argument were heavily worked.

There were two supporting arguments which seemed to the orthodox to clinch their case. One was the 'consensus omnium', the other the witness of conscience in every individual. Many of the anti-atheist writers had recourse to Cicero's assertion that there was no people which did not worship gods of some kind, the more readily as it seemed to be confirmed by Paul in Romans 1: 19ff. The fact that there was a general revelation which underlay even heathen religious practice seemed to afford an impregnable starting-point for the anti-atheist crusade. The consensus of all nations and all ages was encompassed by the consensus of the whole creation, visible and invisible. The attempt to prove by evidence the negative proposition that there was no people without religion, was, however, unlikely to succeed. Jesuits and others, being unable to find in China and among the Indians of North and South America forms of religious practice that they could recognise, concluded that here atheism ruled; both Pierre Bayle (1647–1706) and John Locke (1632–1704) applied a critical intelligence to evaluating reports relating to the supposed irrefragable consensus.

One of the universal ordinances among men had been supposed to be the state, no land being without its prince any more than any family was without its paternal head. Hobbes (according to Christian Kortholt one of the 'three great liars') took all the comfort from this view with his analysis of political organisation as an artificial device to escape a state of nature conceived as a war of everyman against everyman. And in sober fact natural law began to look as contested a battlefield as natural religion. Conscience too began to tremble when Knutzen, the German atheist, declared himself ready to accept it as the highest authority, to which even the Bible and the magistrate should yield. It began to look as though God would have to be rescued by some much more metaphysical subtleties; yet here too the omens were unpalatable. Descartes, 'the dictator of the new philosophy', claimed to prove the existence of God, but for him God was a problem in philosophy not theology, and the only thinker to take him up in the anti-atheist cause was the Dutch philosopher, Burcher de Volder. Leibniz did better. He did not close his eyes to the evil in the world, but argued that God had created the world, and must therefore have realised the best of all possibilities; the evidence or proof of God's existence was the basis of his theodicy and not the reverse as was the case with the physico-theologians. Yet the theologians were cagey even about Leibniz, and their principal new contribution to the debate was the physico-theology, and this pointed the way to the new fashions of the eighteenth century.

Physico-theology

The original hope indeed was that metaphysical principles could be established upon a physical basis. This proved to be impossible and the atheists took most of the rounds. For the working of a divine creator was only to be conceived if the world was not eternal, and to demonstrate this from a point in time was extraordinarily difficult. If the limits of the world could not be established in a metaphysical sense, the theologians could enthuse over the laws of physical creation, and slip into talking of their 'end' and 'purpose'. This change in their frame of mind helped many of them in the eighteenth century to reverse their perspective, and instead of seeking to confute an atheism derived from sources in antiquity, to develop an apologetic based on modern understanding of the laws of nature. Newton proved an admirable antidote to the headaches bequeathed by Lucretius.

Samuel Parker, the time-serving bishop of Oxford (1640–88), set the tone in a treatise of 1678 in which he attacked Epicurus and Descartes, and called his readers away from Aristotle and the scholastics to the observation of nature itself. The splendid design of nature was ground for certainty of the existence of God; it was not now the fact of creation, but its manner and functioning according to law which impressed. This change of stance had the advantage that scientific research need not be left to the critics of orthodoxy, but could be made a bulwark of the defence. This physico-theology grew out of the old natural theology, but it was basically a different thing; the classical natural theology had been interested not in the detail of nature but in the fact of creation as a whole; the physico-theologians proved almost embarrassingly keen to see the evidence of design not just in the systematic motion of the stellar universe, but even in the practical convenience of being able to spot dark coloured fleas upon a white skin. The first writer to make the birds, bees and blossoms into a functioning argument for their Creator was a Jesuit of the early seventeenth century, Leonard Lessius, but by the early eighteenth century this type of apologetic was universal, and had by that time much more scientific material to work on. Fascination with the skills of spiders and ants gave way to awe inspired by gravity. Richard Bentley on the authority of Newton explained that the principle of gravity was insufficient to explain the movements of the stars; but it looked uncommonly like a physicist's shorthand for the omnipresence of God. The marvellous clockwork of the universe implied a celestial clockmaker at the outset; gravity suggested that the original creative principle was continuously at work.

Physico-theology tested

The physico-theologians, however, not only carried anthropocentric inferences of design to absurd lengths, they exposed themselves to criticisms based on alleged imperfections in creation, some of which were very ancient, many being supplied by Lucretius himself. Spizel indeed referred to a certain Franciscus Humblotus who assembled no less than eighty objections to belief in Providence. The physico-theologians found themselves caught in a similar minefield to that encountered by the metaphysicians or representatives of natural theology before them. They 'proved' the providence and existence of God by demonstrating the order of creation; the atheists 'proved' the non-providence and non-existence of God by digging up as much disorder, destruction and evil in the world as they could. The anti-atheists had therefore to go a step further, and argue that the apparently evil was good, and the apparently meaningless was very significant. To Lucretius's argument that nothing was so useless as mountains, forests, wildernesses and swamps, Wesley, following Buddeus of Jena, was prepared to argue that (much as he personally loathed mountains) they were providentially ordained so as to pour the surface water of the world down on to the plains where it was needed. To Lucretius's repugnance for wild beasts it might be replied 'Quid elephantis, rhinocerotibus mirabilius?'

Lucretius's swamps and wildernesses were not, however, the crucial difficulty of the physico-theologians; this was posed by sin and suffering in the life of men. Here the physico-theologians could not escape the law they had attempted to demonstrate. One favourite resort was the Old Testament which was full of examples of judgment upon sin and rewards for righteousness, a symmetry to be observed in history generally. Why, asked the Lutheran Johann Lassenius in 1693, did lightning strike churches, castles, towers, town-halls and private houses? It was not by chance, it was because of the sin practised in them. If the atheist inquired why there were so many shipwrecks, the Reformed theologian de la Serre inquired in turn whether the shipwrecked had not been Godless. The orthodox could not close their eyes to the ostensible facts that the godless often flourished while the godly suffered; but they had a touching faith that the former would not evade judgment for ever, while the latter were being educated by God into a piety yet more profound, a preparation for more apparent justice in the Beyond.

Leibniz at least did not try to prove the existence of God from a demonstrably best possible world; he simply affirmed that if the present world, with its apparent drawbacks, were not the best world possible, God would not have created it. This was not a line which the theologians favoured. The atheists and their critics seemed to have reached much the same point; the existence of God or his non-existence seemed incapable of proof by the methods lately in vogue, and at least Franz Cuper, a Dutch Socinian (1629–92), was prepared to admit the fact. Pascal put the matter the other way up: 'It is incomprehensible that God is, and incomprehensible that he is not'; and expressed his astonishment that theologians should wish to prove God from nature. Only those who already believed would find weight in the arguments of natural theology; those who did not believe would find them trivial. The God of scripture was a hidden God, not to be laid bare by inferences from the detail of his creation. In any case faith was a fundamentally different thing from proof; proof was human, faith a gift of God.

Christianity rational

Still, by the end of the seventeenth century, it appeared, especially to British commentators, that the case for Christianity must be based on what was called 'reason'. It was only too clear to Protestant establishmentarians that 'reason' offered the only effective middle way between the tyranny of external authority represented by the papacy, and the anarchy of the 'inner light' represented by sects of the Quakerish kind. Moreover the more modern apologetic came to rely on evidences produced by the natural sciences the more 'reason' came into its own. When Christian, and especially Protestant, apologetic came to this point its interest shifted from a backward-looking controversy with antiquity, to a forward-looking grappling with new knowledge. When this happened Christian thinkers became involved not merely with the attempts of Enlightenment in the broadest sense to dispute old authority, but with applying its methods to their own business.

Writing from the standpoint of the late eighteenth century, the best contemporary historian of the church, Johann Rudolph Schlegel, laid very heavy emphasis on the unique importance of this period, and also upon 'alterations in states and in the realm of knowledge'. In the late seventeenth century Britain and the Dutch Republic had been gradually asserting a primacy in both; and by the time the Grand Alliance had established limits to the territorial ambitions of Louis XIV by the Peace of Utrecht in 1713, changes in the constitutional standing of the churches were modifying the ways in which they might present their teachings. Absolutism had threatened the cosmopolitanism and the independence of the churches, while the churches themselves as antique vested interests had tended to get in the way of those already looking to the more rational ordering of political life with a view to squeezing more resources for the conduct of war or other ends. Thus the church in France was one of a complex of privileged bodies, able once again after the death of Louis XIV on occasion to supply the chief minister of state, neither fully under temporal control nor fully free of it.

In the United Provinces and Britain by contrast, commercial powers par excellence, a different political and intellectual balance was struck; both were in the forefront of intellectual developments, both achieved a limited degree of religious toleration, both had to experiment with new methods of managing the clergy, and the principal lay restriction upon both consisted in an informal commercial veto upon the forcible proselytisation of native peoples overseas. In England Newton's impressive account of the motions of the stars, with its capacity to predict, owed nothing to his personal faith; and although Locke set out in his *Essay concerning Human Understanding* (1690; 4 edns. before 1700, 20 before 1800) and his *Reasonableness of Christianity* (1695) to define men's indispensable obligations towards God, David Hume (1711–76), the sceptical star of the Scottish Enlightenment, later declared that 'he had never entertained any belief in Religion since he began to read Locke'. Locke himself managed to hold together a good deal of scepticism with a belief in things which were not demonstrable; but what he thought was demonstrable was a very small portion of the traditional field of religion, and though his efforts to harmonise faith and reason comforted Christians, they also inspired numerous atheists and deists. The church was a voluntary society, and the state (which also rested on a contract) had no business to compel people to join it. Locke, indeed, could be used both to justify the rather beggarly concessions made to religious toleration and a free press after the Revolution of 1688, and to justify demands for much more of the same kind.

Limited, however, as was the liberty of the press in England, it permitted the production of religious shockers by the score, and exalted the prestige of British theology, philosophy and ethics in Protestant Europe to a level never previously (or subsequently) attained. The Dutch, who formed the great European centre for the gathering and dissemination of news and opinion, transmitted a good deal and pirated not a little. Protestant Switzerland put a good deal of English work into German for the advantage of both Lutheran and Reformed in the Empire. The Germans exposed themselves to an immense bombardment of British literature, the bulk of it theological or devotional, and much of it, and especially the rather durable Puritan literature, rather outdated at home, but increasingly reflecting the new ways. Thus the German *Aufklärung* had a substantial British input, but it was the Dutch who harboured the two most acute of the early critics.

Spinoza

One of them was the first to attempt a world view including a philosophy of religion without clearly affirming any of the ecclesiastical standpoints of the day, a man who pointed the way to the Enlightenment without breaking free from the systematic habits of thought of a Descartes, and whose own life history exemplified the intolerance to which increasing toleration might lead. Benedictus de Spinoza (1632–77) was born to a Portuguese Jewish family which had settled in Amsterdam, taking advantage of the commercial opportunities and the limited degree of religious toleration available there. That toleration owed much to Jan de Witt, Grand Pensionary from 1653, to whose circle of friends Spinoza later belonged. He fought to maintain Dutch overseas commerce and maritime power, and to strengthen the home base by governing in a republican and liberal spirit. Still for Jews the situation remained precarious.

Like his parents, Spinoza belonged to the Portuguese synagogue, and attended its school from the age of seven. The amazing breadth of his studies, which beside the Talmud and Hebrew included Portuguese, Spanish, Dutch, French, Latin and Greek, together with biblical exegesis, philological and historical analysis, and medieval Jewish philosophy including Maimonides and the cabbala, suggest that he may have been intended as a rabbi; but he worked in his father's business till the latter's death in 1654. Spinoza then expanded his studies to include mathematics and natural sciences, and to do so built up a circle of friends of non-Jewish origin, some of them free spirits, many others deviant Christians, including Mennonites, Remonstrants, Socinians, Collegiants. These connections appeared to the Jewish community to involve clear violations of the Mosaic law, and after repeated warnings Spinoza was expelled from the synagogue in 1656. This disciplinary action was paradoxically related to the spread of religious liberty. In Portugal the threat of forcible baptism had cemented the Jewish community together; now in a context of relatively free and chaotic Protestantism they must maintain their own cohesion, and Spinoza became a victim of that necessity. De Witt was murdered in 1672; the Orange family was always moving in a monarchical direction with the support of anti-patrician sentiments of stricter religious elements from lower down the social scale; religious toleration therefore began to diminish, a double-edged concern to Amsterdam's Jewish community.

Spinoza subsequently experienced the limits of toleration elsewhere; in 1673 he declined a call to the university of Heidelberg, suspecting that he would not enjoy full freedom to teach, and in the following year pressure from the religious establishment and other quarters put a stop to the printing and circulation of his anonymous *Tractatus Theologico-Politicus*. Thus Spinoza encountered authority in its religious, ecclesiastical and political forms.

He tackled the question in seventeenth-century style. In politics he started from the standpoint of Hobbes, that the state of nature was a war of everyman against everyman. Reason must bring men to a mutual contract to establish a supreme power, capable of enforcing a peaceful civil existence. The state of nature, however, persists in civil society in that men obey only so far as they have to, and the state's title to obedience extends only so far as it is able to enforce it. Subordination to the law is sustained by rational self-interest. On its side the state must maintain itself with whatever weapons are to hand, these necessarily including the management of superior church affairs. But reason will again indicate to the state that it will maintain itself only so long as its subjects appreciate that the advantages of the peace it confers are greater than those offered by revolution. It is in its rational interest to govern in a constitutional, even liberal, manner.

Rational freedom required defence against religious tradition as well as against the state. 'The end of philosophy is truth alone, that of faith is simply and solely obedience and piety.' Here Spinoza turned biblical critic. The Bible was a valid account of popular religion, but not a valid source of doctrine. The authority of the prophets rested not on a speculative knowledge of God and nature, but on their exemplary life. The Bible was not a book inspired by God, but written by various hands for men of particular times and political situations. The Pentateuch was not written by Moses, and the Mosaic law was a legal code valid for the Hebrew state, but not for any other time or state. Nor was there any biblical proof for the belief that human understanding was naturally corrupted by original sin, and hence needed direction by religious authority. Belief in miracles was contrary to the essence of God, and also to the Bible, which taught nothing contrary to reason. Spinoza was not in the metaphysical sense an atheist, but as an outsider he recognised that the Christian concept of God as creator and ruler of the universe differed from the metaphysical concept of an absolute, infinite, perfect, eternal and necessarily existing being. The relationship of an infinite Godhead to things could not be determined after the manner of a finite Godhead in terms of plan, purpose and need. Indeed the meaning of the world, if it had one, was not to be determined in human and personal terms. This view of course produced outraged accusations of atheism against him. If, as far as Spinoza was concerned, the Old Testament was a long story of God's accommodation to human weakness, it was a different case with Christ and the apostles. Here it was a question of the foundation of a religion of humanity which had no essential connection with that of Moses and the prophets. From the outset the conventional Christian apologetic was based on the fulfilment of prophecy. Christ was in effect the perfect philosopher who lived in the spiritual knowledge and love of God; to Christ God revealed himself without accommodation. The apostles united the old kind of authority enjoyed by the prophets with that of the doctrine they had received from Christ himself. Their epistles were human creations which, unlike the prophetic words, were not based on some special divine revelation.

Taken as a whole, however, the scriptures did afford seven simple principles by which to live. These began with the proposition that God or the Supreme Being is, with his mercy and justice, the archetype of true life and continued through the proposition that obedience shown in justice and love towards the neighbour is the true service of God, to the promise that God forgives the penitent. It is in the doctrine of Christ that these principles, which are actually the Word of God engraved on the heart of every man, find their fullest expression. Did these principles, reminiscent of those of Herbert of Cherbury, constitute Spinoza a convert to Christianity? The Protestant Orthodoxies of the day were clear they did not. His complete separation of religious faith from the knowledge of the truth was menacing to a religious tradition in which Christianity and the scholarship of the ancient world had cohabited happily for so long; there was no sign of the Christian hope of eternal life. The idea of God as the judge of the world, with Christ seated at his right hand, was disposed of with all the other biblical anthropomorphisms; his view of the Bible as a historical source for popular piety but not a standard of doctrine, could not be redeemed by his touching emphasis on the forgiving grace of God. His deductive metaphysics in the manner of Descartes endeared him to no one, and exposed him to condemnation alternately as an atheist or as a pantheist. Only the humanists of the late eighteenth century with their new understanding of God and nature – Lessing, Mendelssohn, Herder, Goethe and others – and the founders of German idealism – Fichte, Schelling and Hegel – who took possession of his metaphysics, really brought Spinoza back into vogue.

Pierre Bayle

Spinoza was characteristic of his generation to the extent that he proposed a rational metaphysical system into which religious belief could be fitted. To Pierre Bayle (1647–1706) the systems themselves were preposterously overblown demonstrations of what reason could not achieve. The son of a Reformed pastor in the Midi, Bayle was briefly converted to Catholicism in 1669, before taking the dangerous step of abjuring that faith in 1670. He then fled to Geneva where his studies began, never to see his family again. In due course he turned from theology to philosophy, and in 1675 was appointed professor of philosophy at the Reformed academy at Sedan. Here one of his colleagues on the theology side was Pierre Jurieu (1637–1713), whom we have already encountered. When Louis XIV closed the Sedan academy, Bayle obtained employment in Rotterdam for them both, but it came in the end to a complete breach between the two, and to Bayle's dismissal from his appointment in 1693. Jurieu's prophetic conviction of the imminent downfall of the French church and monarchy, and the rise on their ruins of the Reformed church, was the epitome of what the eighteenth century understood by enthusiasm, viz. the pursuit of ends without consideration of means, and it doubtless coloured Bayle's views on the relation of faith and reason. His loss of employment had the advantage to posterity of enabling him to complete his four-volume *Dictionnaire historique et critique* (1697–1702). In this work, while remaining an active member of the Reformed church, Bayle managed to distance himself from virtually all the parties in the field.

Bayle had learned, partly from a world full of competing certainties and partly from Locke, that human reason must be exercised and developed upon experience, and at every stage in its education had only a limited efficiency. The rules of evidence helped, but did not suffice to settle various differences of deep personal conviction, including religious faith. Religion and theology were areas where personal conviction and rational doubt coexisted, or even contradicted one another. He could not find rational grounds for the Christian belief in Providence, or even monotheism, for the principles of good and evil seemed very evenly balanced in the world. It was possible to hold the contrary and to live on grounds of faith, but it was hopeless to support the fact by rational theological explanations. Every religious attitude, his own included, was conditioned by a personal history, which could not establish grounds for general validity.

By thus escaping into the realm of doubt Bayle escaped the standard theological school-questions, sidestepped the clash of religious parties and of Christianity and non-Christian religions, even the war against atheism, and embarked on the first European scientific criticism of religion. He had also provided new grounds for religious toleration, which was from beginning to end one of the great themes of the Enlightenment. Unlike others he did not proceed from the nature of the state. In his view the conscience which followed the true religion and the erring conscience which followed the false could not be distinguished by any rational yardstick. It was therefore an immoral and unnatural use of force for the state to drive men out of one faith and into another. Doubt, in short, went with toleration as well as with religion. This argument was predictably unpalatable to all parties. It gave a civic validity to religious relativism; it extended the right of toleration even to Muslims and heathen; it conceded that there was as good a rational case for atheism as for belief in God, and therefore that there should be toleration even for atheists. Still worse, it separated religion and morality. Moral consciousness depended on rules of conduct derived from natural reason, not faith; this was why religious parties often behaved so much worse than atheists. The great argument in favour of maintaining unity of faith, that religious differences led to uproar, was contradicted by the evidence of the United Provinces, Siebenbürgen and Prussia. It was persecution which led to civil war. This was a doctrine which neither states nor churches were yet ready to receive.

The deists

One of the main sources of knowledge of Spinoza in both the United Provinces and England was the article in Bayle's *Dictionary*, very hostile, and growing longer with every edition. It is indeed an interesting measure of the change of atmosphere in England that Spinoza, who was denounced out of hand by the Cambridge Platonists, savagely opposed by Baxter, and attacked by Stillingfleet and a long list of Bayle lecturers who came to represent the liberal English establishment, had by 1720, when his *Life* by the Dutch Lutheran Colerus was published in English with a commendatory preface, come to be accepted as a hero by a small section of the English literary public, the deists. The deists shared one major presupposition of all the parties to the religious debate at the end of the seventeenth century, that Christianity (or religion more generally) must be, in Locke's phrase, 'reasonable', and that the canons of reasonableness must also be Lockean, that is clear and simple. The deists were dissatisfied with both the political settlement of 1688–89, and its adaptation to the rational canons.

The ground was prepared for the deists by the impossibility of making the doctrine of the Trinity satisfy the current requirements of clarity and simplicity. Nor could the defenders of trinitarian orthodoxy refrain from disputing with each other; this made it harder to insist that the doctrine belonged to the central and indispensable core of Christian doctrine, and created problems with the Toleration Act which conceded nothing to non-trinitarians. A rowdy dissenting synod at Salter's Hall, London, in 1719 voted by the narrowest of margins against requiring subscription to the trinitarian article. Many of the majority were not anti-Trinitarians but Presbyterians hoping to remove a contentious obstacle to comprehension in a national church; and there were others who thought that a disputed article could not be part of the central deposit of faith. Whatever the rationale of the voting, the doctrine of the Trinity was visibly beginning that slow progress towards the periphery of belief which took the bulk of English (as distinct from Scottish) Presbyterians into anti-Trinitarian positions before the eighteenth century was out.

Nor did the Church of England escape the Trinitarian controversy. James Peirce of Exeter, who led the majority at Salter's Hall, had been converted to anti-trinitarianism by Samuel Clarke (1675–1729), who became chaplain to Queen Anne, and was presented by her to the fashionable rectory of St James's, Westminster. After the death of Locke in 1704, Clarke was generally regarded as the country's foremost metaphysician; and he was undone not by metaphysics but by the simple doctrine that the Bible was the religion of Protestants. In his *Scripture Doctrine of the Trinity* (1712) Clarke set himself to examine the 1,215 New Testament texts which might have any bearing on the matter, and came to the conclusion which has never been successfully controverted that the doctrine of the Trinity was not a New Testament doctrine. Since none of the parties to this controversy had the historical sense to argue that the doctrine might nevertheless be adequately rooted in scripture, and since to justify the doctrine on grounds of tradition was, on the premises of the day, popery, it appeared that the doctrine must be untrue. At any rate the big guns of Anglican theology (and especially those of Daniel Waterland (1683–1740)) turned against Clarke, and a rabidly Tory Lower House of Convocation indicted him before the Upper House for substituting his 'private conceits . . . in the room of those Catholic doctrines which the Church professes and maintains as warranted both by Scripture and Antiquity', a charge which made no contact with his arguments. In the end Clarke was brought to make an apology of sorts, and refrained from accepting any further appointment which would involve fresh subscription. The Church of England managed to stave off major agitation on the subject till the 1770s, but the doctrine of the Trinity would not be safe as long as it had to satisfy rational criteria basically derived from arithmetic.

The early deists were more than anti-Trinitarians. Like all the other parties to the controversy they believed that sound politics and sound religion went together, and that sound religion must satisfy the canons of sound reason. They were among those who passed on to the eighteenth century the political thought of the Commonwealth mingled with radical notions from continental sources. Matthew Tindal (1657–1733) and John Toland (1670–1722) indeed stretched radical Whiggery as far as it would go and were destined for ineffective opposition once Walpole had established a degree of political stability on a conservative basis. Such men needed to be careful about their pedigree in order to avoid being dismissed as atheists; the temperate Lord Herbert of Cherbury would do very well, and so would Spinoza, who wasted no time in personal wrangling. The latter affiliation, and a resolute determination to find God exclusively in the processes of nature, gained them a reputation as pantheists (a word said to have been invented by Toland) and, repudiating the latitudinarian Christian *Weltanschauung* along with the religious establishment in which it found a home, they took their place in an alternative Broad Church of their own adoption, freemasonry, and formed close links with freemasons in the United Provinces, especially among French Protestants. The general mood of deism may be sufficiently indicated in the cases of John Toland, Matthew Tindal and Anthony Collins (1676–1729). The group found it prudent to describe themselves as Christians, but let loose a generation of rambling controversy. One of Collins's works provoked thirty-five replies in two years, Tindal's chief work no less than 115. On the deist side the number of petty scribblers was immense, and the variety of views at least as great as the confusion in the official Christian camp.

Toland was the most emphatically political of the group. An Irish ex-Catholic, he became one of the regular pamphleteers on behalf of William III, made a diplomatic journey in north Germany in 1701, and subsequently published a glowing account of it, grossly exaggerating both the amount of toleration and the prosperity of organised religion in Hanover and Prussia. His reputation was made by his *Christianity not Mysterious* (1696). Here he asserted that '*what is evidently repugnant to clear and distinct Ideas or to our common notions, is contrary to reason* which is something the doctrines of the Gospel, if they be the Word of God, cannot be'; nor had God any right to require the assent of his creatures to what they could not comprehend. To demand the adoration of what is above reason was 'the undoubted Source of all the Absurdities that ever were seriously vented among Christians'. Reason thus had the office of testing what was offered as revelation, an office altogether more important than could be allowed by the orthodox, who claimed that while there was nothing in Christianity contrary to reason there were important things in it above reason. To those whose sensibilities came to be programmed by deism, it seemed infinitely ridiculous that God should lay bare his secrets to an uncivilised Chosen People. Moreover, when scripture was read in the light of Spinoza, it did not look like revelation. Scripture was manifestly the work of many hands over a long period, with the inconsistencies inevitable in such a compilation. Finally, the orthodox were fairly delivered into the hands of their critics by the pragmatic argument for religious establishment. This had always been based on the alleged excellence of the officially approved version of the faith in promoting virtue among the people; some defenders of the faith were bound to use this argument against deism. Deists, however, had two compelling replies. On the one hand it became known that Spinoza was a virtuous man; not all 'atheists' were libertines impatient of restraint. And on the other hand Mandeville and Shaftesbury stoutly maintained that Christian morality was not all it was cracked up to be. Toland meanwhile had shot his main philosophical bolt, and, apart from writing copiously for a living, established a political pedigree by editing Milton and Harrington.

Anthony Collins (1676–1729) was an entirely different character, not specially interested in politics, and philosophising from the comfort of a gentlemanly library. He had a strongly Spinozian hostility to the role of free will in conventional religious apologetic. Free will could not explain evil, for evil like everything else must proceed from the omnipotent deity, and its place in the scheme of things must be elucidated by reason. Most devastating was his *Discourse of the Grounds and Reasons of the Christian Religion* (1724). Here Collins displayed a genuine skill in the dating of scripture to discredit the crucial argument that the Messiahship of Jesus could be proved from the fulfilment of prophecy. William Whiston (1667–1752), an honest defender of Christianity, had here played into Collins's hands. In 1707 he had admitted that the messianic prophecies of the Old Testament must be literally fulfilled if the conventional argument was to work; that they did not work proved (in his view) that scripture as it stood was defective, and that canon and text must be reconstructed accordingly. Collins was able to show that to insist on literal fulfilment was 'most destructive of Christianity', while to argue for the allegorical fulfilment was to open the way to entirely arbitrary exegesis.

The deist Bible was, however, yet to come. In *Christianity as Old as the Creation, or the Gospel a Republication of the Religion of Nature* (1730) Matthew Tindal's title said it all. The son of a clergyman and himself a fellow of All Souls, Tindal argued that so-called revelation could gain no more authority than its moral and religious content warranted, and that

New Testament religion gained its force from the fact that it embodied the substance of what reason could infer from nature. Tindal could thus present himself as being not anti-Christian, but as resolutely anti-clerical; it was the hierarchy which filled the Christian world with hatred and ruin by refusing to accept things as they are and must be.

> Natural religion was easy first and plain;
> Tales made it mystery, offerings made it gain.
> Sacrifices and shews were at length prepar'd,
> The priests eat roast meat and the people star'd.

After Tindal the tempo of the deist controversy eased, in part because of political changes. The great threat to established religion had come from Walpole's unscrupulous manipulation of church patronage and his disdain for the church's material welfare, but it proved possible to get him out of office in 1742 by a parliamentary revolt, and the new Leicester House opposition to the court attracted the hopes of a (quite different) Methodist coalition which gathered round the Countess of Huntingdon and George Whitefield. The political prospects of 'true', 'independent' or radical Whigs seemed more remote than ever.

Anti-deism (1) Bishop Butler

Deism also suffered severe intellectual blows from the side of orthodoxy and from within the tradition of radical criticism. Joseph Butler (1692–1752) who became bishop of Durham in 1750 shifted the grounds of debate in his *Analogy of Religion, Natural and Revealed, to the Constitution and Course of Nature* (1736) which (slowly) became one of the most celebrated works of English apologetic and ethics. The burden of his song, not immediately comfortable to either side, was that 'from analogical reasoning, *Origen* has with singular sagacity observed, that *he who believes the Scripture to have proceeded from Him who is the Author of Nature, may well expect to find the same sort of Difficulties in it, as are found in the Constitution of Nature*. And in a like way of Reflexion it may be added, that he who denies the Scripture to have been from God upon account of these difficulties, may for the very same Reason, deny the world to have been formed by Him.' To the deists' shrill protests that God could not possibly expect men to believe more than their reason would accept, Butler argued that there were difficulties everywhere, and both Christians and their opponents must be satisfied with something short of a demonstration. He chose not to argue with the difficulties created by the progress of historical knowledge, simply, like the deists, directing his fire at his enemies' most vulnerable points.

Anti-deism (2) David Hume

The crushing blow to the deists came, however, from within the sceptical tradition, the tradition of Bayle, rather than of Tindal and Collins, from the hand of David Hume (1711–76). Hume was not merely the greatest of all the British contributors to this debate, he is a landmark to a change of atmosphere. If the reception of Spinoza was a measure of the change between 1670 and 1720, the emergence of Hume in the mid-eighteenth century was the measure of another. Not merely did Hume think deism every bit as incredible as revelation, he clearly thought that the political stirrers of the 'true', 'independent', 'radical' Whig tradition among whom deists had often been numbered, had had their day. With the defeat of the Jacobite rebellion of 1745, Britain had obtained a high degree of political stability, and there was nothing to be done about it. He wrote a Toryish *History of Great Britain* (1754–62). It is the radical note of scepticism, and the introduction of a small element of history which enabled Hume to change the course of the debate. Hume did not believe Pope's famous epigram that

> Nature and Nature's laws lay hid in night,
> God said 'Let Newton be!' and all was light.

'While Newton seemed to draw off the veil from some of the mysteries of nature [averred Hume], he showed at the same time the imperfections of the mechanical philosophy; and thereby restored her ultimate secrets to that obscurity in which they ever did and ever will remain.' History was even darker than nature, but there was enough light to put paid to the deists. Hume believed firmly enough 'that the whole frame of nature bespeaks an intelligent author', but history revealed anything but the universal religion of the deist. Religious belief was not universal, 'and no two nations and scarce any two men have ever agreed precisely in the same sentiments'. This situation, which a century later led Newman to search for an authoritarian church to settle disputes, led Hume to abandon the explanation of particular substantive religions to the historian, and to point out that early men were not primitive deists, they were polytheists.

Hume's conclusions were equally bleak for revelation. God might be the Author of Nature, but as an explanation of certain facts He cannot go beyond the facts. Nothing is forthcoming from this hypothesis about the nature of God or the conduct required of men. Hume held that claims to revelation had always been proved by miracles. But the evidence in favour of a miracle could never be equal to the evidence in favour of the natural law it violates. This proposition might not be beyond challenge, but the essence of what Hume was contending was exactly the opposite of what Protestant propagandists had often maintained. To the latter the credibility of a testimony had been proportioned to the credibility of the witness; no promises could be more credible than the promises of God in scripture. But to Hume the credibility of testimony depended on the plausibility of what it asserted, and that was a totally different thing.

The Enlightenment in France

Hume might have been expected to consort easily with the spokesmen for the radical Enlightenment in France. That he did not was indicated by a frequently reported literary legend. The first time Hume attended one of the Baron d'Holbach's dinner-parties, he asserted that he did not believe atheists existed, and that he had never met one; d'Holbach replied that he had been unfortunate, but that he was now surrounded by seventeen. There was indeed a difference between Hume and his companions; the Scot did not care for the self-confident atheism of the French, which was no more warranted than the self-confident theology of the churches. Nor did he care for their mechanical explanation of the universe, which went beyond anything which could be justified by the present state of knowledge. Equally the main content of such religion as Hume possessed was the acceptance of life as it is without presumptuous attempts to go behind it and explain it. But Voltaire and his friends, like the Independent Whigs of an earlier generation in England, felt so injured by the power of antiquated opinions, especially in the church, that they could not accept things as they were. And like the deists they struck first at religion.

Religion was in some ways a greater target in France than in England. The force of public authority behind the religious establishments in England and Scotland had been exercised under the later Stuarts with much greater ambiguity than in France, where Protestants, Jansenists, Quietists and papacy had all felt the violent edge of Louis XIV's understanding of orthodoxy. Moreover, in Britain the established churches and some of the dissenters had shown a prudent willingness to come to terms with 'reason' as currently understood. In France by contrast the Jansenists, who formed the chief force of internal criticism in the church, were locked into an antique battle of their own; so concerned to emphasise the role of grace in conversion, they would not conceive of the possibility of natural law, let alone natural religion. And when progressive intellect was thinking of reasons why miracles could not happen, lower-order (as distinct from scholarly) Jansenists produced them by the wholesale in the cemetery of Saint-Médard in Paris. More persecuted than anyone in eighteenth-century France, the Jansenists were the last to ask for toleration in principle. If, in the jargon of the day, there were fanatics anywhere, they were the Jansenists. And behind their bitter feuds with the Jesuits lay the general Catholic belief that lurking somewhere in the church was the principle of infallibility.

The first phase of the Enlightenment in France was preoccupied, as in the United Provinces and England, with the criticism of revealed religion, and the campaign for tolerance. In the 1740s, when the lead began to swing in France to the group of intellectuals who were to write the *Encyclopédie*, interest began gradually to turn to political, economic and social concerns, and to recruiting rulers and administrators who might implement enlightened policies.

Voltaire

The man who left his personal stamp on this first phase was François Marie Arouet, who adopted the name Voltaire (1694–1778). A successful journalist, Voltaire brought to religious controversy a delicacy of touch and a skilled handling of ridicule calculated to create the impression that he was on the side of light against darkness, of the men of progress against dinosaurs, even if logic was not always his forte. An involuntary stay in England brought him under the spell of Newton, Locke, Shaftesbury and the English deists, not to mention Bayle and Swift. In 1734 he published his *Lettres philosophiques ou Lettres écrites de Londres sur les Anglais*, and in 1738 his *Eléments de la philosophie de Newton*. These works, the first of which was burned by the Paris hangman, marked the beginning of the English liberal impact in France, and signalled that Voltaire's hatred for despotism, Christianity and the church had received a powerful philosophical underpinning. His literary eminence led to his receiving an invitation to Berlin from Frederick the Great (1750–53), which in turn marked him out from his French contemporaries for world repute. Berlin, however, did not confer independence; this Voltaire sought in a country house of his own at Ferney, near Geneva and the Franco-Swiss frontier. Here he resumed his attacks on Christianity and the church prolifically and in every format, only returning to Paris in 1778, too famous to molest, to die shortly afterwards.

There were three great targets for Voltaire's venom. The first was the traditional belief in Providence. In so far as this belief was supported by miracles, he treated it with contempt, drawing mechanistic consequences from the new science much more relentlessly than the scientific pioneers themselves. Life was a meaningless cycle of good and ill fortune; nothing illustrated this more cogently than the Lisbon earthquake of 1755, which supplied Voltaire with the text of a poem, and the most successful novel he ever wrote, *Candide* (1759). This blow to optimism, whether of the Enlightenment or the conventional Christian variety, clearly found a resonance in a wide public. Voltaire's second great campaign was for toleration. It was not that the French *philosophes* suffered anything very dreadful, but toleration would clearly relativise the claims on which religious establishments built their privilege. His *Essai sur la Tolérance* (1763) was acclaimed throughout Europe. His crusade against Christianity and the churches made little distinction as to denomination, though he was particularly virulent against Rome, believing it to be more superstitious than the rest. The historical tradition about Jesus was far too weak to bear the weight the churches put upon it. Jesus was a simple moral teacher, but even his ethical teachings were not preserved unfalsified in the gospels. In any case Jesus was not the founder of the church, which arose through a series of chances, beginning with the lie his first followers told about the resurrection to gain revenge on his Jewish executioners. These early followers took advantage of the ignorance of ordinary people in a way that Socrates and Confucius had refused to do. The work of the original liars and enthusiasts was only compounded by that of others over the years. At the end Christian doctrine is such a tissue of contradictions that faith in it cannot be rational, can only be suppressed unbelief. Small wonder that Voltaire, not himself an atheist, could think it better to be an atheist than to believe in a barbaric god but also tied himself in knots arguing for the social usefulness of religious beliefs which he did not share.

The new science and philosophy which Voltaire had put to such striking anti-religious use were incorporated in a grand map of knowledge, the *Encyclopédie ou Dictionnaire raisonné des Sciences, des Arts et des Métiers* (28 volumes 1751–72 with 7 supplementary volumes to 1780), a bible to set against the scriptures of any revealed faith whatever. This great work, edited up to 1757 by Jean d'Alembert (1717–83) and Denis Diderot (1713–83) and afterwards by Diderot alone, inevitably reflected the views of a considerable variety of authors; it embodied in its earlier volumes Voltaire's scepticism towards all supposed knowedge not based on experience, but in the later ones gave greater weight to atheism and materialism. By this were meant two things: that even spiritual and intellectual phenomena were derived from movements of matter according to its own laws, a mechanical necessity of nature then to be explained, and that the concept of God whether natural or revealed, was now superfluous, since there could be no first cause standing outside the material world. This programme set problems both for the orthodox and for those wishing in some sense to continue in the critical tradition.

The Jesuits

The Jesuits, past masters at the urbane treatment of problems of civilised living, welcomed the first volume of the *Encyclopaedia*, indicating with some relish that more than 100 articles and parts of articles in the first volume had been taken almost verbatim from earlier works, including their own *Dictionnaire de Trévoux* and the philosophical writings of the Jesuit Buffier. The aggressive intention of the Encyclopaedists to replace one religion with another was ultimately too much for Jesuit urbanity, but it remained the case that the temper of the *philosophes* (who demanded toleration) was that of intolerant evangelists, while that of the orthodox defenders of a notoriously intolerant position was comparatively suave. They were in any case in a difficulty. The *philosophes* disbelieved in the supernatural with a zeal which was proof against any amount of evidence, while the continuous multiplication of evidence, whether scientific or historical (and the Jesuit Bollandists were themselves undermining the uncritical acceptance of traditional hagiology by historical investigation), created the impression that the future was with those who challenged the authority of tradition rather than those who accepted it. Two Jesuits, Hardouin and Berryer, attempted the desperate argument that the only ground for Catholic belief was faith in the Catholic Church itself; most apologists attempted another gamble by holding that the revelation which the church claimed to possess was a fact of history to be confirmed by the most rigorous historical inquiry. At the very least, most of the facts in the Bible were possible, though some were only possible by the special action of the Almighty. What history made clear, however, was that even the concept of miracle had evolved, and could not mean the same in biblical times when men who lacked the eighteenth-century sense of the regularity of physical phenomena could have no clear idea of the exceptional and the miraculous. The Catholic apologists of the third quarter of the eighteenth century were in short an unmemorable group; it was Hume and Berkeley who drilled holes in the sensationalist theory of knowledge on which the *philosophes* depended, and Pope Benedict XIV was warranted in his complaint in 1752 that such controversial talent as the church possessed was devoted to less important issues than those raised in the age of the *Lumières*. Perhaps the Jesuit educational system itself had fossilised into an antique pattern.

Rousseau

More striking was a protest (it would be fanciful to call it a revolt despite some bruised personal relationships) from within the camp of the French

Enlightenment. Jean-Jacques Rousseau (1712–78) sprang from a French family long settled in Geneva, but at the age of sixteen he ran away to Savoy and converted to Roman Catholicism. He first visited Paris in 1741 and settled there permanently in 1744, associating closely with Diderot and the Encyclopaedists. From them Rousseau absorbed a great deal, but, particularly after a sort of conversion experience in 1749, became dissatisfied with their mechanistic outlook. This seemed to him to do no justice to the proper status of feelings in perception, nor to the kind of distinctions properly made in the name of moral obligation. 'For us, to exist is to feel; our sense of feeling is most certainly prior to our understanding and we have feelings before we have ideas . . . Conscience! Conscience! divine instinct, immortal and heavenly voice; sure guide of a being who though ignorant and limited is yet intelligent and a free agent; . . . it is you who make the excellence of man's nature and the moral quality of his deeds,' the thing which raises him above the animals. In this cause Rousseau was reconciled to the Reformed Church in Geneva in 1754. It is not surprising that Rousseau fell out with the Encyclopaedists, fell out with the Church of Geneva, fell out with the villagers of Motiers where he had been living under the protection of Frederick the Great in 1765, and, having received the protection of David Hume in England 1766–7, fell out with that sceptical philosopher, and ended his days after 1770 in impoverished obscurity in Paris. While much is elusive about Rousseau, it is clear that in his cultivation of sensibility he spoke for an extensive public, Sterne's *Sentimental Journey* in England for example, or the literary movement in Germany known as *Sturm und Drang* ('storm and stress'). This movement of sensibility was altogether wider than Rousseau, and left an unmistakable mark on one genre of religious literature, the autobiographical notices of its members collected by the Moravian community by the tens of thousands. In the 1770s and 1780s, particularly among the sisters of the community, there was a release from a rigid form of conversion narrative, and dramatic contrasts were drawn between the unworthiness of the narrator and the faithfulness of Jesus; here they were clearly responding to the rage for sensibility in the outside world.

What Rousseau could not accept in orthodox Christianity was the doctrine of original sin. Men must have been created good, because they were God's creation; if they now left much to be desired this must be because of bad social arrangements defying the terms of the social contract. Rousseau accepted the Bible, though he also accepted the supremacy of reason. He believed that a civil religion was indispensable if the social contract and the laws were to be obeyed. That civil religion boiled down to five principles: (1) the existence of a mighty, intelligent, kindly providential God, (2) the future life, (3) the happiness of the righteous and the punishment of the wicked, (4) the sanctity of the social contract and the laws, and (5) the only negative – a condemnation of 'intolerance', by which Rousseau meant the Roman Catholic doctrine *extra ecclesiam nulla spes salutis*. The first three principles, on which all Christians and also Jews and Muslims could agree, were meant to ensure the carrying out of the fourth, and the fifth to put a brake on priesthood. By providing a distilled essence of religion, Rousseau opened the way for men to accept the locally established forms of worship, as he accepted that of Geneva. Here he anticipated something of the mood of the liberal *Kulturprotestantismus* of the late nineteenth century. And like that religious movement he ran into a difficulty he could not solve. There is a difference between a religion believed to be true, and one adopted (as in his case) for its presumed social usefulness. Moreover, if (as began to appear probable at the beginning of the twentieth century to rational historical investigation) the religion of Jesus was of a markedly utopian or chiliastic character, might not this be more socially useful to a would-be revolutionary like Rousseau, than the lowest common denominator of religious belief at which he arrived?

The *Aufklärung*

The Enlightenment in Germany was a different, somewhat more timorous, but from the standpoint of Christian (or even Jewish) faith and practice, ultimately more useful enterprise than that in France. Even Kant, uttering the swan-song of the *Aufklärung*, calling on men to escape from the immaturity of always being led: '*Sapere aude!* Have the courage to use your own understanding', ended on a shaky note in praise of the basic law of Frederician Prussia: 'Reason as much as you wish on whatever you wish; but obey!' The result was that although the *Aufklärung* had a broad impact in philosophy and literature, its political and economic ramifications were less than those of the French Enlightenment until very late in the eighteenth century, and it devoted itself to improving Christianity and the church rather than to disposing of them. In this respect it was like those movements for practical reform which came to constitute Enlightenment all over Europe. Religion was a means and a way to a better life, though only if the religion could be got right. The confidence with which they thought they had succeeded may be well illustrated by the tone of the excellent J. R. Schlegel in 1784:

Enlightened rulers and their equally enlightened advisers have through newly introduced or newly increased freedom of conscience and tolerance of deviant individuals and parties, through permitting liberty of the press and wise institutions, and new ordinances for churches and schools, given a new impulse to the understanding of their pupils. From this arose the enlightenment of a great part of the nation in religious concepts, alienation from superstition, the separation of the essentials of religion from inessential and human additions.

This self-confidence is the more striking when it is compared with the low morale of German Protestantism a century earlier; Protestants felt that they had at last put the Catholic Church on the defensive, and had harnessed progressive forces which would steadily increase the distance between them to their own advantage.

Physico-theology in Germany

This self-confidence is, nevertheless, hardly to be perceived, politically or religiously, in the first quarter of the eighteenth century which German scholars now discuss in terms of early Enlightenment. Not only were the Orthodox battling furiously with Pietism within and a rather antique 'atheism' without, but the newer style of physico-theological apologetic, multiplied by the translation of every grade of English accomplishment in the genre, ran to quite astonishing excess. There was bird-theology, fish-theology, a theology of frogs and tadpoles; there was a theology of European and oriental locusts, of grasshoppers, mussels and snails, of insects, silkworms, bees, mice and caterpillars. Reimarus, better known for radical biblical criticism, wrote physico-theology on the basis of the instincts of animals. Of course there were also plant theologies, flower theologies, grass theology, to prove the existence of God. In the inanimate world there were theologies of mountains, stones and earthquakes, petrifaction, water, fire and snow. The harmony, proportion and movement of heavenly bodies not merely declared but proved the glory of God; even storms did not come amiss. And since the atheists were apt to say that man was a chance collection of atoms, his status as the crown of creation had to be established by treatises on the origin of gender, the structure and statistics of the body, the brain as the hammer of the atheist, the backbone and its elements. Even population statistics and epidemics could be made to prove the existence and attributes of God. By a slight transposition into psycho-theology, the miracle of mental gifts and forces, the affections, love, hate and shame, the relations of body and soul could be pressed into the same cause. And if a century of sermons, catechisms and schoolbooks were not vehicles enough for all this demonstration, Barthold Hinrichs Brockes produced a dozen volumes of physico-theological poems, and there were other poetasters only less fertile. After all this stupendous attempt to coerce consent to the hand and nature of God in the detail of creation,[2] it is no wonder that Tersteegen made it his life's work to assist the faithful to realise the presence of God rather than deduce it.

Christian Wolff

Against the insistent clamour of the physico-theologians, however, 'reason' was steadily being amplified as a concept, and employed more profitably for the benefit of religion. The two great names in this process, those of Christian Wolff (1679–1754) and Johann Salomo Semler (1725–1791), illustrate the increasing role of reason in comparison with revelation.

Wolff was born in Breslau, under the shadow of Silesian religious conflict. It became his hope to establish certainty in theology by applying mathematical methods. In this Wolff can hardly be said to have succeeded; but his addiction to an unconfessional mathematical model proved extraordinarily profitable in career terms, and clearly met a demand among the influential. He was early drawn to the attention of Leibniz, who in 1706 obtained him a chair of mathematics at Halle. Here Wolff's publications ranged far beyond mathematics, and included a long series of *Rational Thoughts* on almost everything, including the ambitiously entitled *Rational Thoughts on God, the World and the Soul of Man, and all things generally* (1720). Wolff was in fact promoting a reform of philosophy comparable with the reform of theological education being pioneered in another faculty by Francke; but the pertness of his pupils towards the theologians, and a lecture he gave as pro-Rektor praising Confucius for developing an ethic from pure reason, led to his being expelled by the king of Prussia at a few hours' notice in 1723.

Wolff, however, was instantly received at the Reformed university of Marburg, where he laboured with great *éclat* till 1740, when he received an offer he could not refuse to come back to Halle. Meanwhile he had received distinctions from the great all over Europe and had become an intellectual cult figure. The tactics of the alliance of Pietist and Orthodox which got Wolff out of Halle rebounded on them in the most painful way; Wolff was a one-man unconfessional encyclopaedia and great was his reward. His follower Gottsched, writing of Wolff's *Logic* (1712), emphasised that it did not break completely with the past: '[It] holds the mean

---

[2] As late as 1824 Heine could genially caricature this story in connection with a chance encounter in the Harz. 'He drew my attention to the rationality and usefulness in nature. The trees are green because green is good for the eyes. I agreed and added that God created cattle because meat soups are good for men, that he created the ass to serve men as a comparison, and that he created Man himself to eat meat soups and not be an ass. My companion was delighted to have found a man of like mind, [and] his face shone yet more joyfully.'

between Aristotelic subtleties, and the loose unconnected manner of Ramus, Descartes and other modern logicians.' Hegel praised him for being the first to naturalise philosophy in Germany, and his pupils ultimately monopolised the higher teaching of the subject.

So far as his ambitions to put theology upon an incontrovertible basis were concerned, Wolff's efforts fell into two very unequal parts. So far as revealed theology, based on the Bible, was concerned, he restricted himself to explanations necessary to rebut attacks on his orthodoxy. On the other hand, within the purview of philosophy he wrote thousands of pages on the doctrine of God, or natural theology. Here he attempted proofs of the existence of God and demonstrations of his characteristics of an abstract and highly unbiblical kind. Returning from the obsessions of the physico-theologians with the details of creation to the Leibnizian style, Wolff affirmed the necessity of an unconditioned basis to the contingency of the world, the argument a posteriori; but the existence and characteristics of God could also be deduced a priori from the concept of a perfect being. What Wolff thus conceived in no way threatened the necessity of revealed religion; reason and revelation were coordinates, and often identical in content. His rational demonstrations were often supported by biblical texts. This foreshadowed a future Kantian 'religion within the limits of pure reason' in which the texts were pushed to a periphery inaccessible to reason. For the concept of revelation was itself subject to rational definition; a revelation might be beyond the limits of reason, but must contradict no necessary rational truth.

The title page of the second volume of Wolff's *Natural Theology* announced that he would controvert the errors of atheism, deism, fatalism, naturalism and Spinozism. In Germany as in England, reason seemed no more capable of settling the disputes of those who would dispute than revelation. Wolff had learned at Halle the expediency of not pushing his arguments to their limits; the result was that even in his lifetime his followers divided into two camps, the Right-Wolffians who used his logic to defend Christianity, and Left-Wolffians like Reimarus who used it to confute Christianity.

Semler

What might happen when the principles of Enlightenment were applied to the documents of revelation itself, albeit in what Hirsch characterised as the worst German ever perpetrated by a scholar of real intellectual stature, was abundantly illustrated in the career of Johann Salomo Semler (1725–91), doubtless the most important Protestant theologian of the eighteenth century; his 171 publications extended to exegesis, church history, the history of dogma and literature, dogmatics and neighbouring disciplines, and a substantial autobiography. The intellectual transition marked by Semler's work was foreshadowed by both his upbringing and his education. Born at Saalfeld in Thuringia the son of an archdeacon, Semler experienced at school the effects of the conversion of the ducal court from orthodoxy to a Pietism which required of every Christian a personal conversion experience. His father's pressure in this direction he resisted and found narrowing. Orthodoxy was impossible and equally narrowing. When he entered the university at Halle in 1743, he found the place in a similar state of transition. The attempt to secure the dominance of Pietism had failed; Christian Wolff had returned; government patronage was in the hands of Frederick the Great. More immediately to the point Semler came under the influence of the historicising Siegmund Jacob Baumgarten. Baumgarten's early experiences in Halle encouraged him to keep his head down in matters of doctrine, and while he contributed enormously to the impact of British historiography in Germany by setting up a translation factory, his contribution to applying this expertise to theological studies was limited. This was to be the life's work of Semler; and he began appropriately with a dissertation on the English textual critic William Whiston. In 1753 he accepted a call back to Halle, determined to bring theology at home up to the level it had attained in Britain, France and Holland.

Semler perceived that Christian doctrine had always had a history, and that therefore neither the Fathers nor the resolutions of church councils had a simple authority to settle disputed questions. More controversially he concluded that both the Scripture and the canon of scripture had a history, a theme to which he devoted the four volumes of his *Treatise on a free inquiry into the canon* (1771–76). In this work he showed that the Christian faith had first spread by oral transmission before the scriptures were written, and long before the canon of scripture was established. Indeed individual church provinces had their own canon of differing scope and authority. The Word of God which describes the order of salvation and effects it in individuals, is indeed contained in the Scripture, but is not identical with it. In the primitive church of the Scripture is to be observed a process which has gone on ever since, that Jesus and the apostles accommodated themselves to the religious ideas of the congregation. In this way Jewish and Gentile ideas had left their mark on the Christian gospel. By the same token the Christian scholar required liberty for his intercourse with scripture, whether on an academic or personal level. The exegetical and historical work on which such conclusions rested threatened the foundations of Orthodox theology. For if the New Testament canon arose relatively late, and was itself historically conditioned, the legal understanding of the canon and the doctrine of the verbal inspiration of scripture were both untenable. And if so, what would happen politically to the establishment of the confessional order? At any rate Semler's enemies laid charges against him before the Corpus Evangelicorum, the Protestant body in the Imperial Diet at Regensburg, which mercifully took no further action.

These conflicts nevertheless strengthened Semler in the conviction that theology and religion were distinct concepts. Theology was the variable and progressive outcome of scholarly work, a labour impossible to require of ordinary Christians; while religion signified the conviction of faith, the piety and love of the neighbour to be proved by all Christians in ordinary life. By the same token Semler broke with his Pietist past. The Halle school had seen the plan of salvation and its purpose, the union of man with God, as the great themes of theology; according to Semler edification was not the business of academic theology. Equally, if academic theology was to be free, it forfeited any claim for the acceptance of its current results to be made obligatory. Semler defended himself against the charge that he was draining popular religion of any dogmatic content by returning to the patristic distinction between Kerygma and Dogma (preaching and doctrine). Preaching included those truths which could be preached in a generally comprehensible form, and which were needed to keep the Christian faith alive. Here Semler and Wesley, two utterly dissimilar characters, came close together; Methodist doctrines were not doctrines invented by Methodists, but doctrines which Methodists found preached effectively. And, like Wesley, Semler was conservative in his estimate of what these were: God the creator, the crucified and risen Christ as our redeemer, and the Holy Spirit as the renewer of the Christian life. Small wonder that when Lessing published (anonymously) *Fragments* of Reimarus's biblical criticism Semler wrote against them (1779), and when Wöllner, the Prussian minister for public worship tried, in his Religious Edict of 1788 to tie the clergy and their preaching more closely to the authoritative church confessions, Semler supported him against many of his liberal friends. Yet it was the greatest of all religious liberals, Friedrich Schleiermacher (1768–1834), like Semler of Pietist origin, and trained in the Halle faculty Semler reconstructed, who held together the two sides of Semler's teaching, and created a vast free reconstruction of Christian doctrine built upon a definition of religious experience.

Lessing

It is impossible within the limits of this chapter to do justice to the fertility of the third stage of the *Aufklärung*, to Goethe's revival of pantheism,

Herder's venture into history and anthropology, to Lessing's plea for toleration and radical biblical criticism, to Kant's attempt to bring together the rationalist and the empirical streams of European philosophy. The latter two, however, well illustrate the progress of reason on the narrowly religious front; while Lessing became a literary icon whose theological views were chewed over by the artisans of Vienna at the time of the French Revolution, Kant had to face the political and religious reaction which the Revolution called forth.

Gotthold Ephraim Lessing (1729–81) was something of a dissenter from the beginning, a man who chose to fail in education for the ministry and for medicine and drifted into theatrical circles. During a stay in Berlin in 1748–55, he found a vocation as a literary critic in the newspapers, and out of this his own creative literary career developed. Precarious it might be, but at least it offered some kind of independence. Not till 1770, when at a time of great financial need he accepted the offer by the heir-apparent of the duchy of Brunswick of the librarianship of the famous Bibliotheca Augusta in Wolfenbüttel, did he become a paid man; and this appointment proved to open at least one door to liberty – the library publications were not subject to the censorship. By this time Lessing had not only acquired a formidable knowledge of the German Protestant tradition and established himself as a dramatist and critic, but had become a striking example to aspiring men of letters of independence and integrity. Moreover about a sixth of his total output was devoted to religious and theological reflection, and the last seven years of his life were largely devoted to the struggle for religious liberty as he understood it. What he wrote then had more enduring interest into the twentieth century than any fruit of the *Aufklärung* apart from the works of Kant.

At the end of his life Lessing made a famous plea for toleration in *Nathan the Wise* (1779), taking up one of the continuous themes of the Enlightenment and admitting that Nathan's 'hostile attitude towards all positive religion was mine all along'; his other two major contributions to the field came in the controversy over the *Fragments* in the later 1770s, and in his *Education of the Human Race* (1777–80). The *Fragments* controversy illustrates perfectly how little toleration there still was in Germany. Hermann Samuel Reimarus (1694–1768) was a member of the important Enlightenment group in Hamburg, a gymnasium professor of oriental studies at the Johanneum, an adherent of Christian Wolff, and a defender of natural religion against materialists and atheists. Reimarus was, however, also a disciple of the English deists, accepting no need for revelation to crown the religion of nature; he also accepted the limits of what could be said in public in Germany, and kept secret an

'Apology or defence for rational worshippers of God' in which he applied his linguistic expertise to undermine belief in the biblical revelation and its miracles, and to explain Christian origins in natural terms. Lessing received a preliminary draft of this work from Reimarus's children, and between 1774 and 1778 published seven substantial fragments (equivalent in size to a 300-page book) ostensibly from anonymous manuscripts discovered in the library, and therefore free of the censorship. The nature of the work is sufficiently indicated by titles such as *The Impossibility of a revelation which all men might believe on adequate evidence*, or *That the books of the Old Testament were not written to reveal a religion*, or *On the resurrection story*, or *The Objects of Jesus and his disciples*. Reimarus set out to produce a compendium of radical criticism of the Bible, and did not spare the inconsistencies, the impossibilities, the allegations of lies. The Reimarus family did not own up to the authorship till 1814, and the work was not published unabridged until 1972; but this did not blunt the effect of what Lessing let out. In the nineteenth century David Friedrich Strauss (the hero of George Eliot) looked on Reimarus as a precursor, and in the twentieth Albert Schweitzer began his *Quest of the Historical Jesus* (German edn. 1906; Eng trans. under this title 1913) with him.

The publication of the *Fragments* involved Lessing in protracted and violent controversy, and it was this controversy which gave the *Education of the Human Race* and *Nathan* their especial resonance. Lessing's immediate object was to put down the old Protestant belief in the Bible. He began by posing as an impartial observer, arguing that the objections to the historical bases of the Christian faith raised in the *Fragments* deserved impartial examination from every side. This examination need not necessarily be damaging to Christianity, for religion depended on its spiritual force and not on the letter of a New Testament which arose by a series of chances after the spread of Christianity had begun. This type of argument had been better put by Semler, whom Lessing regarded as a compromiser; the sting came in his famous assertion that 'the contingent truths of history can never prove the necessary truths of reason'. Thus arguments from miracle and the fulfilment of prophecy were inadmissible, not to mention the resurrection and the inspiration of the Bible. Yet history was not entirely to be put down. Both reason and religion have a history, and history is able to establish what the immediate perceptions of the past were. History may show how the early Christians came to accept the miracles and resurrection of Jesus, and how the Christian religion and church was built upon them. Similarly the power of the Bible was a historical fact though not a proof of its inspiration. The education of the human race had taken place through such stages,[3] and only now was it about to enter upon a period when the educational device of a belief in revelation was no longer necessary. The Bible was rescued from Reimarus's allegations of mendacity at the expense of relativising it and other positive religions.

Lessing's final position is indicated in the parable of the three rings in *Nathan*. The Sultan Saladin asks Nathan on what grounds he adheres to Judaism rather than to Christianity or Islam. Nathan, wishing to appear neither fanatical nor indifferent to the faith of his fathers, tells his story. Three brothers appear before a judge, each claiming to have received from their father the ring entitling them to the inheritance. The rings are so similar and the testimonies of the brothers so credible that the judge cannot decide among them. He reminds the brothers of their claim that the genuine ring has the power to make its owner acceptable to God and man. Therefore each must try through unprejudiced love to men, charity and devotion to God to prove that he has the genuine ring. After many thousands of years a wiser judge will pronounce the true judgment on the rings.

Kant

If Lessing was a man of broad general culture, Immanuel Kant (1724–1804) spent his whole life in Königsberg ploughing his own furrow, a devoted slave to the categorical imperative. Kant's work on the theory of knowledge in effect wound up one set of eighteenth-century debates, and let loose another set which are not yet concluded; these discussions would in any case have affected the way Christian belief and practice were approached. But it was only right at the end of his life when political and religious reaction to the French Revolution set in, and was mobilised in Prussia by Wöllner, that Kant fought his corner with *Religion within the limits of reason alone* (1793). This work could not get past the Prussian censorship, was published in Jena and brought on him a rebuke from the king. But for the deterioration in the political situation, Kant might perhaps not have written this work, which is regarded as somewhat below par by even his legion of German admirers; but it reveals very clearly the dilemma of Protestant or post-Protestant Enlightenment, even in the hands of its most acute exponent.

In the *Critique of Pure Reason* (1781) Kant had set out to heal the

---

[3] 'Education gives a man nothing which he might not have had out of himself; it gives him that which he might have had out of himself, only more quickly and easily. Revelation too gives the human race nothing to which human reason, left to itself, would not come, but it gave and gives it the most important of these things sooner.' *Der Erziehung des Menschengeschlechts*, §4.

age-old rift between the rationalists and the empiricists. The rationalists had maintained, for example in the case of cause and effect, that when we think according to the rules of logic we draw consequences from antecedents; the connection in our mind between antecedent and consequent reveals to us the nature of the connection between cause and effect in the physical world outside our mind. The empiricists on the other hand maintained that the nexus of cause and effect could only be known by direct observation of the outside world; this amounted to the perception of a repetitive pattern which looked as if it were cause and effect. Kant maintained with the rationalists that the mind was constituted in such a way that it connected successive phenomena through a pattern of cause and effect, but (with the empiricists) that this potentiality was only realised in observing the external world. This relationship between the human mind and its relation to reality, the study of the limits of knowledge, was in Kant's view the business of philosophy. Within those limits 'practical reason' must enable us to chart our course. This process was partly assisted, partly complicated, by the fact that there were three great ideas for which there was evidence, but not enough for the mind to grasp or prove, namely God, Freedom and Immortality.

Kant's labours as a moral philosopher in the *Critique of Practical Reason* (1788) consisted in providing practical content for the forms in which the mind operated. The difference between the mind and the external world (where things happened as they had to happen) was the mind's innate sense of moral obligation and the freedom in which it was exercised. 'Ought' and 'is' were two different things. It was the categorical imperative which insisted on the absolute primacy of obligation, and to put some substance into this form of mental activity, Kant arrived at the formula 'Act only on that maxim whereby thou canst at the same time will that it should become a universal law'. What worried Kant about the religious and political reaction of the 1790s was that forms of moral and religious action were being pressed for the convenience of their results, not because they were consistent with the categorical imperative. This was the worse for Kant, because for him ethics formed a basis for religion and not vice versa; it was '*what man himself must do* in order to become worthy' of divine assistance. Ethics led to religion in so far as the realisation of the highest good required a God to help harmonise and realise the ultimate purposes of man and the world. But this religion was natural, rational religion, not the positive religion offered by Christian churches and confessions. These offered no new insights into the requirements of the moral law, simply encouragement to pursue them. Thus positive religion cannot be required by ethics or law, and unlike science and art is not an autonomous realm, simply a branch of ethics.

The task now was to free the rational core of Christianity from the dross, and promote the triumph of this true Christianity in the churches. Jesus was the teacher of the pure rational Chistianity written in the hearts of all men. The four things which took up much of positive religion – works of grace, miracles, mysteries and means of grace – had no place in rational religion, and those who tried to import them wrought havoc by introducing fanaticism, superstition, illumination and thaumaturgy (the hazardous attempt to operate upon the supernatural) respectively. This conclusion suggested that Kant, of all men the most dedicated to the good, had very little religious sense left. Fittingly he was buried at his own wish without religious ceremonial, since the religion of reason required no religious establishment or priesthood, its adherents receiving their 'orders directly from the supreme legislator'. With equal fitness, Goethe and Schiller reckoned that he had conceded far too much to Christianity. But that is a later story.

Frederick the Great

Not the least of the men of letters who employed his pen in the cause of Enlightenment was Frederick the Great, king of Prussia from 1740 to 1786; moreover his long reign enabled him to leave a deep mark on the churches of his domains. The adherent of Wolff, the patron of Voltaire, the correspondent of Diderot and the Encyclopaedists, the writer of innumerable quips against positive religion, the man who complained incessantly about 'fanaticism' and the fact that 'a philosopher, who undertook to preach a simple religion, would . . . run the risk of being stoned by the people', he is almost the caricature of the Enlightened Despot. If, however, Frederick is judged not so much by his posturings in private correspondence as by what he did, he appears much in line with the Calvinism and neo-Stoicism on which his family had prospered for a century and a half; and the problems arising from the fact that the Reformed church to which the Hohenzollerns adhered numbered only three per cent of their subjects at the time of Frederick's accession, were identical with those of his forbears. Moreover, toleration of minority faiths during good behaviour had been an indispensable feature of Hohenzollern policy since their conversion from Lutheranism, and was now more than ever necessary for the recruitment of foreign Protestants for the economic development of the country, and for coping with the large Catholic populations acquired during the Silesian wars. Frederick's intense emphasis on duty, though certainly a foretaste of Kant, was equally a family tradition. After all he had suffered from his father, it is astonishing but true that less than a year before his father's death,

Frederick assured his sister that his relations with the king were as excellent as he could wish. In short Frederick's addiction to Enlightenment was tempered by an acute sense of the limitations of what it might achieve, by family traditions which were well adapted to what he had to do, by Jansenist reading and by other factors. In the war years, 1757–59, Frederick wrote an entirely serious sermon on the Last Judgment in Hallensian style.

Moreover Frederick's conviction that he was the chief bishop of the realm and his determined opposition to pulpit controversy which might lead to disorder implied a limitation of the role of the secular arm; matters of worship and doctrine were left to bishops and consistories. The religious organisation of the army exemplified what Frederick really wanted. As worked out by Military Provost Decker in 1750, the regiment was the superior unit, but provision was made not merely for the troops, but their families and servants of whatever confession. The daily hymn-singing, twice daily devotions, and twice monthly communions were not matched in armies elsewhere. The supremacy of the state was compatible with a high degree of free religious practice. As Otto Hintze pointed out long ago, Frederick's Political Testaments, while adamant against religious discord, Silesian-style, 'in no way conceived the church as an institution of state police, neither Protestant nor Catholic'. In the same way, while welcoming the return of Wolff to Halle, he did not surrender to rationalist influences, nor interfere in their disputes with the Pietists; Pietist influence in school reform continued. Frederick's last great service to the cause of religious toleration jointly sustained by the Enlightenment and by his family tradition came in the preparation of a general legal code (the *Allgemeine Landrecht*) for the Prussian states which was completed just after his death. This guaranteed complete freedom of belief and conscience to every citizen; no one was to be despised or disturbed by the state on account of his religious convictions. The price of this privilege was, of course, that 'every church-society [was] obliged to kindle in its members reverence towards God, obedience to the law, loyalty to the state, and good moral dispositions towards their fellow-citizens'. In eighteenth-century terms this was not a bad bargain. In short Frederick was in some ways a more characteristic example of the *Aufklärung* than were Lessing and Kant; he did a job on behalf of the church.

And his mark on the Prussian churches was profound, for it was in his time that rationalism became one of the hallmarks of the Prussian clergy. It is worth stressing this since Nicholas Hope's great survey of the Lutheran churches creates the impression that the bulk of them were locked into a rural stagnation which insulated them effectively from movements for change whether spiritual or intellectual. It is of course true that the periodising of movements in the Lutheran churches is very variable; the peak of musical achievement in the Orthodox era came only with Handel and Bach when Orthodoxy was a spent force politically and theologically, though it is noteworthy that when Bach died in 1750 he was already considered (musically) old-fashioned and was about to go out of vogue altogether. It is also true that circumstances which affected the rate at which the clergy took up with the new criticism differed considerably in different parts of Germany. In Electoral Saxony, for example, clergy and teachers were bound by a strict oath to the symbolic books of the Lutheran tradition; in Saxe-Gotha by contrast this oath was eased by the amendment 'so far as they are in agreement with Holy Scripture', a concession dearly coveted by Anglican clergy of unitarian propensities. But the fact is that despite all the Enlightenment raving against clerical reaction, one reason why the new ways had a larger popular following than most philosophical fashions was that they were extensively taken up by the clergy, especially in Prussia. Here Frederick the Great came into his own; by various titles he had the patronage of about one-third of the churches in his domains, and there were special privileges for clergy who came up through the chaplaincy to the army, also largely in the king's gift. Again, the principal school of the clergy in Prussia was Halle, and, after the reconstruction by Semler, Halle was firmly in the camp of neology.

Enlightenment in the Protestant churches of Switzerland and Germany

Moreover, as we shall see, there was a marked change in the spiritual atmosphere in Europe after the Seven Years War and the way in which educated people discussed religious issues. The great showdown between Catholic and Protestant now dropped out of diplomatic correspondence and polite conversation; and the intellectual challenge of the Enlightenment theology, whether reason could be made a source for the knowledge of God alongside, or even instead of, revelation, did not seem so compelling. And Enlightenment itself suggested that after such a large dose of imputed righteousness from the Protestant Orthodoxies, a bit more actual righteousness would not come amiss. Where this took the shape on the continent of Orphan Houses, or, in England, of hospitals for particular groups of residents or for the treatment of particular groups of diseases, it required a break with older traditions of endowing parish charities.

At any rate through one channel or another Enlightenment began to make its appearance even in unlikely German churches. In Mecklenburg, for example, it came in very late in the eighteenth century after the reconstruction of the university of Rostock in 1789. In Württemberg, the Stift at Tübingen, where clergy for the Lutheran church in the duchy were trained, famed for its Pietist past, now produced a series of groups of men enlightened in spirit: first, in 1769–71 the historians Ludwig Timotheus Spittler (1752–1810) and Gottlob Jakob Planck (1751–1833), then in the 1780s poets such as Reinhardt, Bardili, Karl Friedrich Stäudlin (1761–1826) and Karl Philipp Conz (d.1827) who revived the spirit of classical Greece; and finally, 1790–93, the philosophical group of the most famous *Stiftler* of all, Hölderlin, Hegel and Schelling. To move further south again into the Reformed cantons of Switzerland, is to encounter an exciting story for which there is no space in a brief study. Protestant Switzerland, always in this period open to English influences, felt the entire canon from Newton to Hume and Gibbon; French Switzerland was subject to the impact of Voltaire and Rousseau; while the whole German *Aufklärung*, literary and philosophical, was received in German-speaking Switzerland. Here Zurich became a major European centre of Enlightenment, lay and ecclesiastical, comparable with Hamburg in the north, and the guardians of Reformed Orthodoxy, Bern, Basel and Schaffhausen, put up a stiff fight against the new ways with only limited success.

Catholic Enlightenment in Germany

If the story of Protestant Enlightenment in Germany is complicated, that of German Catholic Enlightenment is still worse; like much of the Protestant Enlightenment it was not hostile to the church, but sought a better future for it, and mingled with other reforming movements, some of considerable pedigree. Three conclusions spring from the modern work, however, which give some shape to the story. The first is that despite the neglect encouraged by historians who assumed that in this period Austria and Prussia were the only states with a history of any consequence, and despite the doctrinally motivated denials of nineteenth-century inte-gralists that there could be a Catholic Enlightenment, such a thing did exist, and was not simply a consequence of contamination by Protestant Germany, though such contamination also existed. The second is that the Catholic Enlightenment must be dated markedly later than the Protes-tant; indeed it was the misfortune of Catholic Germany that the new movement was barely under way when in the backwash of the French Revolution the spiritual states were secularised. The third is that the periodisation of the Catholic Enlightenment, which was never as much concerned with general ideas as its Protestant counterpart, was largely determined by important events outside the country. The first period has a pre-history extending into the the seventeenth century, but the admixture of modern ideas provoked particularly lively criticism from the 1740s. The second period is ushered in by the suppression of the Jesuit order in 1773, which transformed a longstanding discussion about education into urgent action. And the third phase began in 1780 with the accession of Joseph II to sole authority in the Habsburg lands; the upheaval he contrived gave an impulse to Catholic rulers, lay and spiritual.

Catholic Enlightenment was prefaced by longstanding movements for reform which coalesced and made some use of new ideas. The basic movement in the history of the Church since the fifteenth century had been the triumph of the papacy over its clerical critics (and also over general councils) at the price of expensive concessions to temporal authorities. The temporal authorities, Catholic and Protestant, had used the opportunity to create national churches, or churches otherwise organised to match secular boundaries. The risk was that the worm might turn, and that the local authorities in the church might resist the process by which the papacy and the world had combined to reduce their significance; and that risk was greatest in the Holy Roman Empire where there were mighty prince-bishops who (like the Holy See) combined spiritual and temporal authority, and where the national church was furthest from realisation. And this risk was realised at the precise point when, after the end of the War of the Austrian Succession in 1748, the age-old hostility between Habsburg and Bourbon was put discreetly under wraps. Maria Theresa then knew that she might need French and Spanish assistance to contain the threat from Frederick the Great in Germany. Any *rapprochement* among the Catholic great powers implied peace and stability in Italy, but carried a potential threat to the papacy from the combined action of the very powers to whom it had delivered the local churches.

By this time there was a feeling that some of the policies of church renewal deriving from the Counter-Reformation needed to be more resolutely pursued, while others needed to be rethought. Thus, for example, Germany had been late in implementing the Tridentine policy of creating diocesan seminaries for priests, but caught up energetically in the eighteenth century. On the other hand the Tridentine ideal of episcopacy was ruled out of court in the Empire by the Electoral and princely status of the bishops. Again the Jesuits had been the great missionary force of the Counter-Reformation, and the moving spirit in German Catholicism. But Jesuit missions had probably made more Protestants than they had converted in Bohemia, and they failed to wipe out Protestant communities in Salzburg and the Habsburg family lands, let alone Hungary; thus rulers were beginning to look for alternatives to the Jesuits at the very time when there was a growing chorus of complaints about the inadequacy of Jesuit education. Some of them derived from the intellectual modernisms which in Protestantism went into theology as well as education. Furthermore, as one solution to the pastoral ills of the church was to tighten up church discipline, surviving Jansenists could climb upon the bandwagon, the more easily as it became the habit to describe any one who was anti-Jesuit for any reason as a Jansenist.

By the latter part of the century it was a serious question whether Catholic Enlightenment was any different from Protestant. Certainly Catholic *Aufklärer*, educated in a Protestant university such as Göttingen, could rant against past times when 'the human understanding was not in the least formed' in quite the Protestant Enlightened style. Moreover the Enlightenment began to influence Catholic studies in theology and canon law. Göttingen, the new Hanoverian university built on a mixture of Pietism and Enlightenment, attracted increasing numbers of important Catholics by virtue of its academic reputation; and Christian Wolff proved to be an immensely influential export to Catholic Germany, received even in the Jesuit order. Between 1750 and 1780, long after his influence declined in Protestant Germany, he came to dominate the philosophical instruction in Catholic universities and gymnasia, and his works came to grace the monastic libraries. In the 1780s and 1790s his influence yielded to that of Immanuel Kant.

Episcopalism

The specially unsettling element in central Europe was that Enlightenment entered into much older movements of reform. Episcopalism, a mood of championing the rights of local bishops against the claims of the Holy See, gained the name of Febronianism from the pseudonym, Justinus Febronius, under which Nikolaus von Hontheim, suffragan bishop of Trier (1701–90), published (in Latin) a striking book, *On the state of the Church and the lawful power of the Pope, written to reunite Christians who differ in Religion* (1763). In this work Febronius went beyond the old episcopalism to press for the repeal of decrees of the Council of Trent which were not compatible with the forms of German church life. Here he was digging his own grave, for among these forms were the special privileges of the nobility within the church of the Empire; reforms which did not touch these would not amount to much. More immediately Hontheim represented the episcopalist view that the pope and his nuncios exercised no jurisdiction which competed with that of the bishops. The bishops were not subjects of the pope, but, like the pope himself, were appointed by divine right as successors of the apostles. Here Hontheim spoke for the resentments of a long past, and also offered the prescription for Germany's divided state in religion standard among the Catholic *Aufklärer*; the papal primacy had taken a form unpalatable to Catholics and unacceptable to Protestants. The pope was not infallible, and needed to be kept in check by general and national councils, by reforming churches, bishops and princes. For a time Hontheim looked almost like a second Luther, using the new historical knowledge to reform and unite the church on a national and anti-curial basis. By 1769 the book had acquired practical significance since it formed the basis of the *Gravamina* of the Koblenz congress, directed primarily against the nuncios.

These complaints were resumed in the Punctation of Ems (1786), when the four great archbishops of Mainz, Trier, Cologne and Salzburg turned against all the nuncios in Germany. This quarrel was brought on by the fact that the Elector of Bavaria (like the Habsburgs on a bigger scale) had extensive domains but not a single bishop (Munich was situated in Freising, an independent prince-bishopric). In other words, to get a nuncio to Munich was a way for the Elector of Bavaria to get an archbishop of his own and begin to create a church system within his own boundaries. Appeals to the Emperor and the Diet were not likely to carry the day against a prince; but the bishops reinforced their case by all the other demands which had arisen during the Enlightenment: the improvement of pastoral care and clerical training, the relationship of regular and secular clergy in pastoral care, the simplification of the liturgy, the reduction of processions and pilgrimages, the limitation of popular veneration of saints, the reform of religious orders of both sexes, and the use of capitular clergy in parish and school. In these respects the Punctation of Ems latched on to two of the striking things about the internal propaganda of the Catholic Enlightenment, the extraordinarily hostile criticism of the religious orders, and also the desire to improve education from wherever resources could be found. The ruinous thing about the episcopalist effort at improvement from within was that it involved not only an outright contest with the curia, but also a competition with another form of internal Catholic reform, championed by princes hitherto favoured by the papacy, and interested in a state-church system, which might also involve a clash with the papacy. The two most dramatic examples of this were the two markers in the crescendo of Catholic Enlightenment, the suppression of the Jesuit order and the reforms of Joseph II.

The suppression of the Jesuits

The former event was full of surprises, for in south Germany there were Jesuits enlightened enough to favour even the reforms of Joseph II. The fact that an event precipitated from far away marked a period in the Catholic Enlightenment in Germany illustrates the degree to which the Catholic church was shaken. The very prominence of the Jesuit order ensured that it had Catholic enemies, men prepared to believe that they were politically devious and commercially grasping to a quite unacceptable degree. Moreover there were responsible Catholics who shared the Protestant view that they had been left behind by the progress of knowledge, and wanted to break the Jesuit stranglehold on higher education with a view to introducing modern subjects. These animosities, however, would never have brought the Jesuit order down.

The ball was set rolling by one of the most reactionary governments, that of Portugal. From an early stage in the history of Latin American missions religious orders had taken the view that the natives needed protection from settlers by being organised in reservations, the most famous of which were the Jesuit *Reductions* in Paraguay. The day came when the pressure of settlers would not be denied, and when some settlers and home governments came to believe that the Jesuits were organising independent satrapies, in which native peoples toiled to produce wealth beyond dreams for the Society of Jesus. In 1750 the Portuguese and Spanish governments agreed a treaty defining the frontier in South America which involved moving seven of the thirty reductions across the River Uruguay. To cut a long story short, while everyone in authority in Europe (including two successive Jesuit generals) could see no difficulty in this, the local missionaries held that it was impossible, and when Spanish troops moved in, European governments believed that the Jesuits were causing an Indian rebellion. At this point power in Portugal fell into the hands of the (future) Marquis of Pombal (1689–1782) who made his name in coping with the effects of the Lisbon earthquake of 1755. Determined to modernise an archaic state, he found himself, like other reformers, up against two pillars of the old order, the church and the nobility, and found it convenient that the ill odour of the Jesuits in Paraguay spilled over on to their colleagues at home. In March 1758 the Portuguese envoy in Rome called on Benedict XIV to reform the Jesuit order radically or abolish them and the Pope issued a brief to this effect. The Portuguese government seized the property of the order, dumped 1,000 members of it in the Papal States, and did everything in its power to blacken the reputation of the Jesuits by propaganda. Their campaign could not but strengthen governments in Turin, Milan and Vienna which wanted to reform education. Just at this moment the Jesuits in France were found guilty of commercial malpractice.

Lavalette became head of the Jesuits in the West Indies in 1754, in recognition of his work in turning an unprofitable group of estates in

Martinique and Dominica into a remunerative concern. Then everything went wrong. The French government, mindful of settler interests, forbade him to trade, and in 1756 his Paris agents went bankrupt, bringing him down with them. Creditors began to sue the Society, which speedily faced corporate ruin. The Paris Parlement sequestrated all Jesuit properties in France, while the Jesuits themselves found Lavalette guilty of every conceivable malpractice. That got rid of him but did not otherwise help the Society. In 1762 various French Parlements ordered the expulsion of the Jesuits from France, their schools were closed and property taken over. Then Pope Clement XIII addressed a brief (1762) to the bishops of France denouncing the attack on the Jesuits, but they would not publish it. The number of homeless Jesuits was now nearly 3,000, the largest group of whom seem to have fetched up in Jesuit houses in Spain.

Spain now had every inducement to join in the campaign. She had the same interest in containing Jesuit power in America as the Portuguese, and the same interest as the French in getting hold of their property at home. The Spanish king, Charles III, apparently egged on by France, was against them, and in 1767 demanded the expulsion and expropriation of the Jesuits. Clement XIII pleaded with him not to visit the sins of individuals upon the Society as a whole, and told him that he could not admit the expelled Jesuits (even though the Spanish Jesuits were given a pension from the endowments of the Society) to the Papal States; already supporting Jesuits from Portugal and France, the Pope could not face the burden of becoming a general dumping-ground for the whole of Catholic Christendom. What the great Bourbon powers had done, Naples and Sicily now did, and the tiny dukedom of Parma compounded on 16 January 1768 in an edict banning appeals by the clergy to Rome without permission of the duke and declaring all bulls and briefs from Rome or anywhere else invalid unless they carried the duke's signature. A fortnight later Clement XIII issued the brief called the *Monitorium* proclaiming the Duke of Parma's edict to be null and excommunicating the officials responsible.

This clash between the Pope and the head of a Catholic state produced gloomy prognostications of the fall of the papacy from diplomatic insiders, but in fact it simplified the options all round. The Bourbon powers needed the destruction of the Society of Jesus to justify their anti-Jesuit policies and to modernise their states by reducing ecclesiastical immunities and endowments; the papacy could not take a high line with Catholic states and at the same time defend a Society convicted by inquiries (of a kind) of offending against royal government, commercial probity, and honest missionary method. Moreover if the Society were destroyed huge numbers of useless religious might find secular employment. There were cardinals prepared to support the abolition. The person who would not yield was Pope Clement XIII. He died in 1769, a few days after receiving a formal application from France, Spain and Naples for the suppression of the order, and his death opened the way for the Bourbon powers to seek a more compliant pontiff through their influence in the college of cardinals.

That influence secured the election of a Franciscan, Ganganelli, who took the title of Clement XIV. He was not a pushover, but could not avoid concession. He made Pombal's brother a cardinal; he brought to an end the annual publication of the bull of general excommunication, *In coena Domini*, which let the government of Parma off the hook; after endless procrastination, he ascertained that Maria Theresa, the devout head of the Habsburg house, thought well of the Jesuits but would not oppose his decision if he thought that Catholic unity depended on the suppression of the order. (In that case she reserved the rights of her government to deal with their property.) That sealed the Jesuit fate. The Pope issued the most famous of all his decrees, *Dominus ac Redemptor*, suppressing the order in the summer of 1773. The deed was at last done which no one had contemplated at the outset. The Jesuit order perished without resistance, undone by its own oaths of obedience, and the use of church authority to put down attempts to write an account of the suppression from its point of view. Protestants made a hero of Clement XIV.

The ex-Jesuits

The tactics of the Bourbon powers in expelling Jesuits first and negotiating afterwards, show, paradoxically, why the suppression was a landmark in the history of the German Catholic Enlightenment, for here the problem of informal Jesuit survival was most acute. The most favourable areas for survival were in Switzerland, Britain and in the missions of the British colonies in North America. Here the ex-Jesuits were able to live in community in their old buildings; what they could not do was to ensure the continuity of their tradition by recruiting. In Germany the provisions of the papal bull that the buildings and endowments of the Jesuits were to be used by the bishops for charitable purposes after the payment of pensions to ex-Jesuits in need were generally disregarded by governments in their own interests. Thus the Jesuit house in Vienna became the War Office, and the houses in Prague and Antwerp became barracks. The German Catholic states had now seriously to undertake educational reform; they could not do without the ex-Jesuits but employed them under a variety of restrictions. Some states (including Bavaria and the archbishopric of Mainz), avid for the wealth Jesuit houses might contain, refused to allow their former owners to live in community, but allowed them under restrictions to teach or be parish priests. The government of the Austrian Netherlands, where Jansenism had long been strong, excluded most Jesuits from its schools and parishes. In Poland the Jesuits had been popular, and very many continued in education or parishes. But Poland was in a state of civil war and had just suffered its first partition, unpropitious circumstances for a suppressed order to stick to its property. The result was that the pensions were not always paid and Polish education suffered.

There were non-Catholic governments which regarded the ex-Jesuits as too valuable a resource to waste. Frederick the Great determined to maintain the Jesuit order for the education of the Catholic populations he had acquired in Silesia and western Poland. Here, however, general Catholic discipline proved (not for the last time) too tough for the Prussian state. The bishops regarded the condemned Jesuits as rebels and the faithful began to abandon their preaching and confessionals. The result was that within a couple of years Prussia had retreated to the position taken up at once by German Catholic powers. The ex-Jesuits might keep their schools and colleges, but must abandon their habit and their name. They might train future schoolmasters, but came under the Prussian government in matters of curriculum (which meant they must suffer an injection of history) and the government also managed their finances. Catherine the Great in Russia (who had annexed a large Polish Catholic population) went further. She refused to allow the bull of suppression to be published in Russia, and prevented its being known. The Jesuits continued an equivocal existence, the popes condoning what they could not appear to approve. Pius VII gave his approval in 1801. By that time the lesson taught by this dramatic act of papal power under pressure from Catholic governments had been absorbed by revolutionary governments with scant respect for the Holy See.

Catholic higher education

The suppression of the Jesuit order compelled Catholic governments to make good what were now held to be the faults of Jesuit teaching, the imbalance between their cultivation of Latin and instruction in the vernacular, their inadequate incorporation of historical disciplines, their neglect of mathematics and the natural sciences. The movement was given an impetus and some uniformity by the gross predominance of the Schönborn family in the ecclesiastical politics of the Reich; their great preferments Mainz, Würzburg and Bamberg led the way. In this brief account it is worth concentrating on what happened at the top of the educational pyramid, in the universities. Here some of the specifics of the German Catholic Enlightenment become apparent. The backwardness of the German churches in providing seminary training for priests had meant that clerical training took place in universities, and hence that all Catholic universities possessed theological faculties, which was not the case in France, Italy or Spain. Moreover many Catholic critics held that it was precisely at the university level that Protestant Germany had established a lead, especially in the new foundations at Halle and Göttingen. The characteristics of the changes now made were that universities were to serve the public welfare as focused in the state (even when the head of state was a prince of the church). This meant that although the Catholic Enlightenment was no more hostile to theology than the Protestant, theological faculties lost their old primacy, along with the deductive rationalism which had sustained the claim of theology to be the queen of sciences, and gradually lost also their old right of censorship except in cases of gross offence against religion or the law of the land. Dogmatics and polemics must be 'purified from that scholastic theology which shot up in the Dark Ages'.

The service of the state was promoted in both manner and substance. Universities should produce presentable men of the world, and here Catholic Germany took to its bosom the image projected in the early days of Halle by Christian Thomasius; he had created a sensation not merely by lecturing in German, but by appearing not in academic dress but in wig and sword. The running in the new university oriented to the service of the state was made by a faculty which had shrunk to negligible proportions in the English universities, that of jurisprudence. This included public law, Jus Patrium, feudal law, canon law along with modern practice, civil law and the law of nature; the arts faculty also became slanted in the direction of law. The main pattern for all this had been set in Protestant Germany at Göttingen, but there was one important difference. After all the criticism of the Jesuits for neglecting history, the dominance of Christian Wolff in Catholic universities left little room to do better; so the branch of Protestant legal studies with the largest historical element, which conditioned the growth of historical treatment in many other specialisms, Romano-German public law, did not appear in the reinvigorated Catholic law faculties. The spirit of the new law faculties was exemplified by the pious Maria Theresa, who held that in canon law nothing should be taught which was not in the interests of the state rationally understood. 'What would the rest of the enlightened world say [she asked] if we were again to defend the infallibility of the Pope and his supremacy over a general council, as the official line presents it?' Another testimony to the service of the state was cameralistics, the study in the first instance of estate management in the public sector, and, by gradual extension, of public finance generally; there were chairs in this subject in Protestant Leipzig, Halle, Frankfurt-on-Oder and Erlangen, but they were so immensely outnumbered by chairs in Catholic universities as to make cameralistics almost a Catholic subject. Dedicated to the public usefulness rather than the confessional traditions of the Counter-Reformation, the German Catholic universities were ready to face the new world when they were altogether overtaken by the radical shake-up in the Habsburg lands inaugurated by Joseph II's accession to sole rule.

Josephinism before Joseph II?

Joseph II succeeded as Holy Roman Emperor at the age of twenty-four in 1765. His importance for the Empire (for instance in marking the last period of the German Enlightenment) consisted not in any action as emperor, but in radicalism as ruler of the Habsburg family lands. Here he was only co-regent with his mother, Maria Theresa, until her death in 1780, when he became sole ruler for the last ten years of his life. There has been a long-running international controversy about whether there was 'a Josephinism before Joseph', whether in fact the striking policies of his last years were a personal response to ideas current in the Catholic Enlightenment, or whether they were the ultimate fruit of a longstanding Habsburg propensity to intervention in church matters, going back to Charles VI.

To strip the matter of the complexity and venom it has generated, the truth seems to be this. It was not the Counter-Reformation which saved Catholicism in the Habsburg lands, but Habsburg military prowess directed first against the Protestants and then against the Turks. The Pietas Austriaca which glorified Habsburg victories in the field would not have existed without the military triumph, and, in the nature of the case, by celebrating the services of the dynasty to the Church, it consecrated a role of active intervention. A degree of regalianism which Charles VI shared with Louis XIV is not, however, part of the pre-history of Catholic reform. There was also longstanding friction between the Habsburgs and the papacy. During the War of the Spanish Succession Clement VII backed the Bourbon claims to Spain and allied with the enemies of Austria. When the Habsburg male line died out Benedict XIV recognised not Francis I, Maria Theresa's husband, but the Wittelsbach claimant, Charles VII. And the duke of Parma excommunicated by Clement XIII with such *éclat* in 1768 was Maria Theresa's son-in-law. Moreover the Habsburgs were a force in Italy too near home for the popes' preference. If Josephinism before Joseph existed anywhere it existed in the reorganisation of Lombardy in the 1760s, and Lombardy was not merely a channel to Vienna of Italian reforming ideas of the sort nobly embodied in Muratori, it was chosen by Clement XIII as a theatre of conflict with Maria Theresa, he refusing to help her with clerical taxation and appointing Lombard bishops without consultation. Then there was Leopold, Maria Theresa's son who became Grand Duke of Tuscany in 1765 and who compounded the one felony of embarking on church reform on radical Enlightenment principles by the second of urging his mother to follow suit.

These frictions were, however, the small change of diplomatic existence; the pope was never going to excommunicate the emperor or the queen of Hungary as he had excommunicated the duke of Parma, and Maria Theresa was a devout representative of Pietas Austriaca who expended pains to get Papal approval wherever possible. If she declined to let bishops dispose of the property of the Jesuits, she had the justification that she had hardly any bishops of her own, and the literal fulfilment of the provisions of Dominus ac Redemptor would simply have enabled foreign bishops to take money out of the country. Moreover it is now clear that Maria Theresa was led into the idea of church reform as a last desperate device for exterminating Protestantism when all else had failed or become too expensive.

Here indeed was one of the roots of religious change. The sudden expansion of the Habsburg dynastic empire in the late seventeenth and early eighteenth centuries had been lavishly supported by religious symbols in part triumphalist and in part oppressive, and long afterwards even Joseph II was as clear as to the need for them as any of his forbears. But the sheer cost of the new empire compelled the development of a new frame of mind based on calculation, and compelled the employment of servants like van Swieten from the Netherlands and the Italian Martini, who both had Jansenism in their background. Some strange worms had turned even under the stone of Pietas Austriaca. Prince Eugene's private theological library, to which his intimates were admitted, mirrored the decline of speculative, thomist and scholastic theology, and contained, without respect to the censorship, works relating to all the current movements in the churches. Then there was Maria Theresa's husband, the Emperor Francis I, who in his days as Duke of Lorraine had been a freemason and practised Jansenist devotional methods. He left behind an eclectic 'Instruction pour mes enffans' based on his own rule of life and inculcating these principles. And while in public Francis observed the full court ceremonial on the lines of Charles VI, in private life it was a different story, with no veneration of the Virgin or saints and perhaps freemasonry too. Nor is there any doubt that the state-church system as operated in Lorraine had an influence not only in Tuscany, but in Austria. If this was happening right at the top, the growth of an influential public to whom baroque piety no longer appealed, and who were willing to help execute policies characteristic of the Catholic Enlightenment, becomes easier to understand.

There were doubtless many whose minds moved faster in this field than that of Maria Theresa, but her evolution is important. As we have seen, every time the Habsburg government attacked its native Protestants with its familiar mixture of evangelism, bribery and brute force, it evoked resistance and even revival; moreover its methods were expensive and could not be sustained in time of war. It was time to try another tack. The frontiers of state and church in Austria matched ill; huge areas of the church were subject to the foreign prince-bishops of Passau and Salzburg, who needed to be nursed for political purposes in the Holy Roman Empire; more 'home' bishops were therefore required. Furthermore the parish system was archaic; parishes needed to be divided, and more clergy diverted to pastoral purposes. This required both money and manpower. Since it was difficult to get at the foreign prelates, it was clear that both money and men would have to come from monastic foundations; many of these had been the glory of Pietas Austriaca, and in Bohemia a device for fundamental social engineering by salting away Protestant acres into Catholic mortmain. If the scheme could be brought off, the church in the Habsburg lands could be made more efficient at the point of practical need, to the edification of the Catholic population, and, it was to be hoped, to the elimination of the Protestants.

At any rate one of Maria Theresa's favourite clergy, Fr Pius Manzador, Provincial of the Austrian Barnabites, whom she pushed on to become head of his order, and later a bishop first in Croatia and then in the Protestant stronghold of Hermannstadt (Siebenbürgen), proposed to tighten up existing anti-Protestant policies, and was despatched to Rome in 1753 to negotiate a grand plan for centralising and equalising ecclesiastical revenues for purposes of church reform. A papacy which had not yet got to grips with the Jesuits was not keen on encouraging enterprising governments to finance their ideas at the expense of regular clergy; the Seven Years War broke out in 1756, a war on which Frederick the Great had spent infinite pains to present as a confessional conflict between Catholic and Protestant; there were then members of the Vienna government who did not want to risk the reproach that they were financing the war effort by expropriating church property, and by 1757 the whole project had been dropped.

Here in a nutshell lies the solution to the conundrum about Josephinism before Joseph. Maria Theresa, under pressure from Frederick the Great, had to face bankruptcy – more than the normal pressure on rulers to find resources in men and money for modernisation. And in her case bold talk led to almost no action where the church was concerned outside Kaunitz's satrapy in Lombardy. From the moment when Joseph II became co-regent in 1765, however, the action began, and it began with a simplification of court worship described by a modern Austrian historian as 'the almost total destruction of *Pietas Austriaca*, of Habsburg piety, as it had developed since the beginning of the seventeenth century'. He proceeded with a memorandum on the oppressiveness of the censorship system; the disadvantages of religious intolerance; the weakness of education; and the excessive size, number and wealth of monasteries, many of which he considered useless. By 1769 the government was beginning to consider church reform throughout the Habsburg domains, and to establish a theoretical basis for its right to intervene in every aspect of church life. In the last decade of Maria Theresa's life quite serious attempts were made to check the flow of endowments to the church and to tap its wealth for the advantage of the state and for educational reform. All this was a preface to the dramatic action taken by Joseph II after he became sole ruler in 1780.

Joseph II

Joseph set up a Church Affairs Commission to do quickly what had been talked of for so long. New sees were created to exclude the jurisdiction of Salzburg and Passau. A total of 255 new parishes were created in Lower Austria, 121 in Upper Austria, 180 in Styria, 83 in Carinthia. The new parishes were to have schools, and children were required to attend. The parish priests were to have adequate stipends. At one blow Joseph had ended the torpor of centuries and created the modern Austrian parish system which has given good service ever since. There were three problems with the upheaval. The first was to pay for it. The money could only come from monastic endowments, and the suppression of the Jesuit order by the Pope had by now set an unmistakable precedent. Joseph's commissioners were ordered to make lists of the monasteries and their property, and to abolish those which were contemplative and not following the useful vocations of nursing or teaching. In the event more than one-third of the religious houses in Austria were dissolved and the number of monks and nuns reduced by not far short of two-thirds. Many of the men went into parishes and schools; most of the women went back home. The mass sales of property were not all conducted advantageously, but were sufficient to pension off the ex-religious and benefit Joseph's central religious fund by about 60,000,000 *gulden*. Major new medical foundations in Vienna benefited; 642 brotherhoods were abolished in Austria to the advantage of poor relief and elementary schools; there was no resistance anywhere.

So far Joseph's policies were generally acceptable. But he wanted to avoid training his clergy in diocesan seminaries which were often too small to be useful. He created general seminaries, one for each of his main domains, which should instil not just theological studies but natural science, agriculture, and the art of teaching. Instruction was often in the vernacular. These however did not survive him. They were in breach of the main seminary tradition since the Council of Trent. And, as so often, the students did not help. It was the ordinands of the general seminary at Louvain who set off the revolution which ended in the severance of Belgium from Habsburg rule. Moreover, anxious to slay superstition at one blow, the Emperor encouraged the Commission to interfere in details they could well have left alone. Joseph was in line with Catholic Enlightenment generally in wishing to cut processions and pilgrimages not approved by authority; unfortunately people liked them. They also liked clothes on statues of the Virgin, being buried in coffins rather than sacks, were fond of more relics than was their ruler, and were tenacious of a host of practices which in Joseph's view were at best quaint, at worst superstitions. Attempts to suppress these by law were quietly dropped after his death.

The Patent of Toleration

On even the clearest act of policy Joseph himself was guilty of hesitation and fussiness. That Austria needed religious toleration had been obvious to Joseph for a long time. Toleration would put an end to the awkwardness of Protestant resistance and revival under pressure; it would deprive Prussia of an opportunity to fish in Habsburg troubled waters; it might even (and did in fact) attract Protestant emigrants to return. But Joseph had been prepared to justify toleration to his mother as an anti-Protestant measure, and his first instinct was quietly to suspend persecution without saying anything to undermine the prestige of the church. Enlightenment had become sufficiently politicised, however, for this to be impossible; and Joseph had therefore to issue his famous Patent of Toleration (1781) defining his new policy. Even then, however, he became alarmed at the number of his subjects who registered their adherence to one of the tolerated Protestant creeds, and tightened up the procedure to make registration more difficult. His enduring monument was a Habsburg monarchy which combined toleration with a good deal of informal intolerance.

The third hazard which Joseph had to face was the disapproval of the Pope. As we have seen, the Pope's visit to Vienna in 1782 to persuade Joseph to modify his dash for Enlightenment was a diplomatic disaster but a popular triumph. It showed, as the French Revolution was shortly to show on a bigger scale, that Enlightenment had an Achilles' heel, its lack of popular penetration.

Reform in Tuscany

This moral was further underlined by the last great adventure of Catholic reform, in Tuscany, a duchy long stuffed with reformers and from 1765 ruled by a Habsburg, Leopold, destined to succeed Joseph II in the Empire. He too believed in reform without tarrying for any, and quickly used his church patronage to create a party. His guide and agent was Scipione de' Ricci, vicar-general of the diocese of Florence, a Jansenist in touch with the surviving leaders of that party in France and from 1780 bishop of Pistoia and Prato. Ricci wanted a great deal more than a modernised diocesan and parochial system. He wanted to centre religious life on the parish and its liturgy, which meant getting rid of the competition of the chapels of religious orders, private shrines and the like. The service itself must be made congregational, for the liturgy was 'a common act of priest and people'. The reformers knew that they would not get a liturgy in the vernacular, but hoped to bring alive what they did by plain speaking and vernacular translations. But there would not be corporate participation until the distraction of private masses competing with the parish mass was ended, and until the very infrequent communion of the people was incorporated in the rite and not taken from the reserved sacrament after the rite was over. Financial difficulties could be met by reducing the number of clergy and pillaging the religious orders. Church furnishings should be purged of superstition in the now familiar ways. More advanced training should be provided for a more professional clergy. Edifying literature was provided free for the clergy, including a signal no one could miss, Quesnel's *Moral Reflexions on the New Testament*, the very book which had given rise to the Bull *Unigenitus* in 1713. Some of this could be done by state action, but in 1785 Leopold required all his bishops to hold a diocesan synod, and in 1786 presented them with the famous agenda of Fifty-Seven Points to get through. The slant of these points was clear: they were to consider how to purge the breviary of false legends, how to encourage reading of the Bible, how to defend the authority of the bishops from the encroachments of Rome, how to get St Augustine's teaching on grace into seminaries and universities, and much more of the same. Bishop Ricci summoned his synod to meet at Pistoia in September 1786.

Most of the clergy there were prepared to support their bishop as they were used to proposals of a Jansenist colour, and a smoothness was imparted to the final resolutions by the fact that the principal expert present was the very Jansenist professor Pietro Tamburini of Pavia, who may even have arrived with the drafts in his pocket. The resolutions followed the familiar lines and also condemned exciting parish missions which 'seldom or never produce real conversion', and the wide extension of the prohibited degrees of marriage. In mountain villages where everyone was related to everyone else, this led either to fornication or an endless quest for dispensations. Religious orders should be united into a single order, based on the Benedictine rule and guided by the practice of Port-Royal. Infallibility rested with a general council, not the pope. This programme was so far-reaching as inevitably to stir up controversy. What frightened authority was the popular reaction to the revised liturgies and other changes, culminating in violent riots at Prato in response to the rumour that the bishop was about to demolish an altar dedicated to the girdle of the Virgin. Order was not restored till troops moved in. The duke continued for a time to act by decree, but he had seen the red light. In 1789 Belgium rose against the policies, including ecclesiastical policies, of his brother Joseph, and when Leopold moved off to Vienna to succeed him in 1790, riots broke out again. Leopold advised his successor that Ricci was a liability, that his resignation should be accepted, and rewarded with a good pension. The alliance of prince and prelate which afforded Catholic Enlightenment its best chance had gone; popular devotion ('superstition' in reforming parlance) had set a bound to what princes had been encouraged to think was in their grasp by the papal suppression of the Society of Jesus. The Habsburgs had been defeated by one kind of obstinacy on the part of the Protestants, and another on the part of the Catholics. The rights of man, soon to be proclaimed and trampled on in the French Revolution, were not altogether to be denied in the age of Enlightened Despotism.

Catholic Enlightenment in southern Europe

The Tuscan crisis is a reminder that the Catholic Enlightenment was not solely a matter of the Empire and the Habsburg dynastic area, nor even of ecclesiastical preoccupations. If one of the great theorists of Catholic reform had been van Espen, the Louvain canonist (1646–1728) who had forged together Jansenism and opposition to curial power (episcopalism) and to the Society of Jesus, the other had been the learned and genial

Muratori. Muratori not only accomplished an immense literary work, he was an outspoken critic of excesses in the cult of saints and relics, an opponent of superstitious practices. Most of all he had ensured a proper place for historical criticism in Catholic theological studies. Moreover there were special problems in southern Europe. Portugal was the country in which the Counter-Reformation had penetrated deepest and the Society of Jesus was most powerful. But the papacy knew, the Jesuits knew, and the Portuguese government knew, that Portugal had not the resources to carry out the missionary undertakings it had made in the early days of its empire; and when disaster struck in the Lisbon earthquake in 1755, it did not take long for Carvalho (the future Marquis of Pombal) to create a scenario in which Jesuit resources became the key to the modernisation of the state, and the whole Catholic world was unsettled. The reforms of Charles III in Spain added to the uncertainty. Similarly, while the Italian states escaped the burden of the great European conflicts since the peace of Aix-la-Chapelle, they fell victim to a series of severe famines in 1763–67. These exposed weaknesses of social arrangements which included the wealth and privileges of the church, and invigorated a reform movement in the church as well as in the state. The changes made under this pressure, if small, were sufficient to preserve Italy from famines of such severity again. In the church things were less happy. Benedict XIV had shown signs of coming to terms with his generation, and even spoke of reforming the Society of Jesus. But Clement XIII (1758–69) would face neither the administrative nor spiritual cost of adaptation. The result was that he ran into trouble with not only Portugal but the entire Bourbon caucus, and the excommunicate duchy of Parma became a favoured son of Catholic Europe.

From this crisis changes arose. In Naples, for a time, Jesuit property was even divided among the peasants. But although there was bold talk of carving up the Papal States, it was only in the immediate Habsburg sphere that there was a resolute drive for reform; Clement XIV's dissolution of the Jesuit order was enough to break up the international coalition against him which might have moved the Italian states to radical action. If real reform would have to wait, at least church reform became part of the movement of Enlightenment reform generally. Moreover even church conservatism, the curial opposition to church reform for most of the eighteenth century, began to change. Cardinal Giuseppe Garampi (1725–92) held all the right reforming views, but stuck at the dissolution of the Jesuits and the threat to Catholic cohesion posed by the development of national churches. A stout supporter of Clement XIV, he became nuncio in Vienna in 1776, and ran a regular spy organisation, infiltrating anti-Roman circles, and putting together the basis of an ultramontane network. In the end he created a black international of those who stood for the rights of the papacy and opposed the creation of canon law on a national basis, Febronianism and the antireligious element in the Enlightenment. More than one kind of future was casting its shadow before.

7 The Churches in northern and eastern Europe

Muslim and Christian

The fate of organised religion in eastern Europe was intimately connected with the dramatic rise and fall of empires. The Ottoman Empire, as we have seen, had been pushed back and beaten into permanent decline by the Habsburgs (with Polish and Venetian assistance) by the time of the Peace of Carlowitz of 1699. But that decline was uncommonly slow; the Turks thrashed the Russians in 1711, recovered territory from Venice in 1718 and from Austria in 1739, securing the line of the Danube and the Sava which lasted till 1914. The effect of this was to expose the Protestants of Hungary to the most savage and unsuccessful onslaughts of the Counter-Reformation, and to leave the Christian communities still under Ottoman rule in variegated and often ambiguous positions. In some areas such as Bosnia and much of Albania the population had been converted wholesale to Islam. Moldavia and Wallachia remained Christian and largely autonomous; they paid tribute to the Sultan and were governed after a fashion by hospodars who from the early eighteenth century were always Greeks from Constantinople. The Aegean islands were governed less oppressively than any other part of the Empire, and many Greek communities were almost independent. The recovery of the Morea from Venice in 1718 was assisted by the dislike of the Orthodox population for their intolerant Catholic masters. If to some Orthodox heathen rule might seem preferable to Catholic, to some others it was very profitable. The Phanariot Greeks (so-called from the quarter of Constantinople in which they lived) played a leading role in the Turkish administration, their value enhanced by their wealth, commercial contacts abroad, and linguistic skill. From 1661 they monopolised the influential office of Dragoman (or chief interpreter) at the Porte and regularly governed Romanian provinces. There was, however, a double ambiguity in their influential position. The chief foreign power in Constantinople was the narrowly Catholic power of France, and in general the Balkan peoples became steadily more hostile to their Ottoman rulers (including their Greek coadjutors)

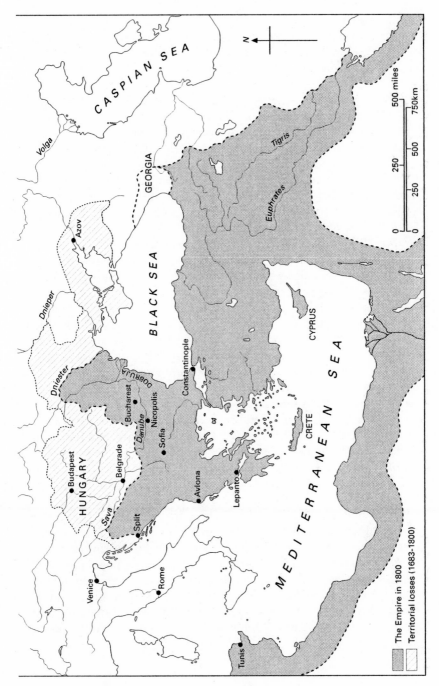

Map 5 The decline of the Ottoman Empire from the end of the seventeenth century

The Empire in 1800

Territorial losses (1683–1800)

during the eighteenth century. This was partly because changes in land tenure worked to the disadvantage of the peasants, and partly because an anti-Turkish middle class began to develop in the seaports. And by the end of the eighteenth century, mostly through contacts with central Europe, national feeling began to develop in parts of the Balkans. There were thus factors which favoured and factors which inhibited the survival of Orthodox communities in the Balkans.

There was much the same ambiguity in the external relations of the Patriarchate at Constantinople; like the Porte it felt the need for periodical French support, but much of the time its attitude to the outside Christian world was hostile. The old hostility of the Orthodox to the primacy of the papacy and the western belief in the procession of the Holy Spirit from the Father and the Son grew no less, and was periodically intensified by eastern sallies against transubstantiation, and the practice of rebaptising Latin Christians, which became a formal requirement in 1755. There was thus little for Uniat Christians (i.e. Christians in union with Rome but practising their own rite in their own language; they were numerous throughout eastern Europe) in the Orthodox system, and 36,000 Serbian Uniat families led by their own bishop got out in 1690 to refound their church in Lower Hungary. But the advance of Habsburg power into Serbia exposed Serbian Uniats to the pressure of the Counter-Reformation, to westernising influences generally, including a 'Serbian baroque', and to squabbles for authority among their own leaders. The emigration inevitably weakened the Catholic cause in Serbia, and the establishment of Habsburg rule in Hungary made the office of Vicar Apostolic and bishop of Belgrade superfluous. Appointments ceased in 1720 in deference to the Hungarian hierarchy. Propaganda Fide kept an anxious eye on the remaining Catholic populations in the Balkans, supplying them with vernacular teaching and liturgical material, and seeing to the training of clergy in Italy. What they could not do in the remaining Catholic strongholds of Croatia and Dalmatia was to end the friction between the Latin and Uniat hierarchies, the antagonism between both and the Franciscan order to which most of the missionary work was entrusted, or between both and the Serbian Orthodox church. Nor had they any power to stop the great displacements of population among Serbs, Croats and Albanians in consequence of the Habsburg incursion into and partial repulse from the peninsula. These were to decide for centuries to come the ethnic and religious division of the area; Propaganda Fide was still more helpless before the enduring hatreds to which these changes gave rise.

The northern empires

The two large states further to the north, Poland and Sweden – the one increasingly ideologically committed to the Counter-Reformation (and dedicated to the Virgin) and the other the great saviour of Lutheran Orthodoxy – went down the hill together, and went against the general European trend by formally consecrating the political power of the aristocracy. Augustus II, Elector of Saxony and the formal head of the Protestant caucus in the Diet of the Holy Roman Empire, had converted to Catholicism in 1697 in order to obtain election to the crown of Poland. This union between a commercial and manufacturing and a rambling, indefensible agricultural power, which might have been a successful complementary match, went wrong from the beginning. Augustus and Denmark commenced war against Sweden in 1700, but Charles XII of Sweden proved strong enough to overcome them both, and at Altranstädt (in Saxon territory) in 1707 dictated to the Habsburgs improved terms for the survival of Silesian Protestantism. Attacking Russia through the Ukraine, however, Charles XII met complete disaster in the battle of Poltava in 1709, had to take refuge in Turkey, and was killed in 1718 soon after his return to Sweden. Poltava at once revived the alliance of Russia, Denmark and Saxony against Sweden, but prefaced no happier fortune to Poland, which was now crossed by Russian and German troops. By the Peace of Nystadt (1721) Sweden lost most of her empire south of the Baltic, principally to Russia, which now became a serious player in the European game for the first time.

This new status was menacing to German powers, but still more menacing to Poland. Russia enforced an agreement limiting the size of the Polish army in 1717, occupied a fief of Poland, the Duchy of Courland, in 1718, in the war of the Polish Succession (1733–35) enforced on the Poles a king they did not want, and another, a former lover of Catherine II in 1764. Meanwhile Frederick the Great's Silesian campaign in the 1740s put a Prussian salient between the Polish and Saxon parts of Augustus's composite state. The weakness of Poland encouraged the local vultures eventually to begin picking over her territory, as they had picked over that of Sweden, in the three partitions which commenced in 1772. The religious fruit of the two dismemberments was, however, entirely different. South of the Baltic (as we have seen) the Swedish retreat put paid to their efforts to root out paganism and assimilate the population religiously (though not linguistically) to the Lutheran Orthodoxy of the Swedish imperial church; and from Halle and Herrnhut forces moved in, as unpalatable as possible to high-church Swedes, but able to capitalise on the work the Swedes had done, and perhaps better equipped

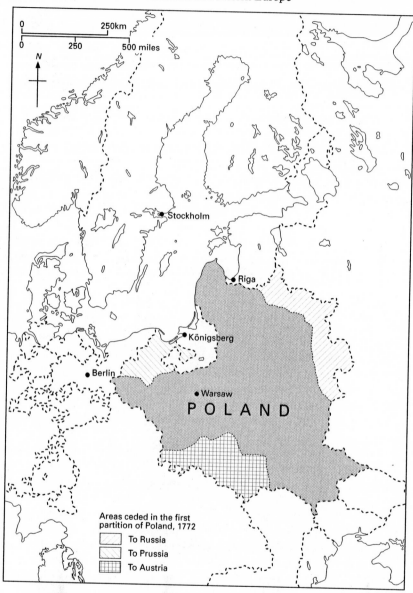

Areas ceded in the first
partition of Poland, 1772

To Russia

To Prussia

To Austria

Map 6 Northern, central and eastern Europe in the early eighteenth
century

to affect the popular mind. Even their dynamism, however, was sapped before long by the strong-arm tactics of the Russian government.

Poland, too, was subject to a good deal of interference, ecclesiastical as well as political, from the Russian side, but the effect of the partitions was to turn Poland from the land of liberty notionally achieved (or least the land where bitter mutual intolerances co-existed), which it still was at the beginning of the eighteenth century, into the Marian kingdom more familiar in recent times. It was not that the Counter-Reformation, by force or otherwise, converted the non-Catholic peoples of Poland, rather that the violence of Poland's neighbours pushed back her borders to the point where the religious dissidents became the assets (or problems) of other powers. Nevertheless a heady mixture of Catholicism and Polish nationalism was already in existence.

Radical changes and much discomfort were also portended for the Russian Orthodox churches. The Russian state was expanding not only into Europe in the west, but into Siberia in the east, where it was often preceded by its own people. This meant that Russian Orthodoxy had to coexist in the west with other forms of Christian profession, and in the east and south with heathenism, Islam and Judaism, all at the moment when it needed new resources for extending its pastoral oversight and administration. Had nothing else happened, this alone would have been enough to change the relations of the Orthodox Church with the Russian state; and Russian Orthodoxy, heavily dependent on liturgical familiarity for transmitting its tradition, and assigning a lower level of importance to the rational formulation of doctrine than the churches of the west, was especially ill-equipped to cope with a state which could no longer dispense with methods of rational calculation. The interrelated problems of organised religion in the declining powers of Sweden and Poland, and in the rising power of Russia are the next inquiries.

Scandinavian Lutheranism

Scandinavian Lutheranism in its two great branches of Denmark-Norway and Sweden-Finland retained a remarkable kinship with the Lutheran churches of Germany, remarkable both in that there was no church-institutional mechanism to preserve it, and that there were political mechanisms which might well have severed it. The rising force in Lutheran Germany was Prussia, uncomfortably headed by a Reformed monarchy, an embarrassment the Scandinavian churches were spared; on the other hand, the Danes were prepared to join the ill-considered coalition of German powers with Russia to pick over the bones of the Swedish empire in Europe, and in the 1730s the only state of any substance in

Europe headed by a Pietist monarchy. This monarchy proved, however, much more of a nuisance to Zinzendorf's Herrnhuters than to the rather high-flying Lutheran Orthodox of the Swedish church.

There was also a kinship between the Scandinavian and the German Lutheran churches in the way in which they were exposed to outside influences. As in Germany, so in Scandinavia, the influence of British works of experimental piety, especially Puritan tracts, was great and much more enduring than it was at home. Not that the influence was direct; Bunyan's *Pilgrim's Progress* was first translated into Swedish in 1727 from German and Dutch versions; one of the first Swedish devotional books to include illustrations, it was an instant success, going through sixty editions. At a distance followed Richard Baxter and Thomas Gouge. But an increasingly anti-Puritan Church of England also played its part, as numbers of Lutheran clergy and ordinands, German and Scandinavian, came to Oxford or Cambridge for part of their studies, especially in the biblical languages. Between 1673 and 1700, 153 Danes signed the Bodleian admissions book, and between 1670 and 1740 every Swedish archbishop but one visited and worked in Oxford or Cambridge. The influence was not of course all in one direction. Queen Anne, on whom the hopes of the narrowest of English high-church Tories were somewhat incongruously pinned, was happily married to Prince George of Denmark. His secretary (1686–91) was Heinrich Wilhelm Ludolf, a friend of Spener and Francke, who became convinced of the need first for Protestant activity in Russia and then for a union between Protestantism and Orthodoxy at Constantinople. His efforts in these causes led him to secure modern Cyrillic fonts for the Oxford University Press in 1695, and the publication of Oxford's first colloquial Russian grammar in 1696. Similar benefactions to Halle followed and Ludolf's persuasions led Francke to found an Oriental college in 1702 in which ordinands could study Russian, Slavonic languages and Arabic. Ludolf indeed had grasped the geopolitical connection between Russia, the Balkans and the Near East more firmly than the governments he sought to influence. But his influence in England was greatly prolonged and extended by the fact that in 1705 he secured the appointment of that able protégé of Halle, Anton Wilhelm Böhme, as secretary to Prince George; and as heir to Ludolf's influence in the SPCK, he kept that body focused on the ecclesiastical affairs of Germany and the north.

The Danish connection was also one of the principal channels for German literary influence upon the whole of the north. The population of Copenhagen grew steadily in the eighteenth century, and many of the incomers were German civil servants, clergy, tradesmen and craftsmen needed for the reconstruction of the town after the great fires of 1728 and

1769, as well as for the bureaucratic development of the state. Many of the former had trained at the Pietist redoubts of Tübingen or Halle, and they encouraged their colleagues to go back to Leipzig or Göttingen to study modern constitutional law or homiletics. In the middle of the eighteenth century Copenhagen became a model Protestant settlement of humane letters, piety and law; and Danish translations did much to spread modern German homiletics and the modern developments in canon law throughout the north.

There was one respect in which the Scandinavian churches differed quite markedly from their German Lutheran brethren. All the European churches, Catholic and Protestant, fought their battles against what they called superstition, according to their lights and resources. The Scandinavian churches, however, were in various respects open to a wider world than the other Lutherans, and were in actual touch with live non-Christian religions. The consequences of this we have already seen in the Baltic lands. The Sami (or in conventional English, Laplanders) and their reindeer ranged across the whole of northern Scandinavia, and in the west were subject to Danish authority. Denmark not only sponsored the Halle mission to Tranquebar but (in a literal sense) had its own fish to fry in Greenland. In 1714 a government department, the *Missionskollegium,* was set up to administer all these interests. The first Sami mission was conceived by a group of young pastors mostly from northern Norway who had studied in Copenhagen. The most important of them, Thomas von Westen, was an Oriental scholar deprived of an academic career by poverty; of a strong Pietist background he was caught up in a revival as pastor of Romsdal in 1711, and gathered half a dozen other pastors, becoming collectively known as the 'seven stars', who wished to tighten up parish discipline and instruction. They submitted proposals for changes in the law to the Danish government without effect; but in 1715 proposals for a mission to the Sami received a backing. The Sami were an extreme case of what the 'seven stars' felt about northern parishes in Norway generally; the people were mostly baptised but clung tenaciously to their old beliefs. Finnmark, one of the Sami grazing grounds, was now a territory disputed by Denmark and Sweden, and the Danish government provided resources for von Westen to go north and learn the Sami language. The outcome was prophetic of the early history of Protestant missions. Westen was well received by the Sami, and was able to build churches and a seminary for the training of colleagues. But he came into conflict with the Danish trade in spirits, the missionary college in Copenhagen seemed to him far too slow, while his own book-keeping and business methods were so hopeless that he had to be replaced by another of the 'seven stars', now bishop of Trondheim. The latter both confessed and guaranteed failure by handing the mission over to the parish clergy. Nevertheless the Sami increased in at least outward churchmanship in the course of the century.

Hans Egede, a Norwegian pastor of Danish descent, had taken part in the preparations for the Tranquebar mission, and had hopes of discovering descendants of the ancient Norsemen in Greenland, and winning them for Christ. Eskimos were, however, all that were to be found. Egede mastered the enormous difficulties of their language, and survived great hardships and accidents. Yet the mission did not prosper. Egede wished to inculcate pure doctrine, but found himself reduced to a civilising mission, and was loathe to administer baptism. In the early years he had a good deal of support from Denmark, but there was opposition from Danish settlers, and in 1733 the Moravians arrived, convinced that they possessed a quick method of conversion, and that Egede was not converted at all. Their hostility did no good locally, and when his wife and closest collaborators died in an epidemic, Egede returned to Denmark. His contribution to the evangelisation of Greenland (supported by his sons) was now to translate the Bible and the liturgical books into the local language.

The Swedish church had hardly this record to boast of, but, apart from its work across the Baltic, had two records of overseas enterprise to its credit not matched by other Lutheran establishments. The brief Swedish colonial presence in America (1638–55) left behind some three thousand Lutherans in New Sweden on the Delaware. Charles XI, king of Sweden (1672–97), found them much neglected and asked Swedborg, later bishop of Skora, to organise a church system there, which, until American independence, was supplied with learned ministers from Sweden, one of them designated provost, with powers of a suffragan bishop. The Swedish provosts of the mid-eighteenth century combined with the agents of Halle to defeat Zinzendorf's attempts to organise the Germans in America, and to create what became (apart from a small organisation in the United Provinces) the only non-established Lutheran church. Under one of the last of these provosts, Carl Magnus von Wrangel (1727–86), the Swedish ministers in America became virtually part of the German ministerium. Wrangel himself, who organised a Swedish counterpart to the SPCK, the society Pro fide et Christianismo (1771), has a toehold in the history of English evangelicalism, preaching to Wesley's approval at the Bristol New Room in 1768, and subsequently corresponding with him.

The other enterprise, though of shorter duration, was of greater importance in Sweden itself, the remarkable effort we have already seen to keep the thousands of defeated Swedish troops who after the battle of Poltava were packed off to Siberia, under regular pastoral oversight. With assistance from Halle this work generated astonishing revivals which had their effect in Sweden when, after fifteen or more years, the troops came home. The immediate impact of the returning exiles was less than might have been expected, death and the opposition of public authorities both taking their toll. Nevertheless the crumbling of strong monarchy in Sweden, and the stern resolve of monarchy in Denmark made possible in the former a revivalist tradition which was uncharacteristic of the German Lutheran churches, and very foreign to the high-church confessionalism of Sweden. When Saxony was becoming too hot for Zinzendorf, he pinned his hopes for a Moravian refuge on Denmark, where he was received with great favour. In the early 1730s, however, this honeymoon ended in one of the celebrated quarrels of the eighteenth century, in Zinzendorf's expulsion and unacceptable terms being imposed on his followers. The Swedish church did not offer a sympathetic reception to religious practice of the Moravian type, but from the inception of the Renewed Unity of the Brethren Swedes had been at Herrnhut (one of them, Arvid Gradin, encountered Wesley there), and from 1731 Moravians began to visit Sweden regularly. Zinzendorf paid a diplomatic visit in 1735 which accomplished nothing at all, but the Brethren were well placed to take advantage of the parliamentary triumph of the 'Hats' over the 'Caps' in 1738.

The new party embodied ideals akin to the Enlightenment, and were concerned with economic development, toleration and a more humane education. This was not a message altogether palatable to the stricter sort of Halle Pietist, but once the political brakes came off the way was open in the 1740s for a vivid Moravian revival, led by the Konrektor of the Stockholm gymnasium, Thore Odhelius, who had been won for the cause during a visit to Livonia. A Swedish shoemaker, Elias Östergren, who had become a Moravian diaspora worker, carried the revival into west Sweden, while in the south, the Provost at Albrum, the patriarchal Johannes Nicolaus Sundius, who had a notable following among the clergy, led a revival in the middle of the century. It was indeed a half-revolution when revival in Sweden could be led by the clergy; and in 1750 Gradin reported to the Moravian synod that clergy had given themselves to the movement in every province in Sweden, to the number of 100 (of a national total of 3,200). It was, however, unavoidable that the emotional excesses of the Moravians' 'time of sifting' in the late 1740s should revive suspicion in Sweden as elsewhere. The church used German anti-Moravian propaganda and political influence to get the revival put down. But, as in Livonia and Estonia, the leaven once fermented continued to work. In the 1760s and 1770s Moravian revival broke out again on a bigger scale than ever.

There were now substantial religious as well as other reasons for the limited toleration conferred in Sweden in 1781. Authority in Sweden was still strong enough to hold at bay the other half-revolution, that of revival led by fishermen and peasants, but Sweden now possessed its homegrown Enlightenment. The famous botanist Linnaeus not only thought up a workable system of plant classification, but as an academic teacher for forty years at Uppsala, he expounded a prophetic theodicy by which nature could be made to prove the existence of God, and natural science supported faith by mediating the true knowledge of the 'majesty, omnipotence, omniscience, and mercy' of the creator. This was doubtless further from the Unaltered Confession of Augsburg and the Formula of Concord behind which the Swedish church had put its authority, than was the enthusiastic piety of the Herrnhuters.

The triumph of Catholicism in Poland

Poland contrived to combine a tenacious belief that she was in some sense a bulwark of the west with extreme difficulties in securing her own survival and with less success than any other major state in attaining domestic religious unity. The paradox was that failures all round contributed eventually to the overwhelming predominance of the strongest confession, Roman Catholicism, which was centred in the west, and to the identification of its symbols with the national cause. This was particularly important for the Polish church, for although the bishops were members of the Senate, and the Primate was regent during an interregnum, the church was not well endowed, and lacked some of the components of ordinary organisation. In some sees the network of parishes was almost non-existent, and at the time of partition, there were more than twice as many (Uniat) parishes using the Greek or Slavonic rite as there were using the Latin rite. Poland was not a party to the Westphalia settlements which formed the fundamental law of the Holy Roman Empire, and before a precarious peace was secured for her by the Treaty of Oliva (1660), she had been overrun in various degrees by Russians, Cossacks, Swedes and Turks. In 1655 at the peak of the intervening crisis, Charles X of Sweden invaded Poland and took Warsaw. But the monastery of Czestochova resisted a siege of forty days and the Swedes had to retreat. This dramatic reversal was perceived as an assurance to the Polish people of the special protection of the black Virgin of Czestochova, the kingdom was dedicated to the Virgin by the Queen, and national enthusiasm overflowed into acts of violence against the non-Catholic populations. Peace could nevertheless only be secured by concessions of territory, and the grant of autonomy to the Orthodox people of the Ukraine.

War with Russia and Sweden resumed, but the symbolism of Czestochova seemed confirmed by the fact that, with the financial backing of the Pope, Polish troops formed an important part of the coalition which saved Vienna from the Turks in 1683. Nevertheless the Great Northern War (1700–21) saw the mixture as before; and if now the power of Sweden was permanently broken, all the participants in the war used religious sympathisers in Poland without scruple, and the peace settlement left Poland permanently vulnerable to Russian interference whenever a Russian government could get its act together effectively. The ultimate partition of Poland to preserve some kind of balance among neighbours, of whom Russia was in principle the strongest, lay in the logic of the situation, Czestochova or not.

The long political agony, however, gradually but fundamentally transformed the religious constitution of the country. At the beginning the Roman Catholic Church was the strongest religious force in the country; at the end it was overwhelming. Yet in both 1660 and 1772 less than half the Poles were Roman Catholics, though in 1660 nearly half the remainder, and in 1772 just over half, were Uniats, that is Catholics of the Slavonic rite. Notwithstanding the relief of Vienna, the Poles were not much given to crusading, and, with rather more than the 'indifferentism' of the participants in the Thirty Years War, had been prepared to hire Tartars from the Crimea against other Christian powers. It was also true (though not a matter of reproach) that the Jesuits figured less prominently in the Counter-Reformation in Poland than (for understandable reasons) they did in Protestant demonology. In the two centuries before 1773 they never controlled more than seventy of the country's 1,200 religious houses, and after the middle of the seventeenth century their contribution to Polish education was greatly outstripped by other religious orders, especially the Piarists. The domestic situation which made it impossible to mobilise Poland for the militant Counter-Reformation, affected the nature of Polish spirituality, in somewhat the same way as the Silesian situation affected that of Protestants there. It was the inner life which counted, the life witnessed externally by pilgrimages, reliquaries, confraternities devoted to the rosary, by marathon prayer-meetings, and by the fashions which had been internationally reinforced by the surge of Catholic missions, public displays of repentance, and mutual flagellation. Indeed the religious life of Poland depended very heavily on the missions conducted by Jesuits, Lazarists and other orders, the Jesuits alone taking up to 1,000 a year and hearing hundreds of thousands of confessions. The cults of Polish saints were pushed, exactly as the Habsburgs had pushed the veneration and canonisation of St John of Nepomuk in Bohemia. But most of all the Marian cult was pressed on a very extraordinary scale.

In seventeenth-century Poland and Lithuania more than 1,000 Marian shrines, each with its miraculous ikon, were thriving. In the ecclesiastical competition for the possession of the national tradition the cult of the Virgin offered three advantages over that of the national saints. It had an international currency which the local saints did not, and thus could better profit from the notion that Poland was the bulwark of the west; it more clearly distinguished the Catholic community from the penumbra of Protestants, Orthodox and Jews than any other symbol; and the tender piety which it fostered had, at Czestochova, been indissolubly welded to the public issue of national survival. When in 1717 the Polish Diet silently received a new constitution and a limitation of military strength under the auspices of the Russian ambassador, the ceremonial coronation of the Virgin as Queen of Poland was celebrated at Czestochova; the moral could hardly have been stated more clearly, and it carried the implication that the channels of the influence of the ancient world, humanising or secularising, which had been opened in the west by the Renaissance, would count for less in Poland.

Religious minorities in Poland (1) The Orthodox

Of the leading religious minorities in Poland, each had problems of its own. The Polish Orthodox were subject to the Metropolitan of Kiev; he in turn became subject to the Moscow Patriarchate when that institution was created in 1589. This suited neither the kings of Poland nor the Metropolitans of Kiev who came to live in Vilna. The Orthodox had been constantly at odds with each other, and in 1633, when the Orthodox hierarchy was established after thirty-seven years of persecution, it began to feel the impact of new policies in Moscow which anticipated the greater stir later to be made by Peter the Great. Already there were efforts to bring the Orthodox liturgy up to date, to turn Russian Orthodoxy into a state religion, and to establish its primacy in the Orthodox world. This was the pressure to transform the ancient Greek Orthodox church of the Slavonic rite into the Russian Orthodox church. Between 1648 and 1667 parts of the southern, Ukrainian, provinces of Poland were severed by Cossack and Russian armies and the Orthodox church there was subjected to state rule. They had now to choose between submitting to the new Nikonian liturgy and the Russian discipline that went with it, or staying with their old beliefs and becoming in Russian eyes schismatics. The result as we shall see was the great *Raskol* or schism, which had enduring effects. Poland was directly affected because the *Raskolniki* or Old Believers tended to move west away from the centres of Russian authority towards or even inside the shrunken eastern frontier of Poland. A similar decision confronted the Polish Orthodox who had not been stranded by the change of frontiers. If they adopted the new Russian reforms and discipline, they could not easily avoid the suspicion that they were prospective fifth columnists looking to eventual incorporation in the Russian Empire. From the standpoint of the kings of Poland the best solution was for the Polish Orthodox to adopt a union with Rome first negotiated in the fifteenth century and put into effect in 1595. This enabled them to keep their Slavonic liturgy; and at the beginning of the eighteenth century the old Greek bishops of Poland-Lithuania joined the Uniat church. But this church never received the political support in Poland which had been originally envisaged; it was a cause for concern in Moscow; it never overcame the hostility between the Polish leadership and the Ruthenian rank and file in the parishes; and it left Poland with two Orthodox churches. The Orthodox, again, had the same difficulty as the Polish Protestants in acquiring or retaining the one thing needful in that age, aristocratic support. Some prominent Orthodox remained indeed loyal to the Republic and to the fractious religious pluralism which had marked its past; others, for time-serving or other reasons, went over to Calvinism in the sixteenth century and then to Roman Catholicism in the seventeenth.

Religious minorities in Poland (2) The Lutherans

The Protestants were also in contention on several fronts. The Lutherans were mostly established in towns, and their position was protected by borough charters as well as by royal promises; under this aegis they had developed a university at Königsberg (Prussia) and gymnasia of regional significance in Danzig, Thorn and elsewhere. During the brief occupation of Poland by Charles XII the circumstances of the Lutherans naturally improved and church-building began again. This was sufficient for the enemies of the Protestants to brand them as Swedish collaborators, and when Russian dictation was accepted at the Treaty of Warsaw (1717) the restoration of old Protestant churches was forbidden and those built between 1704 and 1709 were to be pulled down. A campaign began for the destruction of Protestant churches which went on for fifty years, supported by a series of measures to persecute Protestants or put them in the position of second-class citizens. The venom and duration of this campaign may be judged from the fact that even in 1733 the Diet proclaimed that 'in this realm we detest foreign cults' (as though practically every religious community in Poland were not a foreign cult) and determined to bar non-Catholics from all civil office; but its most revolting expression came in the celebrated and widely reported affair at Thorn in 1724.

In this Protestant town which now contained a successful Jesuit gymnasium (as well as a renowned Protestant competitor) disorder of a not very serious kind broke out on 16 July 1724, the feast of the Virgin of Mount Carmel, when her image was carried through the town. There was some damage to church furnishings for which the Protestant mayor offered satisfaction to the Jesuits. They, however, were now out for much bigger game, appealed to Warsaw, and for four months got an entirely Catholic commission of inquiry into the town at the town's expense, while they whipped up a campaign of mingled xenophobia and class consciousness:

The Holy Mother of God . . . protected Poland against the Tartars but has now fallen to a Tartarish heathenism in Thorn . . . The wickedness of the Jews against the crucified Lord has ceased to rage at Golgotha, only the blind frenzy of the citizens of Thorn . . . God gave the image at Czestochova 1,000 wounds because it was twice cut by a heathen hand. Should not the town of Thorn requite her honour to the Mother of God by the cession of her churches which they misuse to the blasphemy of God? . . . Is not Thorn a real London, subject to English and not Polish laws?

If there was any vestige of justification for the Jesuit campaign it lay in the fact that Prussia had fished for the loyalty of German towns in Poland, and now all the Protestant powers stood together in a pamphlet war like that occasioned by the Revocation of the Edict of Nantes, but to no avail. The academy was closed, the one remaining Protestant church handed over to the Catholics who were given parity on the council; worst of all twelve burghers including the mayor were beheaded in a public carnage of quite peculiar crudeness and brutality. The Jesuits had conformed to the Protestant stereotype, and Poland was well launched on the road which led from mutual intolerances to a single intolerance.

Religious minorities in Poland (3) The Reformed

The Reformed in Poland had met trouble earlier, partly because they were successful in recruiting a considerable aristocratic following among nobles of moderate status looking for independence and also the opportunity to divert Catholic tithes into their own pockets, or among great men anxious to circumvent the power of the clergy. But the Reformed movement in Poland never overcame the variety of its origins, and never had sufficient aristocratic patronage to make a real push for power. The result was that the doctrinal disintegration which set into the Reformed churches in the west in the course of the Enlightenment set in in Poland at a very early stage in the sixteenth century. These differences encouraged the Reformed movement to concentrate on defence and the propagation of their views through education and publishing, weapons which as we have seen were very vulnerable to Jesuit pressure. The schismatics among the Polish Reformed have remained of permanent interest because of their radical development of anti-Trinitarian views (which would have involved them in trouble with any of the Protestant establishments), their demand for free thought and their skill in social experiment. Many of the radicals gathered at Raków under the protection of Michael Sienicki and established a commune which abolished distinctions of rank and estate, and withdrew from the community at large, denying allegiance to the state, achieving fame through a famous academy and the press. Latin versions of the Raków catechism circulated in the west, and one was burnt by order of the English Rump Parliament. The Arians were expelled from Poland on political grounds in 1658. Some went north to East Prussia, some went south to the tolerant principality of Siebenbürgen (Transylvania), where unitarianism still survives and where it acquired a following among the labouring classes of a sort it acquired nowhere else. And Samuel Crell (1660–1747), the resourceful grandson of the celebrated Polish Socinian theologian Joseph Crell, and the son of one of the expelled, who was himself brought up in the United Provinces, was the doughty opponent of Spener in the last great theological controversy of his life.

There were also in Poland other refugees in pursuit of liberty, Anabaptists, members of the Unity of the Brethren from Moravia, Schwenkfeldians from Silesia; all shared the common fate. Among the minorities the least uncomfortable were the non-Christian groups, Muslim Tartars who were recruited into the army down to the Second World War, and who in the seventeenth century had over 100 Polish mosques, and Jews who enjoyed some peace and quiet as long as they observed strict religious segregation. The one thing not to be was a witch; witches were burned by the thousand, and the peak of the witch craze was not reached in Poland till the first quarter of the eighteenth century. Thus in the end the limited social base of all the Protestant fellowships, and genuine decay on the part of the Orthodox, enabled a minority Roman Catholic Church to annex the national tradition, and establish a militant Catholic kingdom; the question was how it would fare in its relations with the military kingdom to the east.

The Orthodox churches in Russia

The problem confronting the Russian church even in the eighteenth century was the problem which would have confronted the Catholic church in Poland, had the Polish state succeeded. The Russian church had an enormous work of organisation to perform; the vast empire, which in the later seventeenth century was already two-and-a-quarter times as large in Asia as in Europe, increased by a further sixth in both continents in the eighteenth, and it was already not difficult to foresee the day when the Orthodox would be in a minority in the empire as a whole. While this situation was bound to lead to a revision of the curiously informal relations of church and state in the old Moscow, it led also to a steady increase in the weight of the Russian church among the Orthodox churches as a whole. Indeed John Mason Neale, the Cambridge ecclesiologist and hymn-writer, published an estimate in the middle of the nineteenth century which gave the Russian church more than a quarter of all the metropolitans, archbishops and bishops in the Eastern churches, and considerably more than three-quarters of the entire lay following.

Thus intrinsic to the situation of the Russian church were points of conflict as well as cooperation with the state. The international pretensions of the church, its continually strengthening claims to be the Third Rome, did not dispose it to accept changes in status at home; equally, tsars who needed to take the domestic organisation of the church in hand also needed its international standing for diplomatic purposes, and hoped to use it for the Russification of new provinces. The great upheaval in the affairs of the Russian church took place in the reign of Peter the Great (1694–1725), but that reign itself was affected by the impact of changes which had begun earlier in response to the general situation. Already the Metropolitan Nikon had carried through a revision of the liturgy which had led to the *Raskol* or schism of Old Believers. It was difficult for a church which depended as heavily as the Russian church on the liturgical transmission of its tradition to find a basis for rational discussion for liturgical change, especially when the church presented itself to the state as a force of conservatism; the *Raskolniki* wounded the church at an emotionally vulnerable point, and in its turn the church devoted a disproportionate amount of its total energy to attend to the struggle against them, and did so unsuccessfully. Peter could see quite other defects in the church – the gross neglect of the education of ordinary parish priests, the need for new church building, and the creation of new church provinces. But it was not these defects which principally moved Peter. Like every other ruler in Europe he could see in the church a great endowment inefficiently used for purposes of either church or state; and unlike everyone else in Russia, Peter and his right-hand man in church affairs, Feofan Prokopovic, had acquired western doctrines of sovereignty from Pufendorf, Grotius and Hobbes, and were not content with the informal dyarchy which had characterised relations of church and state in Muscovite Russia. Prokopovic, moreover, as a young man had been a Uniat, had trained at Jesuit colleges in Poland and in Rome, and later, as a biblical theologian, depended much on the Lutheran Johann Gerhard (1582–1637).

However Peter might appear in the demonology of his critics, he was not an irreligious man. Brought up from an early age on the psalms, gospels and Acts, he delighted in quoting scripture wholesale. He venerated ikons and the Mother of God, kissed relics, and liked going to church and singing in the church choir. When he returned from abroad or from a battle he would seek out the Patriarch. He undoubtedly wished to use the church, but churchmen could hardly complain of his struggle against superstition, hypocrisy and blasphemy or his refusal to countenance schemes of union with the Roman Catholics. All this was very Russian, but Peter was very un-Russian in his insensitivity to the metaphysical (as distinct from the ethical) content of religion, and his view of the church as a device for making men useful to the state; since he could not drag Russia up to date without the professional services of Protestants, especially Germans, from the west, he could hardly think otherwise, nor could he avoid the risk of foreign contamination. And as Peter clashed with his Patriarch Adrian (1690–1700) over the wearing of beards and the introduction of German clothing, and speedily learned the depths of the hostility of hierarchy and monks who did not scruple to to pamphleteer against him as Anti-Christ, he was not attracted by the dyarchy of the past. The tsarist state had been gradually developing, but had been imbued with the idea that the tsars had inherited the rights and duties of the Byzantine emperors. Muscovite Russia became the authority which guaranteed Orthodoxy in all its rights and duties, and was bound to maintain not only divine justice, but the forms and institutions, the churches and monasteries, of Orthodox life. The tsar might be autocratic, but he normally governed easily with the Patriarch, and in 1656–57 when the tsar was away in the Swedish and Polish wars, the Patriarch governed autocratically in his name. The tsar normally appeared in a sort of sacerdotal dress.

It was this system which Peter brought to an end for the rest of the tsarist monarchy. When Adrian died he blocked the election of another Patriarch; he normally appeared in military uniform; and it was in the military statute of 1716 that he announced that he was a sovereign monarch accountable to no one, and had full power to govern as a Christian (not Orthodox) monarch. The formal subordination of the church soon followed. In 1718 it was clear that Peter was victorious over Sweden, and he began the reordering of the administration of the central and district governments on collegial principles, the new institutions deriving their authority from his ukase. Since the death of Adrian he had managed with a provisional church government, but in 1721 he applied the general collegial principle to the church in creating the Holy Synod. Peter did his best to get the approval of the Patriarch of Constantinople for the act, but it was plain that by ending the Patriarchate of Moscow and handing the government of the church over to a department of state he was reducing the connection of the church with the Orthodox world at large to one of doctrine and worship alone. To rub the point home, this same Holy Synod was to deal with the affairs of other Christian confessions and of non-Christian communities. The Holy Synod took over many of the religious duties of the old Moscow tsars, church extension, the nomination of bishops, the preservation of faith and morals against superstition, heresy and the *Raskol*, the examination of relics and lives of the saints, the preservation of correct ikon painting and the preparation of new liturgical texts. But Peter fell out with the first president of the Holy Synod, got rid of him after a year, and thereafter relied on Feofan Prokopovic to advocate his views. Small wonder that the Old Believers thought that Peter intended to become head of the Church.

A quite new subordination of the church to a newly defined state was not the end of the grievances which churchmen and schismatics conceived against Peter. The new subordination had its counterpart in a financial dependence of the church upon the state which was unknown to the old Muscovite Russia. If church extension was to keep pace with the growth of the state (and although the number of church buildings increased in the eighteenth century by about two-thirds, the number of church provinces always lagged) the church was always likely to become financially dependent on the state, and the Russian hierarchy showed no particular interest in financial autonomy. But what began with the Holy Synod taking control of revenues from monasteries and churches and supplementing them with state subsidies led logically to the secularisation of church lands carried through by Catherine the Great in 1764, and that in its turn implied the nationalisation of institutions and administrative offices which had been maintained by church property. Few of the parish clergy benefited from the state subsidies, and, the year after the secularisation of church property, the casual fees which were the mainstay of their income became subject to tax for the the the first time.

Bishops and monks

Moreover, under the Petrine system long-term changes began in the episcopate and in the monastic life on which it was based. The old Russian system had been that bishops were chosen from among the monasteries (the parish clergy, by contrast, being allowed to marry). This tradition was broken by Peter who had no reason for gratitude to the bishops and the monks from among whom they were chosen. He appointed bishops from among the so-called 'learned monks' who were distinguished from the rank and file by having very little connection with the conventual life. In the seventeenth century a stronghold of the 'learned monks' had developed in the Ukraine, and their educational level was well ahead of that of the Great Russian monks because they were almost all graduates of the Kiev Academy. They were also attractive to Peter as they disliked the Patriarchate (which he suppressed) which had been forced on them only in 1686. They proved to be less keen on reform than he hoped, but by the middle of the eighteenth century the Holy Synod was almost entirely composed of Little Russian bishops who were very unpopular in the church provinces. A great number of Little Russians were also called in to manage monasteries. From early in the century they were becoming teachers in clerical schools and rectors of seminaries, and finding in these appointments a fast track to the episcopate. The fast track was moreover lucrative, for annexed to these offices was usually the headship of an often very distant monastery, a nominal office, but one carrying with it the monastic revenues. Monks who had never seen a monastery were at a young age being entrusted with responsible office, and the whole system was sanctioned by the Holy Synod in 1767, when the incomes of the learned monks were fixed by the state along with the clergy teaching in institutions. In the latter part of the century Catherine the Great, who was highly skilled in negotiating the minefields of Russian prejudice, reduced the monopoly the learned monks had come to enjoy, but she made little difference to the Russian version of a problem which existed over much of Europe, that there was a deep gulf between the bishops on the one side and the lower clergy and church people on the other.

Nor did Catherine do anything to halt the speedy decline of the old Russian monasticism. In 1724 there were still 25,207 monks and nuns; by 1762 the number was down to 12,395. In 1700–1701 there had been 1,201 religious houses, about one-quarter of them for women; after the secularisation of church property there were only 536, of which only 225 were supported by the state; and the slide was not halted till the middle of the nineteenth century. This decline was brought about by the state in two ways. Huge numbers of monks were expelled from their monasteries on political charges and condemned to forced labour in Siberia or the Urals. This draconic enforcement of service to the state was reinforced by state prohibition of, or restrictions upon, recruiting, which were only relaxed in the southern (or Ukrainian) sees, and in the middle of the century when the whole system seemed to be facing collapse. By that time some monasteries were empty, others had so few and such aged monks that services could not be held, and many abbots were in exile or in prison. No wonder that there seemed to be surplus monastic funds for use by the state.

Successors to Peter the Great

Moreover, once church and state were yoked according to Peter's principles, more royal tact was needed in dealing with the church than the dynasty could often provide. The Empress Anna (1730–40), formerly Duchess of Courland, gave the church a bad time. Taxation was increased to pay for Anna's wars, her court was filled with Balts and Germans, and bishops and metropolitans who had been looking to the downfall of Feofan Prokopovic, Peter's right-hand man in the church, found themselves in exile or in prison. The accession of Elizabeth (1741–62) after two depositions was greeted by churchmen with such extravagant enthusiasm that it was not clear whether the diabolical influences to which the late regime was held subject were exercised directly or through foreigners battening on the empire. Piety and faith (it was now held) had been the victims of campaigns to uproot superstition, and every Russian of learning and education had been persecuted, tortured or destroyed. The fallen regime now appeared so dreadful that by contrast the rehabilitation of even Peter the Great began. But Elizabeth had no more intention of abandoning or mollifying the system she had inherited than had Anna.

Her successor Peter III (1762) was, if the legends which have entered the books may be credited, still worse. The son of the Duke of Holstein, he supplanted great Russian families by Germans, and treated the Orthodox interest with such contempt that it was easy to get up a cry of 'Lutheranism' against him. He prepared for the secularisation of monastic lands, required the secular clergy to register their sons for military service, and ordered the archbishop of Novgorod, Procurator of the Holy Synod, to clear Russian churches of all ikons except those of the Saviour and the Mother of God. The clergy were to shave off their beards and dress like foreign pastors – orders not carried out. He stuck out his tongue at Orthodox priests, and in church services talked loudly, walked about and received visitors. Peter of course did not last long, and was displaced by a palace revolution in favour of his wife, who acceded to the throne as Catherine II. Catherine was virtually as much a German as was her husband, and had not merely been born a Protestant, but had been educated in Orthodoxy by the Archimandrite Simon Todorskij, the Russian translator of Arndt's *True Christianity*. This experience had left

her with the conviction that there was little to choose between Lutheranism and Orthodoxy. The financial situation ensured that the secularisation of Church property would go ahead. And it was Catherine who
imported Protestant settlers into the Ukraine who exercised an important influence all round. Yet Catherine was a capable politician who
flattered Orthodox susceptibilities in a way that Peter III and Anna had
not. The result was that in a great measure she had her way with the
church. Equally clearly the expansion she led in the south and in the
partitions of Poland, brought Orthodoxy up sharp against the fiercest of
her anti-Russian enemies, the Muslims and the Roman Catholics. The
adaptation of the state to meet these problems was not, in the long run,
likely to suit the Orthodox church or the antique conception of monarchy it cherished.

Cultural accommodation

Moreover, the crude xenophobia to which the church had so frequently
lent itself obscured the complexity of the adaptation required of it in
coping with her 'own' people. Church-Slavonic was the *lingua sacra*, and
at the beginning of the eighteenth century the formal literary language
too. It was not the everyday language of any social group, and it was
becoming incomprehensible even to the clergy. Feofan Prokopovic had
attempted to ensure that the Russian used in preaching and the confessional was comprehensible and was free not merely from literary fancy
but also from fashionable Polonisms and other foreign intrusions. The
practical problem was that spoken Russian could not do without the
intrusions. German was the source of the new administrative terminol-
ogy; Holland and England supplied a naval vocabulary; French gradually
came to supply diplomatic and military terms and the language of
fashion. Mikhail Lomonosov (1711–65) believed that Church-Slavonic
still had advantages as a linguistic unity which German did not yet
possess, and thought that the best protection of a national culture lay in
keeping the living Church-Slavonic elements which were commonly
understood and using them in proportion to the medium in which they
were to be employed – the high, middle or low style. The problem here
was the social prestige of the various styles. Before the eighteenth century
was out the gentry had already developed a literary culture which gave
expression to its separate identity as a class and a nation, and one
moreover which had been in contact with the foreign importations of the
dynasty. But there had also been a Russian version of Ossianism which
led to a romantic veneration of the folk and its lore as the true embodi-
ment of the nation; from this in the nineteenth century a peasant national-

ism might develop. Meanwhile Russian Orthodoxy had to face the problems not only of co-existence with non-Orthodox and non-Christian faiths, but with the considerable headaches of discovering how, in the new world, to be either Russian or Orthodox.

8   Religion after the Seven Years War

Confessional Armageddon forgotten?

In 1782 the Baron von Schrautenbach handed over to the Moravian archive a sympathetic life of Zinzendorf written from the standpoint of the Enlightenment, a book which did not appear in cold print till 1851. Zinzendorf had died only in 1760, but already the glory days of his youth appeared to his biographer to belong to a remote heroic past.

In the times in which we now live such a community institution would develop with difficulty, and entail much joyless toil upon its creators and promoters. How astonishingly different from today were those times which have scarcely passed from us. Education, light, generally diffused knowledge, were much less than they are now. There was less international friendship among men across the globe . . . Habits were rough, always a step nearer nature, fierceness too, irritability, energy . . . A general longing among all men for fellowship, with a whole caboodle of opinions and very uncertain foundations.

This testimony clearly owed much to the conviction of men of the Enlightenment that their own happy generation had broken decisively with an obscurantist past, but it can be paralleled from various standpoints, and it is in some respects clearly true. When the Seven Years War began, the long-expected Armageddon between Catholic and Protestant seemed to have arrived. The town council of Zurich closed the gates and brought out the cannon and munition trains in the belief that confessional warfare in Switzerland had actually begun; Whitefield preached patriotic sermons; Howel Harris, the Welsh evangelist, for the 'defence of the precious word of God, the Bible, against Popery' took a company of volunteers to the English east coast; Samuel Davies, the Presbyterian revivalist in Virginia, tried to out-recruit the Anglican gentry with a view to putting down the popish menace from Canada. None of this was to happen in the same way again. The heroism of confessional hot war went into cold storage till the next century.

This was in part the result of the war itself. Military operations in the Rhineland did no good to evangelical religion there, and, as Goethe vividly recalled in his autobiography, produced the kind of division of spirits ruinous to religious fellowship. In Europe it was in Britain alone that religion received an impulse; Wesley, who had almost despaired of his cause as recently as 1753, found his work buoyed up by the great rallying of national sentiment as the tide of victory set in and revivals followed. The young George III's resolve in 1760 to govern above party was not just a cliché; old irreconcilables had been coming back to court for a few years, and now they came in increasing numbers. Methodists found their critics not merely less voluble (the number of anti-Methodist pamphlets seemed to diminish every year) but less virulent; and there is no reason to suppose that other forms of religious fellowship did not benefit from the new spirit of national unity.

Even in Britain, however, where borrowing was easier and cheaper than for any other great power, the strain had been felt, and the war had occasioned a series of campaigns to cut the cost of government while there was yet time, and to small-scale encroachments on what was left of the confessional state with a view to facilitating the recruitment of Irish Catholics to the armed forces. Concessions of this kind could not but encourage the more radical friends of Enlightenment; attempts in 1772–73 to end subscription to the Thirty-Nine Articles at ordination and graduation failed in Parliament, but failed signally to encounter defenders who would stand up for them on principle.

On the continent the financial strain of the war confronted many of the great established churches with the reality of the Leviathan which had so graciously found work for them to do. The Seven Years War was the immediate preface to the nationalisation of church property in Russia, to the almost united campaign of Catholic Europe against the Jesuits, to the Febronian crusades of the Catholic grandees of the Empire against the papacy. And everywhere the state was showing less and less inclination to wait on the constitutional processes of the church before dragging it up to date by more or less direct action. We have already noted striking examples of this in the Habsburg sphere of influence. In France too the state authority, decaying in vigour as it was, got into the way of intervening to settle disputes over ecclesiastical authority. The assembly of the clergy in 1765 admitted the obligation of the clergy to obey the king in political and temporal matters, but insisted on the reciprocal obligation of the king to obey the pope in matters spiritual. This, however, brought censure from both the Paris Parlement and the royal council, which claimed the right to examine decrees of the church to see whether they conformed to the maxims of the realm.

The decline of confessional absolutism in France

A constitutional quadrille developed, in which the king in normal times used the papacy to control the bishops, a body now almost completely taken over by the nobility, with a view to securing allies against Parlement in critical times. The tactical nature of all these disputes and the utilitarian outlook of many of those concerned illustrates very sharply the way in which the Ancien Régime in France had been sapped by the coalition of forces which had been brought together by the opposition to the Bull *Unigenitus*. The conflicts of the 1720s and early 1730s had brought French absolutism to its formal peak; the Declaration of 1730 made *Unigenitus* part of the law of the state as well as of the church. In 1725 Louis XV had married the Polish Marie Leszczynska, who brought with her an active devotion to the Sacred Heart of Jesus, and attracted the formation of a *dévot* party in the episcopate. Thus in a political as well as ecclesiastical sense an anti-absolutist Jansenist party confronted an absolutist, Jesuit, ultramontane party. By the mid-1730s the latter had emerged apparently victorious, but by the mid-1750s disputes over the refusal of sacraments to those who were opposed to *Unigenitus* and the tenacity of Jansenist strength in the Parlements had undone the religious symbols of absolutism. Parlements forbade the refusal of sacraments in these cases, and by exiling *curés* who obeyed their bishop in this matter, and requisitioning resident priests in their stead, undermined the subordination of the parish priests to their superiors. The other symbols of the system, a Jesuit confessor at court, the active persecution of Protestants, even the support of *Unigenitus* itself, fell on hard times. If monarchy, even episcopacy, was to regain the lost ground, they must find a fresh platform, and utilitarianism offered the most convenient alternative. Jansenism too paid a price for the political advantages of its long cohabitation with Parlementary allies who had a genius for transforming differences about doctrine into disputes about jurisdiction, in an increasing displacement from theology to ecclesiology and public law. Many old Jansenists poured into the *parti patriote* which defended the Parlements against the onslaughts of the court in 1771. But in the general disintegration the church was caught up in a maelstrom in which tactics increasingly displaced inherited ideology.

The Commission des reguliers

After 1765 Parlement found a way of using a period of high food prices and attacks against religious institutions to bring all the Gallican forces together. The opportunity was created by an appeal of twenty-eight

Maurists in residence at Saint-Germain-des-Prés against their rule. They thought their vestments ridiculous and their night devotions and fasting prejudicial to their scholarly work. The Assembly of the Clergy which met on 25 May 1765 was overwhelmed with complaints about the decline of religion and these it passed on to one of its own committees. Loménie de Brienne, archbishop of Toulouse, the *rapporteur* of this committee, eventually proposed on its behalf that an appeal should be made to the Pope, setting forth the condition of the religious orders in France, and asking him to appoint a commission of cardinals and bishops with his authority to re-establish order and regularity. But the negotiation with the Pope should be handled by the king. Meanwhile the Assembly fell into conflict with the Parlement, over its attempts to interfere in doctrinal matters, and was prorogued by the king till 1766. In the interim the government negotiated with the Parlement and created not a pontifical but a royal commission composed of prelates and members of the royal council with authority to take cognisance of the statutes and regulations of the parties concerned. Brienne, a man close to the *philosophes*, was to be *rapporteur* of this commission also. This suggested a bias in favour of innovation rather than just reform. The first measure of the commission embodied in an edict of 1768 put back the minimum age for taking vows to twenty-one for men and eighteen for women (provisions thought certain to reduce the number of vocations) and began to reduce the number of religious houses. Houses were to contain not less than nineteen men or fifteen women, nor might the same order have more than one house in a single town. The statutes of houses subject to the Ordinary were to be drafted by the bishop, the others by chapters of regulars assisted by royal commissioners. The reactions of the institutions were striking. Some were divided and allowed themselves to be manipulated; some refused to budge; others gave way. Pope Clement XIII protested that he had not been consulted, and in any case national authorities could not alter the entire statutes of international institutions. Nevertheless, the commission continued to put its slide-rule over one order after another, gathering new powers virtually to end exemption from episcopal oversight, till it ceased work in 1784. By that time it had shut down 426 religious houses, including 108 of the Benedictines and 69 of the Augustinians. And from all causes the numbers professed in the main men's orders are reckoned to have declined from 22,500 in 1768 to under 15,000 by 1790.

It cannot be held against this exercise of power that it afforded a splendid precedent for the work of the later revolutionary Constituent Assembly, the existence of which no one could foresee. But it was hardly part of a grand design for improving the pastoral efficiency of the church like the changes of Joseph II, and it modified the official quadrille.

Parlementary Gallicanism was now anti-episcopal; but a sort of episcopal Gallicanism was now in being which had taken advantage of royal support, the vacuum created by the suppression of the Jesuit order, and the appointment of the *Commission des reguliers*, to establish a new supremacy. The great advantage of the commission from an episcopal viewpoint was that it kept the Parlements out of the affairs of the regulars, and permitted encroachments on the rights of the Holy See and of the regular clergy to be described as episcopal protection. The quadrille was further modified in 1770–71, when a government which had allowed the Parlement to destroy the Jesuits temporarily abolished the Parlements. Thus episcopal Gallicanism, encouraged by the weakness of both monarchy and papacy, went into the French Revolution believing that the religious houses were in essence simply auxiliaries to the secular clergy whom the bishops controlled. This was an early sign of those revolts of the privileged which were to bring the monarchy down. When that happened the French establishment would have to look to quite different sources of support; and the paradox even now was that it was the state, not the bishops, that in 1768 and 1786 secured increases in the stipends of the parish clergy.

The rise of the parish

For this shift in attitude the bishops had some reason. Ever since the middle of the seventeenth century that part of the machinery of the church operated under episcopal oversight by the secular clergy had been improving. In Montpellier, a former Huguenot stronghold, for example, new parishes were created to assist in the evangelisation of the new flock and between 1677 and 1689 the number of parish schools was doubled, so that all but the tiniest communities had one. The aim was modest, to teach reading, writing, a little arithmetic and the basics of the catechism and Christian ethics, but it was a mechanism which had not been at the disposal of the church before. There was a great deal of church building and reconstruction, and by the beginning of the eighteenth century the losses incurred by the church in the Fronde had been made good. The bishops themselves resided and succeeded, more or less, in stamping out non-residence among parish priests. Those priests themselves became more numerous and better educated. In short the religious life of the flock became more dependent on the parish and less dependent on the missions, the charity, and the private places of worship, of the religious orders. French Catholicism was moving slowly towards the strategy which had animated the Protestant churches since the Reformation, and had left them absolutely dependent in the parish as a device for the Christianisation of the people. This shift was encouraged in Montpellier and many other parts by a striking decline in the numbers of regular clergy. In Montpellier Franciscans of various sorts numbered eighty-four at the beginning of the eighteenth century, but on the eve of the French Revolution only twenty-three. Many Benedictine houses were almost deserted. Indeed right through France the decline in the number of regulars was most marked among the ancient and most heavily endowed orders for men. It was hardly surprising that many, bishops included, thought that their underused property could be put to better use.

Significantly, the women's orders, on the whole newer, poorer, and more often devoted to socially approved works like teaching, nursing, poor relief or the assistance of fallen women, were much more flourishing, and were much more highly appreciated by the public; indeed their popularity continued into the revolutionary period, when governments felt almost morally bound to make incursions into church property not less than those previously made by the monarchy. What is apparent in all this is not Enlightenment, but a general shift in values in a utilitarian direction which was readily compatible with Enlightenment. Whereas life according to a rule and the celebration of the Mass would once have been considered sufficient ends in themselves, now it was thought that the religious must demonstrate a social or ecclesiastical utility. And bishops who had acquired the habit of issuing general instructions around their diocese were as disposed as others to make their own policies the criterion of usefulness.

The decline of parish life

Unfortunately the criterion of usefulness could be applied by the public to the secular as well as the regular clergy. Ordinations reached their peak in 1745, and after the Seven Years War the numbers and the quality of the secular clergy also diminished, and not surprisingly the general esteem for a profession which had often been a whipping-boy of government, but much more often its willing tool, diminished with that accorded to the establishment as a whole. In Montpellier as in Oxford, Cambridge and the cathedral towns of England, the presence of heavily endowed religious institutions, in this case abbeys and monasteries, seemed to have a locally depressing effect on religious enthusiasm. Dances and general merry-making were allowed to go on during Lent and during divine service, and the civil power was not active in supporting the efforts of the clergy to put them down. Police reports suggest that there was little respect for religious processions in the streets, and shrines along the route of processions were allowed to fall into decay. And in a curious reversal of roles, the vicar-general, the bishop's deputy, demanded that the intendant demolish the shrines because they 'harboured malefactors and libertines'. Not all the disrespect sprang from irreligion or even contempt for the establishment; some was doubtless occasioned by changes of religious taste to the disadvantage of religious practices or institutions which had served well in the past. The active opponents of religious processions and pilgrimages in the eighteenth century had long been not Protestants nor conoclasts, but Catholic governments. And those same governments and their local agents had too voracious an appetite for buildings to house barracks, hospitals, orphanages, and yet more bureaucrats, not to mention for sites for development, to view the under-used property of the religious orders with any degree of complacency; and their appetite could only be whetted by the further depression in recruiting to religious orders created by the commission on the regulars itself; to take perpetual vows within institutions which might not be permitted to last was not an inviting prospect.

Both the successes and the failures of episcopal activism evoked hostility. In France, as everywhere in Europe, the population increased vigorously in the eighteenth century. This meant that institutions like the parish had continually to work harder even to maintain their impact upon the parishioners, and that in the towns where some of the most dramatic increases took place the parochial structure could get completely out of date. Even in the Church of England, where the parochial organisation had escaped the upheavals of both the Reformation and the Counter-Reformation, there were devices for alleviating some of the modern inconveniences; but in France, where episcopacy had secured improvements in the past, no general progress was made on the question of parochial boundaries between the Seven Years War and the Revolution, and bishops contented themselves with juggling the number of *vicaires* to assist very large parishes. Too many entrenched vested interests stood in the way.

The parish clergy

On the other hand in that same generation there was a growing sense of solidarity and a willingness to combine among the parish clergy, whether in the hope of greater fairness and transparency in the distribution of preferment, or in the defence of parish charities, or still more in self-defence against the way the burden of clerical taxation was divided by their seniors in the hierarchy. *Richérisme*, the old seventeenth-century doctrine that the church ought to be ruled by the whole company of its pastors, had been given a new lease of life by the arbitrary powers which prelates had obtained by royal edict in order to hunt down Jansenists, and it revived in a fresh form in the grievances conceived by the ordinary clergy in the later eighteenth century. In this division of spirits whatever the bishop did or did not do might lay up trouble for the future. Professor McManners comments on Angers, where Mgr de Vaugirault was succeeded as bishop in 1758 by Mgr de Grasse:

Virtue and zeal [against the Jansenists] made Jean de Vaugirault dictatorial: sloth and worldliness inclined Jacques de Grasse to make crafty, friendly advances to his lower clergy. Thus one prelate stirred up a united opposition and his successor called for united support, both in their own way assisting the curés of Angers to move into a closer alliance for the furtherance of their common interests.

The French Revolution was to show both the depth of this division between the upper and the lower clergy and also the professional solidarity which the clergy retained when once they perceived that the fundamental interests of the church were at hazard. Meanwhile they betrayed their accommodation to the spirit of the political establishment in general; in a context of increasing political feebleness, sectional interests pushed with inadequate heed to the survival of the whole. Indeed, where taxation was concerned, the parish clergy found individual abuses so entrenched at law that the only way to break through hierarchical domination seemed to be to appeal to natural law on a general issue. When members of the most privileged social order took this route, the omens were clearly stormy, and the only group to reap a short-term profit were the Protestants. Left relatively unpersecuted for a generation, they regained the right to marry according to their own custom (though not full liberty of conscience) in 1787 and even began to be elected to the Estates-General. It was characteristic of the inextricable involvement of the church in the establishment at large that in 1787 that worldly prelate, Loménie de Brienne, archbishop of Toulouse, became first minister when the nobility refused to bail out the monarchy in its financial crisis; his idea was that the clergy should fill the gap. When they refused for the same self-centred reasons, there was no escape from a quasi-revolutionary appeal to the Third Estate.

Marian congregations

And, in one important respect, the bishops' trust in the parochial organisation of the church worked to the disadvantage of a source of spiritual vitality which was to be of inestimable value in the revolutionary crisis ahead. It is now clear that Jesuit enterprise from an early date had not been limited to missions at home and abroad, nor to the education of the upper classes. Its colleges were very active centres of apostleship from which preachers, catechists and missionaries streamed out into the town and neighbouring countryside. Their work among men of all social ranks was consolidated by enrolling them in associations under the patronage of a Virgin very militantly imagined. These Marian congregations were intended as a means of rolling back the Protestant tide by training the members to live as good Catholics on the principles of the Council of Trent. In this aim they were not unique among Catholic associations, but they had the benefit of the world-wide Jesuit organisation behind them, and in the seventeenth century united adherents from the Emperor Ferdinand II and the Duke of Bavaria down to prisoners in Neapolitan jails. In the days before diocesan seminaries established themselves the training available in these sodalities was a fruitful source of clerical recruitment. The Marian congregations speedily became much larger than the colleges, and seem to be the explanation of the very large churches built by the Jesuits in connection with colleges in small places; the church had not just a collegiate funtion, but was a meeting place for the Marian congregation. In towns like Cologne and Antwerp they numbered some thousands of members in the mid-seventeenth century, and in the Jesuit province of Champagne (which covered the secular provinces of Champagne, Burgundy, Lorraine and Alsace) they went on growing throughout the life of the Jesuit order, and at the end numbered almost three times the enrolment of college pupils.

Whatever the Jesuits did attracted some kind of Catholic opposition, and in due course the congregations fell under the displeasure of kings of France who employed the Turks against the Habsburgs when the Jesuits were seeking to promote Catholic unity against the infidel; they incurred the censure of others when they took sides in social conflicts or interfered with the marriage plans of particular families. Parish priests often regarded them as competitors, and Jansenists could be relied on to be hostile. Like so many institutions created in the glory days of the Counter-Reformation, the Marian congregations in many places entered a long decline in the eighteenth century, and could not but suffer as the political campaign against the Jesuits gathered force. Indeed, in the jurisdiction of the Parlement of Paris the sodalities were put down in 1761 before the condemnation of the Society itself. The suppression of the Society by the Pope in 1773 entailed the disappearance of the institutions with which it was linked, and this should have been the end for the Marian congregations.

In fact no such thing happened. The history of the congregations in the last quarter of the eighteenth century showed two things. The first was that ecclesiastical decline, like revival, was a patchy affair, and in Munich and south Germany it seems never to have happened at all. In eighteenth-century Bavaria fraternity life seems to have experienced an extraordinary surge of energy, confraternities of all sorts, including the congregations, reaching extraordinary numbers and embracing many of the ordinary clergy.

It was a similar story in Alsace, where there was a strong Protestant presence. Strasbourg was a Lutheran town only open to Catholic immigration after its capitulation to Louis XIV in 1681. He saw to it that the entire machine by which the bishop had run the area as an ecclesiastical principality was displaced by another on the French pattern and run from Versailles. The Jesuits in particular were commissioned not only to Catholicise, but also to Gallicise the town, and turned to with such effect that St Ignatius speedily became the great curer of animals on the left bank of the Rhine. Twenty years after capitulation Strasbourg had a Catholic majority, and it was the Marian congregation which gave some unity to the inward migration. Here the congregation was entirely undisturbed by the suppression of the Society of Jesus, and continued its work with vigour. The second and more striking thing is that, whatever had happened earlier in the eighteenth century, the congregations now demonstrated a new vitality, establishing themselves in the countryside in areas hitherto barely affected, extending their purview to include the whole family and not simply men, widening their range to compass every stage of life, and, in the nineteenth century, to include social as well as spiritual action. Thus an institution conceived as a weapon of counterattack against Protestantism in the end proved its value as a defensive bulwark against the inroads of revolutionary Enlightenment. It demonstrated that Catholicism, which had neglected the countryside for so many centuries, was now alive there, and, like the Protestant versions of the *collegia pietatis*, provided an informal means for sustaining it when other mechanisms failed. Yet these cells of new life had always incurred the bitter hostility of bishops of Jansenist tendency, and had been neglected by other bishops once they had acquired under their own control a parish clergy much superior to that which had been at their disposal at the beginning of the seventeenth century. In the day of trial in the Catholic as well as the Protestant world, popular affections and informal mechanisms achieved a result which was beyond the reach of the churches institutionally conceived. On the way they helped to explain one of the oddities of the French book market. In France as elsewhere in the eighteenth century, theology, the professional purchase of the clergy, declined sharply as a proportion of a rapidly burgeoning publishing market; on the other hand provincial reprints of works of devotion retained an overwhelming importance right down to the Revolution. If in some quarters the 'practice of piety' flagged, in others the piety of the Counter-Reformation took deep root.

What neither the formal nor the informal mechanisms could adequately cope with were the moral effects of a population increase which outstripped the economic means to support it in spite of the beneficent secular upswing in the price curve. At the beginning of the century the illegitimacy rate for France as a whole was only one per cent of all births; this deteriorated right through the century, and towards the end was between four and seventeen per cent in towns. Marital break-up (and it seems, prostitution) also increased towards the end of the century, when prolonged recession set in again. If this was mainly an urban problem, the family was also under strain in the countryside; in the later eighteenth century the care of the elderly deteriorated and there was a heavy growth of infanticide and the abandonment of children. Here social strains were proving too much for the impressive internalisation of Catholic family ethics in seventeenth-century France, and more than a reshuffling of *vicaires* was needed to counteract it.

The church and the French Revolution

Yet religious decline in France, palpable though not universal, was no explanation of the fate which came upon the French church in the Revolution, a fate which the clergy in a great measure brought upon themselves. The defeat of the monarchy at the assembly of the notables in 1787 was led by several archbishops. The financial crisis which it heralded was intensified by an acute recession which reduced the yield of the turnover taxes on which the revenues of state depended. There was now no alternative but to call a meeting of the States-General. The elections were held in a new form, doubling the representation of the Third Estate, and this gave a crushing majority to the lower clergy in the local clerical assemblies. Yet still, with the aid of compromise, the bishops got their way in the drafting of *cahiers*. In general the *cahiers* showed that church reform was on the map, much in the style of the previous generation. No one wanted to involve the pope or abolish religious orders, but they did want further reform of the regulars and better pay and resources for the *curés*. But the props to privilege weakened when the States-General decided to vote by head instead of by estate. It was also true that the Constituent Assembly did not want to destroy the church, was filled mostly with well-meaning Catholics, and had no doubt that the political order needed a religious establishment. But the Constituent Assembly could not be passive. It inherited the full force of the financial crisis from which the church had declined to save the monarchy, aggravated now by rural revolt.

The result was that as early as 2 November 1789, less than six months after the Estates General had first met, the Constituent Assembly, led by a bishop, Talleyrand, put church property at the disposal of the nation, undertaking to provide a reasonable sum for the maintenance of worship, the support of ministers, and the care of the poor. All this was so much in line with the regalian traditions of the past that purchasers of church lands included clergy and the future leaders of the Catholic and royalist rebellion in the Vendée. It was also clear by this time that without the wholesale dissolution of religious houses not enough property would accrue to the state to meet the budget deficit. The taking of vows was provisionally suppressed, and the municipal commissioners went round the religious houses. They found that many of the much diminished numbers of men wanted to secure release from their vows, and still more would do so if they would otherwise be moved to another house. The women, for whom society had much less to offer, were more steadfast. But it was the next step which created the great division in French life.

The Constituent Assembly had, against the background of the religious indifferentism of the Declaration of the Rights of Man, to create a new framework for the church. It was assumed that the Pope would agree to this (as so often in the past), that the bishops were trying to avoid schism, that the *curés*, for whom the Civil Constitution of the Clergy promised much, would not desert the constitution; and this assumption was justified by the fact that, even among the clergy, the Civil Constitution obtained a degree of acceptance. But the ordinary clergy wanted to be elected to their parishes by synods, not districts and departments, the Pope's consent was not forthcoming, and the way modern diocesan-seminary training had helped to create a sense of professional solidarity among the clergy of all grades was illustrated by the frequency with which they now turned to their colleges for advice whether to take the oath to the Civil Constitution or not. Indeed, this advice, together with the local degree of enthusiasm for the church, seems to have been the thing which turned so many clergy into non-jurors. The French church now faced a much more severe test of political loyalty than the Church of England at the Hanoverian accession in 1714.

The Assembly had obtained the resources to fight its first wars at the price of increasing coercion in religious matters, and ultimately of bitter political division. The Gallican church had perished along with the complex of political privilege of which it had been part. Religious establishments everywhere must face the risks of relying on the arm of flesh; while the arm of flesh in France, the revolutionary governments which had pulled down the Gallican church with such ease, were to find that it was beyond them to replace that church with anything more convenient. When the question at the heart of every *Kirchenkampf* was unmistakably put – the question 'what is the church?' – the Catholic faithful and the rest gave irreconcilable answers. It was not now (as in the 1680s) the Protestants who fled France, but 30,000–40,000 non-juring priests, who fetched up principally in England, Spain and the Papal States.

Catholicism outside France

If the religious life of France has been under scholarly scrutiny, both microscopic and methodological, the same cannot be said of any other part of Catholic Europe. Even the history of theology in the eighteenth century is substantially unknown territory, a failing the more unfortunate in view of the lingering tendency to see Enlightenment everywhere and to equate it with decline. But that some of the marks of medieval and Counter-Reformation Catholicism were in decay is hardly open to question. One of the great devices for lay participation in church ritual and at the same time a reinforcement of local sociability were the fraternities which had organised processions, pilgrimages and religious ceremonies of all kinds. Over much of Catholic Europe there is circumstantial evidence that at any rate the religious significance of the fraternities was in decline, and that at least in Italy the number of fraternities was declining also. The simplest explanation of this change is that urban institutions were unable to assimilate all the rural migration that came their way; this, however, does not explain some of the qualitative changes to be observed in areas as far apart as Germany and Portugal, of fraternities taking up with secular objects. But everywhere Catholic authorities had been turning against some of the evidences of popular piety, such as pilgrimages, and eventually fraternities turned against others which were acceptable. Many of the confraternities of Seville failed to take part in religious processions after 1778 and the same was true of artisan guilds in Catalonia. Equally the efforts made in Rome to break superstition led to frequent skirmishing against devotions popular among the lower orders; Benedict XIII put on the Index all the litanies not officially approved, and Benedict XIV struck at all those which did not celebrate the Virgin or the saints. Even devotion to the Sacred Heart fell under the disapproval of the Congregation of Rites between 1729 and 1764.

There was general backing in the Catholic world for more frequent communion among the flock; and although there was a good deal of local disparity in what was understood by frequent communion, participation seems to have become more frequent at any rate among an emerging elite of *dévots*. The officially approved approach to the flock in the Italianate missions went on, especially in Italy, under very high pressure till late in the century; but here too the tide of taste was turning. Italian critics of the

Redemptorists raised their voices in the last quarter of the eighteenth century; Catholic subjects of the Habsburgs began to want something different, and Protestants were fairly readily resistant. It may be that by the time of the generation which followed the Seven Years War the dramatic missions which had made such an impact over the previous 200 years had accomplished most of what they were able to accomplish until psychological circumstances changed in the nineteenth century.

Religious orders

Since, to the Catholic, life according to a rule was the Christian life *par excellence*, the health of the religious orders was a matter of consequence. Part of the problem with the religious orders was the enormous increase in size and number which they had enjoyed since the Counter-Reformation. Old orders had been reformed and subdivided, and fresh efforts to bring old orders back to their primitive observance were made afer the Thirty Years War. The pursuit of sanctity in so many different styles defies brief assessment, but two things may be said. The first is that the great endowments of monastic property were made in the Middle Ages; if an order was wealthy it was likely to be an old one. Whether wealth was corrupting to the monastic ideal (as some Catholic historians have alleged that scholarship was) is arguable; what is hardly open to dispute is the fact that wealth was very damaging to the monastic ideal as a whole given the change in taste (or in need) to which the monastic ideal had successfully adapted in the seventeenth century. The trail had been blazed by the great missionary orders of the Counter-Reformation; they were followed by new orders devoted to education at every level, pastoral care (not least of the unfortunates known as *filles perdues*), famine relief, nursing, orders for men and women, Theatines, Piarists, Eudists, Ursulines, Daughters of Charity, Montfortains and a host of others. Rome itself had to plan in the purposive style of the new orders, once it was fairly launched into the business of overseas missions. The Congregation of Propaganda was organised in its definitive form in 1622, and by 1640 it was claiming the right to direct all overseas missions. The great obstacles to progress were the mutual rivalries of religious orders and the uncooperativeness of Spain and Portugal. Propaganda thereupon proceeded to identify resources by a process of elimination. Central Europe was still taken up with the struggle against the Reformation on one wing and the Turks on the other; eastern Europe had the preoccupation of drawing the Uniats closer. That left France, and France now qualified as a missionary dynamo by the possession of overseas bases, by native missionary enthusiasm, and by greater willingness to cooperate with Propaganda than the Iberian kingdoms. If Propaganda could thus proceed rationally (in the Weberian sense), the religious public could do the same. The new religious orders set out to attain ends of approved public welfare, and their recruiting held up far better in the eighteenth century than did that of the old and venerable orders. But the total disparity between the wealth of the old orders and their lack of approved public function, a disparity only aggravated by their inability to recruit, not only exposed them to rapacity of the state, but created problems for the newer, on the whole much less generously endowed orders. They too were showing signs of lethargy in the later eighteenth century, and it is a question whether their rationally purposive ends could be satisfactorily harnessed to those of personal sanctification which they shared with the older orders. If the supreme Catholic value of life according to a rule was working less happily for those who professed a vocation to it, the failure to recruit and the impatience of princes suffering from over-stretched budgets become easier to understand.

Policy in the Church of England

Problems with religious orders were one headache spared Protestant communities which had staked their entire prospect of Christianising future generations on the parish, reinforced from time to time by itinerant preaching and house-to-house visiting. The political setting of the Church of England changed very substantially between the first and the last generation of the eighteenth century. The great Tory slogan of the former period, 'the Church in Danger', implied a threat to the establish-ment from militant and newly tolerated dissent; this threat, always illu-sory, had been publicly proved to be so by the middle of the eighteenth century, the Church having gained much more in secession from Dissent than it had lost to it in separation. The real threat to the Church at this stage was from an armed Jacobite uprising in favour of the Catholic Stuarts, perhaps with French backing; by the middle of the century this threat had been defeated, and by the end of the Seven Years War the players in the great international game no longer kept up a pretence of playing on confessional principles.

Unfortunately all the major policy prescriptions for the Church had also been defeated. William Wake, archbishop of Canterbury in 1716–37, had tried to halt the Counter-Reformation, save the Church from isola-tion, and compensate it for its failure to achieve comprehension at home, by the formation of a Protestant bloc or at least an alliance with the French Gallican theologians. The latter policy failed because it was based on the illusion that the Gallican theologians would throw off allegiance to the pope; the former strategy became irrelevant, basically because European statesmen grasped very quickly after the fiasco in the Palatinate in 1719, that the forward march of the Counter-Reformation had at last been stopped. For this and other reasons Wake speedily became a complete political nonentity. Wake's successor as informal strong man of the Church, Edmund Gibson, bishop of London in 1720–48, started from the premise that the Church must fully accept the Protestant constitution in its present shape, and the Whigs as its only reliable defenders; under their aegis the Church must solve its own problems by improved discipline, by administrative reform and by improved clerical training. By 1736, however, Gibson had been convinced that the government had reneged on its side of the bargain and was encouraging a persistent vein of anticlericalism in Parliament. He therefore broke bitterly with Walpole and his influence was at an end. The third policy, that of the liberal theologians, was that the Church must shake off the shackles of scholasticism and regain its vigour by fertilising contact with the pure streams of modern knowledge. This policy also failed before Queen Anne's death. It led to endless embarrassments over the doctrine of the Trinity which almost everyone wished to avoid. Anti-Trinitarianism now became the policy of political and theological outsiders, Independent Whigs, deists and the like. Even Latitudinarianism is now thought to have played a smaller part in the eighteenth-century church than the older books assumed. There was finally the view that since the arm of flesh in the shape of whole-hearted support by the state had been of limited effect, churchmen should see what could be done by private enterprise.

In so far as there was any general policy in the church after the Seven Years War this was it; and it took three main forms. There was the squirearchical practice of employing worldly deference to the advantage of the Church; in fiction this was exemplified by Sir Roger de Coverley ensuring that his tenants turned up in church, sang properly and kept awake in the sermon, a practice far more effective than the statutory restraints favoured under the Restoration and Queen Anne. There was also the practice of religious revival which began to make some noticeable difference by the 1780s. And there was an unsung but effective method of adapting a rigid parish system to a growing population by enlarging, and to a much lesser extent, building, churches by private generosity. This shows clearly enough that there were a good many places where people wanted to make their churches useful and were prepared to find the means to do so. Moreover the Seven Years War itself gave a psychological boost to a Church establishment which seemed to have put paid to all its old rivals. Military success induced a national rally of opinion, and began the process by which old irreconcilables (and not least clergy) came back to court and had by the end of the century produced a new conservative political establishment for which the Church, in the earlier part of the century a frequently disgruntled, and in parts treasonable, institution, was a valuable symbol and constituent. Add to this the fact that the Church profited enormously from the enclosure movement and its un-earned increment from the wider enterprise of the British economy, and the last generation of the eighteenth century should have been, and in many ways was, a golden age for the Church of England.

Political and social problems in Britain

Before the century was out, however, it was clear that neither the political nor the social weather was as set fair as it had appeared after the Seven Years War. For both the success and the cost of that war laid up problems of imperial reorganisation which ignited sharper divisions of opinion than could be bridged by religious symbols. Both America and Ireland turned against the new imperial system; the American War of Independence was in effect a civil war in which the old Dissent was militantly arrayed against the establishment on both sides of the Atlantic, and Ireland proved to be a similar case. For once, Wesley's personal problems mirrored those of the establishment as a whole. He did his movement a great deal of good in England by coming out strongly on the side of the government; the result was that he substantially lost control of his movement in America, and was put to curious shifts in Ireland in the effort to discover *how* to be establishmentarian there. Still worse, when the French Revolution took a radical turn in 1792 there was a sharp polarisation of English opinion which was the preface not only to divisions in Methodism but to a mass turning of ordinary English sentiment away from the Church establish-ment. Never since that date has the Church of England functioned effectively as a symbol of national unity.

The sudden revulsion brought on by political division had been pre-pared in a subterranean way by social developments in the previous generation. The enclosure movement which had profited the clergy so greatly was part of a general commercialisation of agriculture which led to the proliferation of Lord's Day business, and to a reluctance by farmers to get their servants to church. It also generated a good deal of ill-feeling in the countryside as labourers lost access to the commons, at the same time as parvenu clergy moved out of the village and built themselves the rural palaces which were a millstone round the necks of their successors until sold off recently to urban parvenus. At the same time the clergy in many counties took charge of the bench of magistrates and for half a century instituted a clerical dominion which had never existed before and has never existed since.

The increase in population which underlay the prosperity of agriculture in those years also prepared problems for the Church both financial and pastoral. The Church was an endowed institution; and when Queen Anne had returned to it the revenue of first-fruits and tenths taken by Henry VIII, for the relief of poor livings, the Bounty Commissioners had divided their annual income into small capital endowments in the reasonable belief that by turning revenue into capital they would one day be able to overtake the ancient problem of clerical poverty. Unhappily this approach to the problem of funding a public service was wrecked in perpetuity when the market for that service began indefinitely to expand. There was no possibility of providing both the capital for church and school building and the further capital for endowing the service for a nation which grew as remorselessly as the English nation began to grow in the middle of the eighteenth century. Nor, as the Church was too slow to realise, could a state confronted by the rise of mass dissent and Catholicism do much to make good the shortfall. And since endowment and establishment seemed to be twins threatened by voluntaryism and the foes of establishment, it was difficult for the Church to continue with either the quiet voluntaryism which had served it well in the eighteenth century or to enter new schemes for concurrent endowment of churches which with minor exceptions were still-born in the nineteenth. The event was to show that the second-class establishment created by the Toleration Act, even when reinforced by the evangelical and Catholic revivals, was never quite capable of replacing the original endowed establishment with a voluntaryist version of its own.

The narrowing of the Anglican mind

The introversion of the Anglican mentality which this story reveals was also prepared by lengthy developments in the eighteenth century. In the early eighteenth century the repute of the English Church stood high among the Protestant churches abroad. What they valued, however, were the tracts of Puritan devotion, on which the English church had turned its back in the Restoration period, and biblical studies in which the Dissenters were as eminent as the church. Recent study has been emphasising that there was a coherent and unbroken chain of teaching from the Caroline divines and the Non-jurors of the late seventeenth century to the Hutchinsonian school of Bishop Horne and Jones of Nayland of the mid-eighteenth and on to divines like Daubeny, Sikes and the Hackney Phalanx in the pre-Tractarian Church. What in short was happening was that the Church was severing itself from its own Reformed roots and the main Protestant traditions of the Continent in a way that was alien from the undogmatic Protestantism which was now the only Christianity which the bulk of the English nation knew, and would win no sympathy from resurgent, let alone imported, Roman Catholicism. And this shift in *mentalité* was alas! publicly illustrated in two of the adaptations to church order effected in response to the increase in population. Since that increase guaranteed that that larger numbers would fall through the net of pastoral oversight than in the past, one solution was to adopt the kind of systematic itinerant ministry on which Wesley's followers had stumbled, with a view to going into the highways and hedges and compelling the lost to come in. This adaptation was as foreign to the church order of the Dissenters as it was to that of the Church, but both took it up, and in the 1790s not a little was done on an undenominational basis. Equally, the growth of population brought with it a youth problem of a new severity, and from the 1780s onwards this was tackled on a huge scale by Sunday schools organised mostly on an undenominational basis. In each case, when the political crisis became acute over the turn of the century, the church establishment sought to prove its counter-revolutionary credentials by pulling out of the combined enterprises at the cost of its links with the nation. Unhappily an even narrower and less palatable introversion was to be the nostrum of the most vocal Anglican ginger-group of the nineteenth century, the Anglo-Catholics. What is not known is whether the new spirit of exclusive clericalism did anything to remedy one of the major spiritual and organisational weaknesses of the late eighteenth-century establishment, the failure of prestigious and wealthy sees like London and Winchester to replenish their stock of clergy from local recruitment.

The Kirk and assimilation

Some but not all of the problems facing the Church of England were also faced by the Presbyterian church establishment of Scotland. The Scottish church had to fight its way into the Highlands in the early eighteenth century and rooted itself deeply there by a combination of ruthlessness and religious revival. Though the Kirk was never the sole bearer of the national tradition – the lawyers and the universities saw to that – it was closer to this in the eighteenth century than the Church of England ever became, and acquired a certain toughness from its fight at the outset. It also retained a sense of being part of an international fellowship of Reformed churches, and of ecclesiastical claims which not only put paid to modern doctrines of sovereignty, but preserved it from the embarrassments encountered by the Church of England in the doctrine of the Divine Right of Kings. On the other hand there were great ambiguities not only in the relation of the Kirk to the national tradition, but in what the essence of the Kirk itself was in terms of doctrine and order. The Act of Union with Scotland had given the Kirk every conceivable guarantee, but there was no altering the fact that the act existed primarily for English convenience, and that the Kirk became one of the instruments of management employed by English governments. Queen Anne's last Tory government had seen to it that patronage in the Scottish church followed none of the various hallowed principles of Presbyterian tradition, but was in the hands of the crown and landlords, like so much of English patronage. This was a sore point for much of the eighteenth century. It was also the case that Calvinism poured out of the Scottish church at a great rate from 1690 onwards, to fetch up, along with scruples about patronage, in the steadily swelling tide of Scottish dissent. The Moderate party were dominant in the Church Assembly for most of the eighteenth century; not always generous in their Moderatism, they contained the evangelical revival and damped down the level of Scottish ecclesiastical discord. The price of their triumph was the almost total demise of Scottish theology (since they would neither accept the Westminster Confession, nor admit to the fact), and a triumph of Enlightenment in the ruling quarters of the church entirely unparalleled in England. In lay culture the Scottish Enlightenment was the nation's glory; in the church it left sour memories, as in Lord Cockburn's recollection that Moderatism 'tended to divide our ministers into two classes; one, and that by far the largest, had no principle superior to that of obsequious allegiance to patrons; the other devoting itself entirely to the religion of the lower orders'. This recollection admittedly came from the far side of the events in the nineteenth century, when the evangelicals who devoted themselves 'to the religion of the lower orders' first of all seized control of the fund-raising machinery of the Kirk and then drove it into a collision with the law which forced a disruption on an unprecedented scale; but it acknowledged clearly enough that in Moderatism the forces of order and the impulses of life had been imprudently unbalanced in favour of the former.

The fruits of security in Protestant Germany

In Protestant Germany no unity of response to the situation after the Seven Years War was possible, but one fact was abundantly clear. Frederick the Great had spared no pains to represent that war as a confessional conflict of the old style and had won a Protestant response from far afield. After the war, in which he had been almost undone, with the energies of Roman Catholic powers now being venomously turned against Jesuits, idle monks and even the curia, the atmosphere changed radically. The Westphalia settlement was now safe, even from the century of niggling conflicts to which its implementation had given rise; Protestantism was secure from confessional aggression even in the divided Empire. The new sunshine transformed the old timorous conservatism into a satisfaction with present ways which had curious results. Ecclesiastical topography, indeed global ecclesiastical geography, became all the rage as vision rose above parochial survival, and it proved in no way incompatible with a lofty religious patriotism. Carl Friedrich Stäudlin (for purposes of church-history teaching at Göttingen) catalogued all the religions on earth, and had no doubt of German superiority: 'They have made Christianity more moral and carried further the views of of its founder. They have not made a religion of sticking with old forms and determinations but they have not gone over to unbelief or a new superstition.' There seems indeed no doubt that some famous sons of the Pietist manse carried over the frame of mind in which they had been brought up into a new nationalism, a process which was made easier by the fact that German nationalism, lacking a state or dynasty upon which to focus, began to form around a set of cultural traditions. Carl Friedrich Moser (1723–98), for example, the son of Johann Jakob Moser, a doughty exponent of the public law of the Empire, a deeply convinced Pietist, and pillar of the Pietist cause in Württemberg, turned away from legal studies and began to address the whole nation in the cause of Christian patriotism, his book *The German National Spirit* (1765) establishing his reputation throughout Germany. Unlike his father, he even accepted imperial employment in Vienna in 1767, but the experience quickly convinced him that dynastic rather than imperial interests were what counted there, and he returned to serve the national cause in Hesse-Darmstadt. For him, patriotism, the cause of the kingdom without, came to replace that of the kingdom of God within cherished by the Pietist, but it attracted the same mystical vocabulary and evoked similar emotional responses.

In the case of Johann Gottfried Herder (1744–1803) the repudiation of a Pietist background was a good deal sharper. In his *Ideas on the Philosophy of the History of Mankind* (1784) he set out to show the harmony between science and education on the one hand and religious faith on the other. Nature and history, history in the especial sense of the shaping of the human race in nations of individual character and quality, reveal the handiwork of Providence. If this sounds uncommonly like pantheism, Herder remained a zealous working Lutheran pastor, heavily preoccupied with the person and teaching of Jesus as revealed in the gospels, and hoping, when he left Riga, his first preferment, to escape from Baltic provincialism and do a job for the nation. His theatres of practical activity proved to be even smaller than those of Moser, but he was one of the very few to establish himself both as a professional theologian and a man of letters. There were innumerable connections between Moser and Herder on the one hand and Goethe and Lessing on the other; but there is a perceptible contrast between the nationalism of the one and the comopolitanism of the other.

If some ex-Pietists, lay and clerical, began to look to a fatherland which did not yet exist, other clergy in considerable numbers began to voice the feeling that the religious establishment of *Kleinstaaterei*, from which they derived their social standing and often much of their income, was professionally demeaning in that (in the eyes of the state) it transformed ministers of God into petty bureaucrats, giving public notice of legislation and collecting statistics. Clearly the further the Enlightenment went in amalgamating religion with reason, the more the clergy were likely to be regarded by the state as additional parish schoolmasters charged with promoting economic growth, or whatever was the policy of the moment, and the more their education would be threatened with reform in the interests of social utility. There was a large grey area in which clergy might easily miss their way. Even in Württemberg, where a relatively weak state was confronted by what would have been called in England a powerful 'country' movement, there were in the eighteenth century twenty-four rescripts governing eighty-three aspects of the clerical office. The text and content of sermons, their duration and construction (including penalties for preaching too long), right up to the prohibition of quotations in Greek and Hebrew, were all regulated by the state. To clergy who had been used to this degree of regulation, it was not difficult to obscure the dividing line between traditional responsibilities in poor relief, and modern dedication to economic growth. Yet even in Württemberg complaints poured forth: 'Why are we poor pastors loaded with so many burdens? Why must we be petty governors? Why are we plagued with dealing with prostitutes, quarrelsome marriages, peasant properties, parish poor funds, affairs of orphans and matters of assessment?'

Collegialism

The clerical office could hardly be defended by the kinds of arguments used by the old Lutheran Orthodox, since the old view of revelation itself had been undermined by historical studies. But the old Empire was a not unfruitful balance between centralising and decentralising tendencies, and while the German Protestant pastors could not mutiny as the priests in France ultimately did, they could find a home and a doctrine in the decentralising camp. This camp proved expert in using the imperial courts against the territorial powers. Pfaff in Tübingen and Mosheim in Göttingen produced doctrines of collegialism, based on the premise that the church was a society with inherent rights and was not, as Thomasius had alleged, simply a subordinate body deriving its rights and duties from the territorial power. The appeal to revelation and the appeal to the courts fitted neatly together. In the not very long run, events turned against both the collegial and the territorial parties. No clergy had been more fully regimented by the state than those of Prussia, and none had more exclusively worn the territorial badge of rationalism. None paid the price of their subordination more fully, when immediately after Frederick's death, his successor and nephew, Frederick William IV rejected his religious policies, and in the edict of 1788 Johann Christoph von Wöllner tried to close the door on Enlightenment, reintroduced religious censorship of books and university study, and increased the disciplinary powers of the consistories. On the other hand the anti-utilitarian, anti-centralist party in the German pastorate took fright at the French Revolution and still more at Napoleonic invasion. Independence of the state now took second place to the preservation of establishment; the arm of flesh had its attractions after all.

Church attendance

There is no satisfactory way of measuring the loyalty of the German Protestant public to their established churches. Clerical complaints at being treated as registrars for secular statistics did not mean that ecclesiastical statistics were efficiently kept. In very few states were there efforts to compile a census of church attendance, and it would seem that the best series of communion statistics were kept where there were political menaces to Protestant survival. They are nevertheless of some interest. In Saxony they illuminate the perils of establishment. Participation in communion declined suddenly at the beginning of the eighteenth century, at the precise point when the dynasty took the heart out of the establishment by converting to Roman Catholicism. The decline steepened in the 1740s at the time of the War of the Austrian Succession. In mid-century the Saxon church paid the penalty of having forcibly suppressed Pietism without having generated any other religious appeal, and went over wholesale from a very dead Orthodoxy to a Rationalism with little popular appeal; the communion statistics decline even faster. By 1800 communion attendance had dropped by about half over the century, and was to decline by more than half again by 1880. The Saxon church had become an establishment without a constituency. The same could not be said of Silesia where until the Prussian conquest in the 1740s Protestantism had been menaced by Catholicism, and reinforced by revival. Here the figures were high and remained steady. Yet there was a falling away after the Seven Years War, which may even have been accelerated by Pietist exclusion of sinners from communion after the manner of Jansenism in France. Communion figures for Württemberg mean little since attendance was obligatory down to the middle of the eighteenth century; but complaints that in the later eighteenth century services on special holy days were ill-attended, and the facts that after the middle of the century class-meetings led by simple working men multiplied greatly, and that in the last generation of the century separatism rapidly increased, suggest that the establishment was being gradually hollowed out.

The Deutsche Christentumsgesellschaft

If the old church establishments were now creaking audibly, it would be a mistake to suppose that in the cold climate after 1763 there were no opportunities for fanning the flames of religious zeal, nor that there was no one to take them. Underlying the great Protestant revival movement of the early nineteenth century was the gradual decay of old forms of communal dependence in rural and town parishes over much of central and northern Europe. This gave an opening to those who were prepared to act in new ways, disregarding the old barriers of parish, confession and nation, and to apply the principle of joint-stock and contract, dominant in the world of commerce, to the affairs of the kingdom of God. This principle brought to prominence the pious bourgeoisie of Basel, and generated an alliance of Orthodox and Pietist against the reign of Enlightenment which anticipated a great deal that was to happen during the French Revolution. Much of the initial impetus, however, was to come from Germany.

Johann August Urlsperger (1728–1806) was the tenth son of that celebrated Samuel Urlsperger who had organised and tended the refuge for the Salzburger exiles in Georgia. Like his father he served in Augsburg, ending up as Senior there. Also like his father he became in 1765 a member of the SPCK with special responsibility for the Georgia settlement. In 1778 he became a member of the Swedish society 'pro fide et christianismo' founded by Wesley's friend Wrangel, and went on a great tour of German towns advocating the formation of societies on the English and Swedish pattern. These tours continued over the next two years and took in, among other places, both Basel and London, where he met the pastor of the German congregation in the Savoy who was receptive to the idea of forming a society on Urlsperger's lines. Urlsperger himself was a conservative Lutheran theologian known principally for an eccentric defence of the doctrine of the Trinity. In Basel, however, he encountered societary action for other purposes. For a generation disciples of the celebrated Pietist pastor, Hieronymus Annoni, had been meeting under various titles for mutual encouragement and the furtherance of the cause, and had cast the net in correspondence as far as Halle and Augsburg. What Urlsperger was able to give the Baselers was organisation, a much wider range of international contacts, and a very telling conservative name – the German Society for Furthering Pure Doctrine and True Godliness. At any rate by 1780 the society had its statutes; these pledged the members to mutual love irrespective of social status, and committed them to daily prayer, the sanctification of the Lord's Day, regular attendance at public worship and family devotions, and attendance at class-meetings, monthly meetings for prayer and Bible study, weekly self-examination and daily Bible reading. If all this was very Pietist, it also betrayed a church spirit, inculcating respect for public authority, and discountenancing dependence on favourite pastors. The one thing which was not mentioned at all was doctrine, not even Urlsperger's favourite concern of the Trinity, though he himself made no bones about 'the decline of the pure faith, the spreading Babylonian confusion, and the general spirit of giddiness'. The reason for this was presumably that the contracting parties felt at one in the old Protestant Orthodoxy, with one important exception, the strict doctrine of double predestination, to salvation or damnation. To have raised this issue would have undercut the basis for cooperation between Reformed and Lutheran; to be silent on it breathed the irenic spirit of English evangelicalism in the 1790s, and indeed after spreading like wildfire on the Continent, the Society obtained a new impulse during the worst days of the Revolutionary and Napoleonic Wars by close personal contacts with the English evangelicals and their missionary societies and with the forces of a Catholic revival of a very undenominational character in the Allgäu.

No one doubted where the Deutsche Christentumsgesellschaft (as it became known) stood in regard to the Enlightenment; the enlightened *Berliner Monatschrift* attacked them as Protestant Jesuits, while they were delighted by Wöllner's Religious Edict of 1788.[1] Nevertheless, conservative as were their views, they had hit on a very successful and progressive formula for the rerooting of Protestant Christianity throughout the west;

---

[1] The edict of Johann Christoph von Wöllner recalled men from Enlightenment to tradition and custom and denounced the undermining of the authority of the Bible, the clergy and the Lutheran understanding of atonement and satisfaction. It also reintroduced religious censorship of books and university study, and enhanced the powers of Lutheran and Reformed consistories. It was in many ways out of harmony with the uniform code adopted for all the Prussian churches in 1794.

a combination of foreign and home missions (which in the case of the Society included the support of the newly tolerated Protestants in Austria), giving unity and purpose to an immense range of local societies in which middle-class laymen and -women were prominent, and a skilful exploitation of societal organisation which enabled, for example, a Basel Missionary Society to undertake distinguished missionary work in Africa, where there was no Swiss flag for them to follow. For a generation or two Protestant Christianity exhibited astonishing new vigour by going over wholesale to unconfessional, international, societary means of action, in which the laity paid for and often ran great machines which had no place in the traditional church orders.

In the longer run they would be challenged by high-church parties of Lutheran, Anglican and Reformed varieties; but in the still longer run those very high-church parties could only sustain their 'church' Christianity on the basis of ecumenical bargains between ordained ministries. The difference between all this and the success of both Catholic and Protestant in tapping new sources of lay support at the end of the eighteenth century is very striking. The confessional and establishmentarian spirit is not dead in Europe, just sufficiently desperate to be seeking survival by turning its back on the means by which modern Christianity was propagated across the globe and by retro-action across much of Europe. Meanwhile astonishing results continue to be reported by adaptable organisations like the Society of Jesus and by the endless unreconstructed offshoots from the evangelical stem.

Suggestions for further reading

Fifty years ago my tutor J. M. Thompson wound up a notable treatise on the French Revolution by a list of the fifty best books on the subject. The present state of research and the breadth of the theme of this book hardly permit that bold and elegant solution to the question of further reading; but the following books and papers in the tongues most accessible to readers whose first language is English will be found to be useful, and will give further indications of the sources and literature. Before the Oxford History of the Christian Church began to produce its modern volumes, English contributions to the subject were sparse, but Owen Chadwick, *The Popes and European Revolution* (Oxford, 1981), and Nicholas Hope, *German and Scandinavian Protestantism 1700–1918* (Oxford, 1995), are distinguished volumes, and a major treatment of the French church in the eighteenth century by John McManners is forthcoming in the same series. My own *Protestant Evangelical Awakening* (Cambridge, 1992) attempts to treat one theme in Protestant history on an international basis. The French series, *L'Histoire de l'Église*, ed. A. Fliche and V. Martin (for whom the Church was the Roman Catholic Church), is now becoming dated both in scholarship and viewpoint, but remains useful for the breadth of its treatment and its indications of the older literature. The volumes for this period are E. Préclin and E. Jarry, *Les Luttes politiques et doctrinales aux XVIIe et XVIIIe siècles* (Paris, 1955–56), and J. Leflon, *La Crise revolutionnaire 1789–1846* (n.p., 1949). A useful textbook of the same type is the English translation of H. Jedin and J. Dolan, *History of the hurch*, vol. 6: *The Church in the Age of Absolutism and Enlightenment*; vol. 7: *The Church between Revolution and Restoration* (London, 1990). The Catholic world was also treated with much distinction and cosmopolitan grasp by Gustav Schnürer in *Katholische Kirche und Kultur im 18. Jahrhundert* (Paderborn, 1941). Like all cooperative works *Church and Society in Catholic Europe of the Eighteenth Century*, ed. W. J. Callaghan and David Higgs (Cambridge, 1979) is uneven, but contains much valuable modern material. The student of Catholic Europe cannot avoid testing his stamina against that of Ludwig von Pastor, *The History of the Popes from the*

Close of the Middle Ages, especially vols. 33–6 (Eng. trans. London, 1941–50) (the faint-hearted may attempt E. E. Y. Hales, *Revolution and Papacy, 1761–1846* (London, 1960)); Michael Walsh, *A Dictionary of Devotions* (London, 1993), by contrast, compactly explains a huge range of devotions now forgotten by practising Catholics. A theological reference work to end all reference works, the *Theologische Realenzyclopaedie* (Berlin, 1977–), having reached vol. 25, is now making stately progress towards its conclusion, increasing in value with every volume that appears. Much briefer, and almost exclusively thematic in its treatment, but still valuable, is the *Evangelische Kirchenlexicon* (Göttingen, 1986–97).

Regional reading may include the following.

France: An interesting recent attempt at synthesis is made in *Histoire de la France religieuse*, ed. J. Le Goff and R. Rémond (Paris, 1988–92). The contribution of Jansenism to the undermining of the Ancien Régime is seminally worked out by Dale Van Kley in three books, *The Damiens Affair* (New Haven, 1984), *The Jansenists and the Expulsion of the Jesuits from France, 1757–65* (New Haven, 1975) and *The Religious Origins of the French Revolution. From Calvin to the Civil Constitution, 1560–1791* (New Haven, 1996). On this subject see also A. Gazier, *Histoire générale du mouvement jansénist* (Paris, 1922) and R. Shackleton, 'Jansenism and the Enlightenment', *Studies on Voltaire and the Eighteenth Century*, 57 (1967). Major revision of an entirely different kind has been achieved by Louis Châtellier, *The Europe of the Devout. The Catholic Reformation and the Formation of a New Society* (Eng. trans. Cambridge, 1989) and *The Religion of the Poor. Rural Missions in Europe and the Formation of Modern Catholicism* (Eng. trans. Cambridge, 1997). See also his *Tradition Chrétienne et Renouveau Catholique dans le Cadre de l'ancien Diocèse de Strasbourg (1650–1770)* (Paris, 1981). A monument to the enormous effort expended upon testing the religious pulse of the old France is given by B. Plongeron and P. Lerou, *La Piété Populaire en France. Répertoire Bibliographique* (Paris, 1984–). There are examples of it in different styles in Michèle Ménard, *Une histoire de mentalités religieuses aux XVIIᵉ et XVIIIᵉ siècles. Mille retables de l'ancien diocèse du Mans* (Paris, 1980), Bernard Dompnier, *Enquête au pays des Frères des Anges. Les Capucins de la Province de Lyon aux XVIIᵉ et XVIIIᵉ siècles* (Saint-Etienne, 1993), and Yves-Marie Bercé, *Des mentalités populaires du XVIe au XVIIIᵉ siècle* (Paris, 1995). Older work not to be missed includes R. Mandrou, *De la culture populaire aux XVIIᵉ et XVIIIᵉ siècles. Le bibliothèque bleue de Troyes* (Paris, 1965), and J. McManners, *French Ecclesiastical Society under the Ancien Régime* (Manchester, 1960). Also by McManners are 'Jansenism and Politics in the 18th century', *Studies in Church History*, vol. 12, ed. D. Baker (Oxford, 1975), and *Death and the Enlightenment* (Oxford, 1981).

The **Iberian peninsula** is less well served, but there is valuable material in the following: William J. Callaghan, *Church, Politics and Society in Spain, 1750–1874* (Cambridge, Mass., 1984); Samuel J. Miller, *Portugal and Rome c. 1748–1830. An Aspect of Catholic Enlightenment* (Rome, 1978); Jean Sarrailh's two studies, *L'Espagne éclairée de la seconde moitié du XVIIIᵉ siècle* (Paris, 1954) and *La Crise religieuse à la fin du XVIIIᵉ siècle* (Oxford, 1951) are subject to later criticism in *The Ibero-American Enlightenment*, ed. A. Owen Aldridge (Urbana, 1971). See also Richard Herr, *The Eighteenth-Century Revolution in Spain* (Princeton, 1958).

Italy, including the papacy, affords an embarrassment and a dearth of riches. On Propaganda Fide see *Sacrae Congregationis de Propaganda Fide Memoria Rerum*, ed. J. Metzler (Rome/Freiburg/ Vienna, 1971–76). For the Italian missions, see G. De Rosa, 'Sainteté, clergé et peuple dans le Mezzogiorno italien au milieu du XVIIIᵉ siecle', *Revue d'histoire de la spiritualité*, 52 (1976), 245–64, and F. M. Jones, *Alphonsus de Liguori. The Saint of Bourbon Naples, 1696–1787* (Dublin, 1992). For the Italian Enlightenment see Franco Venturi, *Italy and the Enlightenment. Studies in a Cosmopolitan Century*, ed. S. Woolf (London, 1972), and 'Church Reform in Enlightenment Italy: the Sixties of the Eighteenth Century', *Journal of Modern History*, 48 (1976), 215–32; see also Dino Carpanetto and Giuseppe Ricuperati, *Italy in the Age of Reason*, (London, 1987). Charles A. Bolton, *Church Reform in Eighteenth-Century Italy: The Synod of Pistoia, 1786* (The Hague, 1969) is valuable. The change in atmosphere at the end of the century is treated in Dries Vanysacker, *Cardinal Giuseppe Garampi (1725–92), an Enlightened Ultramontane* (Brussels, 1995).

On **Germany** has been lavished the extraordinary productivity of German scholarship with not much attempt at synthesis. An exception to this rule is provided by the first two volumes of the *Geschichte des Pietismus*, ed. Martin Brecht (Göttingen, 1993–95), which mobilise and introduce the enormous literature on this subject, not entirely, it must be said, to the satisfaction of Johannes Wallmann, whose *Philipp Jakob Spener und die Anfänge des Pietismus* (1st edn., Tübingen, 1970) is one of the basic texts of the new work. See also the work of Wallmann's pupil, Udo Sträter, *Meditation und Kirchenreform in der lutherischen Kirche des 17. Jahrhunderts* (Tübingen, 1995). I attempted a brief survey of the literature in 'German Pietism, 1670–1750', *Journal of Ecclesiastical History* , 44 (1993), 476–505. Orthodoxy as a subject in its own right has fared less well in recent years, with Martin Greschat, *Zwischen Tradition und neuem Anfang. Valentin Ernst Löscher und der Ausgang der lutherischen Orthodoxie* (Witten, 1971), outstanding. The Landeskirchen are well provided with histories, including Karl Schmalz, *Kirchengeschichte Mecklenburgs* (Schwerin/Berlin, 1935–52), the rather inaccurate H. Hermelink,

Geschichte der evangelische Kirche in Württemberg von der Reformation bis zur Gegenwart (Stuttgart/Tübingen, 1949), and Walther Hubatsch, *Geschichte der Evangelischen Kirche Ostpreussens* (Göttingen, 1968). Hartmut Lehmann struck out on an independent line of social history in *Pietismus und weltliche Ordnung in Württemberg vom 17. bis zum 20. Jahrhundert* (Stuttgart, 1969), a work which has stood the test of time. Of the works treating popular practice in Catholic Germany, L. A. Veit and L. Lenhart, *Kirche und Volksfrömmigkeit im Zeitalter des Barock* (Freiburg, 1956) is bigoted, Richard van Dülmen, *Kultur und Alltag in der frühen Neuzeit*, vol. 3: *Religion, Magie, Aufklärung* (Munich, 1994) is very interesting, and *Religion und Religiosität im Zeitalter des Barock*, ed. D. Breuer, 2 vols. (Wiesbaden, 1995), is fascinating but overwhelming in detail. The two latter works also contain Protestant material. Recent discussions on the Catholic Enlightenment in Germany are effectively thrashed out in *Katholische Aufklärung – Aufklärung im katholischen Deutschland*, ed. Harm Klueting (Hamburg, 1993), which also contains an extensive bibliography. Much of the rest of the Catholic work had gone into regional studies such as Heribert Raab, *Clemens Wenzeslaus von Sachsen und seine Zeit*, vol. 1 (Freiburg, 1962), and two works by Alfred Schröcker, *Ein Schönborn im Reich. Studien zur Reichspolitik des Fürstbischofs Lothar Franz von Schönborn (1655–1729)* (Wiesbaden, 1978), and *Die Patronage des Lothar Franz von Schönborn (1655–1729). Sozialgeschichtliche Studie zum Beziehungsnetz in der Germania Sacra* (Wiesbaden, 1981). See also T. C. W. Blanning, *Reform and Revolution in Mainz, 1743–1803* (Cambridge, 1974), and Joachim Whaley, *Religious Toleration and Social Change in Hamburg, 1529–1819* (Cambridge, 1985).

The general church histories of **Austria** and the Habsburg lands, such as Ernst Tomek, *Kirchegeschichte Österreichs* (Innsbruck, 1935–59), are depressingly reactionary; however, a modest Marxist tonic was administered by Eduard Winter, *Barock, Absolutism und Aufklärung in der Donaumonarchie* (Vienna, 1971), and an attempt to breathe new life into the subject on the basis of French models was made in *Katholische Aufklärung und Josephinismus*, ed. Elisabeth Kovács (Vienna, 1979). She also produced *Ultramontanismus und Staatskirchentum im Theresianisch-Josephischen Staat* (Vienna, 1979), and with Rupert Feuchtmüller prepared an exemplary two-volume catalogue for the exhibition at St Florian in 1986 under the title *Welt des Barock*. Anna Coreth expounded part of this subject in *Pietas Austriaca* (Vienna, 1959). On the building Hans Sedlmayr, *Österreichische Barockarchitectur 1690–1740* (Vienna, 1930), and John Bourke, *Baroque Churches of Central Europe* (2nd edn., London, 1962) are still useful; so is Robert A. Kann, *A Study in Austrian Intellectual History. From Late Baroque to Romanticism* (London, 1960). Rudolf Reinhardt, 'Zur Kirchenreform in Österreich unter Maria Theresa' in *Zeitschrift für Kirchengeschichte*, 4s. 77 (1966), 105–119, discusses intentions for church reform, and H. Ferihumer, *Die kirchliche Gliederung des Landes ob der Enns im Zeitalter Kaiser Josefs II* (Linz, 1952) explains what actually happened. In English there are Derek Beales, *Joseph II*, vol. 1 (Cambridge, 1987), T. C. W. Blanning, *Joseph II* (London, 1994), and W. W. Davis, 'The origins of religious Josephism', *East Central Europe*, 1 (1974). The Institut für protestantische Kirchengeschichte in Vienna has seen to it over the last generation that the Protestants of the old Habsburg domains are better served than the Catholics, notably in two works edited by Peter Barton, *Im Lichte der Toleranz* and *Im Zeichen der Toleranz* (both Vienna, 1981), Gerhard Florey's *Geschichte der Salzburger Protestanten und ihrer Emigration 1731/2* (Vienna, 1977), and Oskar Wagner, *Mutterkirche vieler Länder. Geschichte der Evangelischen Kirche im Herzogtum Teschen* (Vienna, 1978).

The Institut has also cast its net into **Hungary** with Mihály Bucsay, *Der Protestantismus in Ungarn, 1521–1978* (2 vols., Vienna, 1977–79). The bloodthirsty annals of Hungarian religion may also be followed in Béla Obál, *Die Religionspolitik in Ungarn . . . während der Regierung Leopold I* (Halle, 1910), Béla K. Kiraly, *Hungary in the Eighteenth Century* (New York, 1969), and Béla Köpeczi, *Staatsräson und Christliche Solidarität* (Vienna, 1983).

Switzerland is blessed on the Protestant side with one of the classics of modern church history, Paul Wernle's *Der schweizerische Protestantismus im 18. Jahrhundert*, of which the first three volumes (Tübingen, 1923–25) cover this period, and a much inferior Catholic counterpart, T. Schwegler, *Geschichte der katholischen Kirche der Schweiz* (2nd edn., Freiburg 1943). Kurt Guggisberg's *Bernische Kirchengeschichte* (Bern, 1958) is vastly superior to the ordinary seminary textbook. Rudolf Dellsperger is expounding the national and international importance of Swiss Pietism; begin with his *Die Anfänge des Pietismus in Bern* (Göttingen, 1984).

Scandinavia, Poland and **Russia**. Nicholas Hope (see above) provides the best guide to Scandinavia, but Poul Georg Lindhardt, *Kirchengeschichte Scandinaviens* (Göttingen and East Berlin, 1983) retains its value because of its quite different approach to the subject. *Aufklärung und Pietismus im danischen Gesamtstaat*, ed. H. Lehmann and D. Lohmaier (Neumünster, 1983), is valuable for Denmark. On Poland Norman Davies, *God's Playground*, vol. 1 (Oxford, 1982), is excellent, and useful material may be dredged from Karl Völker, *Kirchengeschichte Polens* (Berlin/Leipzig, 1930) and Julian Pelesz, *Geschichte der Union der Ruthenische Kirche mit Rom* (3 vols., Würzburg/Vienna, 1881). On the Baltic area, *Baltische Kirchengeschichte*, ed. Reinhard Wittram (Göttingen, 1956), is valuable. The Russian church is systematically treated by Igor Smolitsch in *Russisches Mönchtum* (Würzburg, 1953) and *Geschichte der Russischen Kirche, 1700–1917* (Leiden, 1964), while cultural factors are the theme of Hans Rogger, *National Consciousness in Eighteenth-Century Russia* (Cambridge, Mass., 1960). See also James Cracraft, *The Church reforms of Peter the Great* (London, 1971), and Isabel de Madariaga, *Russia in the Age of Catherine the Great* (London, 1981).

The church history of Britain's near neighbours in the **Netherlands** presents more language difficulties than most, but *Pietismus und Reveil*, ed. J. van den Berg and J. P van Dooren (Leiden, 1978) contains more in German and English than Dutch. Jan van den Berg has made major contributions to the subject in English, as in his 'Orthodoxy, Rationalism and the World' in *Studies in Church History* vol. 10 (1973), in 'The Evangelical Revival in Scotland and the Nineteenth-Century "Reveil" in the Netherlands', *Scottish Church History Society. Records*, 25 (1994), 309–37, and (with G. F. Nuttall) in *Philip Doddridge and the Netherlands* (Leiden, 1987); and also in German in Martin Brecht's *Geschichte des Pietismus*, vol. 2, pp. 542–87. There is also Wilhelm Goeters, *Die Vorbereitung des Pietismus in der Reformierten Kirche der Niederlande* (Leipzig, 1911; repr. Amsterdam, 1974).

British church history is a subject which remains to be recognised, let alone written, though pioneer efforts by myself (in German, forthcoming) and by Sheridan Gilley and W. J. Sheils, eds., *A History of Religion in Britain* (Oxford, 1993, with bibliographies) mark a beginning. The benchmark remains the work of Norman Sykes, summed up in his *Church and State in England in the Eighteenth Century* (Cambridge, 1934); unhappily the quality of his work has intensified the natural insularity of the writing of English church history, and limited the imagination of his successors as to the questions which may fruitfully be posed to it. *The Church of England c. 1689–c. 1833*, ed. J. Walsh, C. Haydon and S. Taylor (Cambridge, 1993) attempts a balance sheet of the work, post-Sykes. At the other extreme J. C. D. Clark's *English Society 1688–1832* (Cambridge, 1985) is admirably learned and provocative, but has mostly provoked disagreement. Six other works, utterly differing in approach, are for various reasons indispensable: Peter Virgin, *The Church in an Age of Negligence* (Cambridge, 1989), Viviane Barrie-Curien, *Clergé et pastorale en Angleterre au XVIIIᵉ siècle. Le Diocèse de Londres* (Paris, 1992), F. C. Mather, *High Church Prophet. Bishop Samuel Horsley (1733–1806) and the Caroline Tradition* (Oxford, 1992), Michael R. Watts, *The Dissenters from the Reformation to the French Revolution* (Oxford, 1978), David Hempton and Myrtle Hill, *Evangelical Protestantism in Ulster Society 1740–1890* (London, 1992), and David Hempton, *Religion and Political Culture in*

Britain and Ireland (Cambridge, 1996). For Scotland A. L. Drummond and J. Bulloch, *The Scottish Church 1688–1843* (Edinburgh, 1973) and A. Fawcett, *The Cambuslang Revival* (London, 1971) are still useful. The bibliography of the **Enlightenment** has reached desperate proportions and spread into every variety of literary studies; a necessarily desperate effort to convey its recent flavour in a brief space is made by Knud Haakonssen in the introduction to *Enlightenment and Religion. Rational Dissent in Eighteenth-century Britain* (Cambridge, 1996) which he edited. For the great atheism debate H. M. Barth *Atheismus und Orthodoxie* (Göttingen, 1971) and A. C. Kors, *Atheism in France, 1650–1729* (Princeton, 1990–) are both valuable. Two primers, neither of them recent, help, by being eminently sensible, to show how views of the Enlightenment in France and Germany have shifted, viz. Norman Hampson, *The Enlightenment* (London, 1965) and Franklin Kopitsch, *Aufklärung, Absolutism und Bürgertum in Deutschland* (Munich, 1976); compare them with Roy Porter, *The Enlightenment,* (London, 1990), *The Blackwell Companion to the Enlightenment* ed. John Yolton and others (Oxford, 1991), and Dorinda Outram, *The Enlightenment* (Cambridge, 1995). See also Robert Shackleton, *The* Encyclopédie *and the Clerks* (Oxford, 1970) and R. R. Palmer, *Catholics and Unbelievers in Eighteenth-century France* (Princeton, 1949). The shifting interest of the German work is most conveniently followed in the admirable occasional series published by the Wolfenbüttel library over which Lessing presided, the *Wolfenbütteler Studien zur Aufklärung* (1971–). Views of the British Enlightenment have been much influenced by the work of J. G. A. Pocock, for example his *Virtue, Commerce and History. Essays on Political Thought and History, chiefly in the Eighteenth Century* (Cambridge, 1985). See also Margaret C. Jacob, *The Radical Enlightenment: Pantheists, Freemasons, and Republicans* (London, 1981), and *Living the Enlightenment. Freemasonry and Politics in Eighteenth-century Europe* (Oxford, 1991). On Scotland see R. B. Sher, *Church and University in the Scottish Enlightenment* (Princeton, 1985). Literature on the Catholic Enlightenment appears above under national headings. The multiplicity of national Enlightenments is the theme of *The Enlightenment in National Context,* ed. Roy Porter and Mikulás Teich (Cambridge, 1981), and S. Jüttner and J. Schlobach, eds., *Europäische Aufklärung(en)* (Hamburg, 1992).

Index

Baumgarten, Siegmund Jacob, 175
Bavaria, 54–5, 58–60, 68, 187, 190, 233
Baxter, Richard, 88, 143, 160, 208
Bayle, Pierre, 71, 151, 158–60, 165, 167
Bayreuth, 54
Beccaria, Cesare, 49
Behmenists, 88–91
Belgium, 45, 197, 199
Belgrade, 204
Benedict XIII, pope, 30, 237
Benedict XIV, pope, 30, 41, 50, 169, 188,
  193, 200, 237
Benedictines, 41, 70, 149, 199, 228, 230
Benediktbeuern, 58
Bengel, Johann Albrecht, 127–8
Bennet, John, 145
Bentley, Richard, 153
Berchtesgaden, 105, 109
Berdyaev, N. A., 90
Berkeley, George, bishop, 169
Berleburg Bible, 20, 91
Berlin, 77, 98, 109, 167, 177
Bern, 27, 87–8, 103, 124–5, 184
Bernese Oberland, 88, 125–6
Bernières-Louvigny, mystic, 129
Berthelsdorf, 113–5
Bielitz, 96
Blois, 22
Bohemia, 4, 55–6, 58–60, 68, 93, 96–8,
  110–11, 114–5, 132, 185, 195, 213
Bohemian Brethren, 97, 114–115, 211,
  217
Böhme, Anton Wilhelm, 81–2, 133, 137,
  208
Böhme, Jakob, 24, 89–91, 134
Bollandists, 169
Bologna, Archbishop of, 47
Bosnia, 202
Bossuet, Bishop J. B., 14, 22, 25, 30
Boston, 82
Bourignon, Antoinette, 18, 24–5, 79, 87
Braga, 38
Brainerd, David, 140
Brandenburg, 15, 55, 77–8, 80, 91, 93, 98
Brandenburg, Electors of, 4, 5, 15
Brazil, 38
Bremen, 85–6
Breslau, 6, 93–4, 173
Brice, Edmund, 90
Brieg, 6
Brienne, Loménie de, archbishop, 228,
  232
Brinkenhof, 119
Bristol, 142, 145, 210
Brockes, Barthold Hinrichs, 172
Bromley, Thomas, 90

Bruno, Giordano, 150
Brunswick, 177
Buddeus, Johann Franz, 153
Buffier, 169
Bunyan, John, 130, 208
Burgos, 35
Burgundy, 233
Burnet, Gilbert, 21, 65
Butler, Joseph, bishop, 164

Cabbalism, 89, 156
Calvin, John, 9
Calvinism, 64, 84, 135, 143–4, 181, 215,
  244
Calvinistic Methodists, 138, 145
Cambridge, 36, 208, 230
Cambridge Platonists, 90, 160
Cambuslang, 141–2
cameralistics, 192–3
Cameronians, 141–2
Camisards, 17–18
camp meetings, 94, 119
Campanella, Tommaso, 150
Canada, 225
canonisation, 2, 35, 48, 50–1
Canstein, Baron Karl Hildebrandt von, 78
Capuchins, 42, 52, 93, 108
Carinthia, 62, 98, 107, 110, 196
Carlowitz, Peace of, (1699), 202
Carpzov, Johann Benedikt, 77
cartesianism, 24–5, 78, 85, 87, 149
Castell-Remlingen, Sophia Theodora of,
  113n.
Catalonia, 237
Catherine II, the Great, of Russia, 191,
  205, 220–2
Catholic Enlightenment, 184–201
censorship, 11, 192
Cévennes, 16–18, 94, 126
Champagne, 233
Charles I of England, king, 9
Charles II of England, king, 9–10
Charles III of Spain, king, 37, 189, 200
Charles VI, emperor, 56, 62, 65–6, 193–4
Charles X of Sweden, king, 212
Charles XI of Sweden, king, 210
Charles XII of Sweden, king, 18, 94, 97–8,
  205, 215
Chatellier, Louis, 68
Cherasco, Treaty of, 34
children, 17–18, 25, 63, 94, 108, 115, 119,
  125, 134
chiliasm, 15
Chillingworth, William, 71
China, 151
Christian perfection, 130

NEW APPROACHES TO EUROPEAN HISTORY

Printed in the United Kingdom
by Lightning Source UK Ltd.
109831UKS00002B/264